THE JURY SPOKE:
THE COURT REPORTER MURDER CASE

Written by:

James D. Jordan

Former District Attorney and Judge

Publishing Coordinator – Sharon Kizziah-Holmes

INDIE PUB PRESS

Printed in the USA

ISBN -13: 978-1-7366409-0-6

CONTENTS

My book is based on official court records, newspaper reports, personal notes and my personal memory.

Introduction

Have you ever wondered what District Attorneys do with their time?

Have you ever wondered why some laws get enforced and others just don't?

Have you ever wondered what hypnosis is, and how it works, or how law enforcement uses it, or what the experts have to say about it?

One time while I was District Attorney, a horse had been tied up and left to almost starve to death. I certainly believe that animal cruelty needs to be addressed seriously. A local lady got to wanting everything prosecuted seriously that even looked like it might be unkindness to animals. The problem was that I had so many serious crimes against people, and far too few resources. Read on and you will discover some of what goes on in the life of a District Attorney.

President Donald Trump recently could tell that confidential information was leaking out of his office. I, too, could tell that information was leaking out of my office. President Trump had a lot more resources and talent available to stop the leaks, but he found it very difficult. From time to time during the development of this case I could tell that confidential information was leaking out of my office in Okmulgee, OK, but I could never be certain who was doing the leaking or how the leaks happened.

I understood that the father of the defendant in this case owned the building across the street from my office. I wondered a few times if someone had placed a parabolic antenna in or on that building, or had a microphone in my office and was listening in to what was said. One day I ran up a trial balloon; I told one of the agents of the Oklahoma State Bureau of Investigation in confidence in my office something that sounded important to the defendant. Within a day or two this came back to me. I didn't know if this O.S.B.I. agent was dirty, or careless, or if he had shared the information with a supervisor or other agent who might be dirty or careless, or if someone was eavesdropping – hearing whatever was said in my office. Thereafter, I did all my own trial preparation at home and never found another information leak.

I found the vast majority of law officers I worked with to be totally honest. There were a few questions, but never any proof of anything wrong.

Court Reporter Murder Case

Defense attorney Steven W. Taylor wanted to take the deposition of Dr. Bernard Diamond in Corte Madera, Calif., on the admissibility of the testimony of a formerly hypnotized witness.

Dr. Diamond's deposition was scheduled on Monday morning in Corte Madera, Calif., and the deposition of Martin Reiser, Ed.D., Director of Behavioral Sciences Services, Los Angeles Police department , and Director of the Law Enforcement Hypnosis Institute, was scheduled in Los Angeles that afternoon.

I arrived at my hotel in Corte Madera north across the bay from San Francisco on a Sunday. It was a very nice hotel and should have been. I understood it was one of the highest income areas in the country.

I had been talking with every prosecutor across the country I could find who was involved with the issue of admissibility of the testimony of a previously hypnotized witness. One of the persons with whom I had spoken was an Assistant Attorney General for California who was arguing that very issue before the California Supreme Court the next day. The plan was for me to drive to Sacramento to visit him on Sunday afternoon to be sure I was fully briefed, and that he knew everything I had learned.

I checked into my room and called him about driving up. I could not see the hall door because of the bathroom, which extended into my room. I was sitting on my bed cross-legged, looking down at my notes, talking on the phone to the California Assistant Attorney General, when an attractive oriental lady walked up to the foot of my bed. She was wearing a nice-looking dress fastened with three buttons.

I knew how the game was played. There would be a photographer standing just out of my sight. Her dress would fly open, and pictures would be taken to incriminate me or at least slow down my vigorous prosecution. I knew that if I participated, they would have exactly what they wanted. I knew that if I ran, they would have a picture of me running from a naked woman looking like I got caught in the act. I ducked my head as I sat on the bed looking at my notes and talked with the Assistant Attorney General for 45 minutes before she finally left.

I never saw the photographer or any pictures to incriminate me. The next morning, we took the deposition of Dr. Diamond, a psychiatrist who had used hypnosis as catharsis when working with veterans who had returned from serious combat and were severely traumatized. He believed that no truthfully accurate information spewed out while under hypnosis but that they just dumped out a bunch of garbage to clear their minds. He was very vocal and persuasive to courts, and the use of hypnosis was severely restricted.

Dr. Martin Reiser, the L.A.P.D.'s first staff psychologist, founded the Law Enforcement Hypnosis Institute in 1976 to use hypnosis to solve crimes that might not have been solved without carefully securing lost memories. His group worked on a number of notable cases. One case involved a busload of school kids who were kidnapped. The bus they were on was driven into a pre-dug trench and buried. The bus was found and the kids recovered, but they were so traumatized that they could not tell anything about their abductors. Through hypnosis, enough information was secured to find and prosecute the perpetrators. A movie was later made dramatizing the incident. They were successful in another case where a low-level drug dealer did not pay his supplier. Rather he used the drugs with his girlfriend. She was so doped up that she had passed out and didn't even know that the supplier had arrived and killed her boyfriend. When the police interviewed her, she couldn't tell them anything. Through hypnosis they were able to get enough information from her to find and convict the killer. As a grade school student, I would rush home to hear my favorite radio programs, which included "The Shadow." In it the good guy, if I remember correctly, could walk through a room and people could not see him because of hypnosis. This intrigued me.

In Junior High School I was a member of the YMCA Boys Choir, which practiced on Wednesday evenings after school. After practice an older guy would hypnotize some of the boys. I knew one of the boys and had wrestled with him, so I knew he wasn't very strong. One evening he was hypnotized and told to stand stiff like a board; he was lifted up like a board and his heals were placed on the back of one chair and the back of his head on another chair and everyone simply walked off and left him for several minutes; I knew he was not strong enough to do that on his own. Right then I realized that hypnosis could be used to do a lot of things that seemed incredible.

One of the instructors at the Law Enforcement Hypnosis Institute from which I was graduated would run a needle through his hand and ask people which side of his hand they wanted to see blood come out. They would select a side and that was the side that bled. Later he would ask if they would like to see blood come from the other side. When they agreed, the blood would dry up on the side that had been running and start running out the other side. Mind over matter.

THE START OF THE STORY

The way I heard the story, Ray Courtemanche arrived in Okmulgee, Okla., as a well-qualified Court Reporter, but without a pot to piss in. By the time he died, Ray was the chairman of the County Excise Board, owned the Tag Agency and Welfare Office buildings, was an owner of convenience stores, other real property, mineral interests and various stocks, was a director of a bank, and apparently had no debt. He seemed to be liked by everybody and had been very effective behind the scenes helping people win elections.

Okmulgee was and is the county seat of Okmulgee County, in eastern Oklahoma. Henryetta was and is a nice sized town south of Okmulgee, separated by the Deep Fork River, but still in Okmulgee County. For many years there was no bridge from Okmulgee to Henryetta, so when Henryetta lawyers needed to do business at the County seat they had to make an all-day trip by train out of county from Henryetta and back to Okmulgee in the county, and repeat the trip after they had finished their business. Hence, a Superior Court was established in Henryetta so that court business could be completed without leaving town or the county. When I arrived in Henryetta to conduct court business, the court room was large with a coal stove in the center of the room. A bridge was built and the highway improved so it was only a 15-minute trip from Henryetta to Okmulgee. Thus, there was no longer a need for a Superior Court there. Finally it was closed, and all court business was moved to the county seat in Okmulgee.

About this time, the story was, some of the lawyers in Okmulgee seemed to be so argumentative that they could never settle any cases, so every case had to go to trial. The lawyers in Henryetta worked together and could settle some cases without going to trial.

Ray was quiet and effective. He got the credit for working behind the scenes and getting cases settled. Also behind the scenes, he became effective in getting candidates elected to public office. A well-known District Attorney from Tulsa, David Hall, ran for Governor. The story related to me by one of Hall's close operatives well after the event was that the Hall people came to Ray and asked what he wanted to deliver Okmulgee County to the Hall camp. Ray told them he wanted to appoint the judges, and they agreed to that. Hall won. Later Hall was convicted on Federal extortion and bribery charges and sent to prison, although he steadfastly maintained his innocence.

K.D. Bailey had come from coal miner stock and was a Golden Glove Boxer before he became a lawyer. K.D had been a State Senator but lost re-election to Kenneth Butler, who shared office space with Ray Courtemanche.

I arrived in Okmulgee on Labor Day weekend in 1970 to serve as an Assistant District Attorney. K.D. had had an injury or illness, and the story was that the doctors had gotten him hooked on narcotics. He would come to court, but other lawyers stepped up and helped him with his arguments. To his credit, K.D. seemed to recover from his problem.

K.D. had a son, Kenneth Dexter Bailey, Jr. Dexter, as he was known, was a bull rider and a strong young man. He had to be to hold on to those bulls, which were bucking and jerking and twisting and turning. His wife Sue had to be strong to live with him; one time she shook my hand, and I thought she was going to break it.

I was elected District Attorney for Okmulgee and McIntosh Counties in eastern Oklahoma for a four-year term running from Jan. 1, 1979, to Jan. 2, 1983.

Harry Pitchfork had been the County Attorney for Okmulgee County. The town fathers felt he was not trying enough DUI cases so they wanted a new District Attorney. The state legislature had just recently changed the law. Rather than have a County Attorney for each county, one District Attorney would serve two or more less populous counties.

Odie Webb had been the County Attorney for McIntosh County for years. He had the reputation of being a whiskey drinking, crossword working, womanizer. He had operated a machine gun in Europe during World War II and was a coon hunter. I heard him talking on the phone one day telling a friend that he had better be "packing" when he comes down to his area.

One day I went to lunch with Odie at a crowded restaurant on Main street in Okmulgee. He walked up to an attractive lady, probably in her 30's, and loudly asked her if she would like to play hide the wiener. She was obviously embarrassed and didn't know what to say. I never knew if she was a former girlfriend or a total stranger.

I was told that the Okmulgee town fathers made a deal with Odie. Since most of the votes were in the city of Okmulgee, they would get Odie elected as District Attorney if he would agree to stay south of the Deep Fork River; I was told he agreed. I was hired by the First Assistant District Attorney and didn't even see Odie until I had been on the job about a month. After serving as Assistant D.A., I served three years as Special Judge hearing all criminal matters other than felony trials; I got a lot of experience in both of those positions.

When I came to Okmulgee, there were law officers who could not read or write, but they could chase down cattle rustlers. I established a new rule when I became D.A. I insisted that I would file a felony case only if I had a written report.

One day I came to work early and walked past the Sheriff's office where I saw one of the deputies doing paper work. Several times I passed the office that day and noticed the intense work going on. I was late leaving the courthouse that evening when that deputy stopped me and gave me his very first written report. That was the only time I ever saw a written report that contained no facts. We grew from there.

At that time the Sheriff didn't have a camera so the news reporter was called to make pictures of serious accidents or crime scenes.

Ed Boatman had been County Attorney years before I came to Okmulgee. When I got to Okmulgee, he practiced law in a nice office just across the alley from the Okmulgee County Courthouse.

Charlie Steel had practiced law in Okmulgee years before. I am told he left because of incriminating pictures that had been circulated in the area. He made a career in the army as a Judge Advocate General officer. At the end of his career, he returned to Okmulgee. I assume that he believed that the old pictures had long been forgotten, but someone was sure to tell me the story and they did. About the same time he returned to Okmulgee, Charlie Steel was appointed to fill a vacant position as Associate District Judge. I appeared in his court several times, and I believed that I could do a much better job in that position than he was doing.

I resigned as Special Judge and ran for Associate District Judge against Charlie Steel. At the last minute, Pete Richardson jumped into the race. Pete was a respected lawyer from Henryetta who had previously served in the state legislature. I beat Charlie, but Pete beat me. So, I went into the private practice of law in Okmulgee.

After I lost that election, Ed Boatman asked me to stop by and visit with him. I did, and he showed me his fine office and library and told me that he knew how hard it was to start a law practice. It takes time for clients to start asking for legal services; a library was needed and that was expensive. He came across as very friendly, offered to send some business to me, and told me that I could use his library anytime I needed to.

Before coming to Okmulgee, I had spent nine years in the claims division of American Fidelity Assurance Company in Oklahoma City. In that job I learned that there was always someone who was trying to pull on my ankle or step on my fingers as I tried to climb the ladder of success. I realized that I needed more education than I had to develop the freedom I wanted in my work. Bob Gritz, a cousin, was Mayor at Hennessy, Okla. Bob came to me and told me about a special program under which they would pay my way to medical school if I would agree to practice medicine in Hennessy for four years following graduation. By this time, I was married and had a baby daughter, and I had heard just how hard it was to attend medical school. I could see no way I could make that work and keep my family together. But clearly I needed to do something to develop the freedom I wanted in my work. There was a law school just a few blocks from our office, the Oklahoma City University School of Law. I applied and was accepted. At the same time, a young man who had tried to get the claims adjustor job when I did went to work as a salesman for American Fidelity Assurance Company. He also started law school at O.C.U. at the same time I did. If my memory is correct, management found out that he was enrolled in law school and they fired him on the spot. C.W. Cameron, so the story went, was graduated from High School at Altus, Okla., and went to work as a bank teller. He watched to see who was making the money, and when he realized that it was the insurance people, he went into the insurance business. He was successful and moved his insurance agency to Oklahoma City. As the business grew, he set up his own premium, underwriting, and claims departments and ultimately set up his own insurance company, American Fidelity Assurance Company, which in recent years has been recognized as one of the best places to work in the nation; that was after we built it on sweat, blood and tears. C.W. was a real salesman. Part of his success was that he frequently hired people who could perform but had some problem. One salesman was a real whiz-bang, selling lots of policies; about every three or four months C.W. would get a call on Saturday night because his whiz-bang was drunk in jail. C.W. would get him out and clean him up and send him out to sell more policies. C.W. didn't like claims because we were sending money out of the company, but as long as we kept things in order, he left us alone. His focus was on the things that brought money into the company. I worked full time in the demanding claims job, left work at 5:00 p.m., ate a bite and spent evenings at law school. The hardest thing about law school was needing to study at home; my little daughter couldn't understand why I would no longer play with her as she banged on my door and said "Daddy, Daddy, Let me in!" That still hurts to the core. Dean Foster advised us to take a full load and finish it because it was going to take every waking moment anyway. As hard as it was, that was good advice.

After I lost the election for the office of Associate District Judge I set up a private law practice in Okmulgee. By this time, I had some experience in the world and had seen the kid's movie, Uncle Remus, where I learned about Tar-Baby. There are some things you hold onto that hold you fast and won't let you go. Ed Boatman looked to me like Tar-Baby, so I never took him up on his offer for assistance with starting my law practice.

I saw other young lawyers come to town, and though I never observed any contact between them and Ed Boatman it became my strong belief that he had called each one to his office and made the same pitch to them, and they had to have taken him up on his offer. Then they fell into support for Ed, which could have been for appreciation for his help. However, it became my strong belief that he asked each one to do a favor for him. I strongly suspect that it was something not exactly above board but not too bad, and after all Ed was a successful lawyer in town and had been for years. Then it became my strong belief that he would ask for more than one favor, each a bit more across the line, and soon these young lawyers felt they had been trapped by Tar-Baby, and they were no longer free to make their own decisions.

I will paint a fuller picture of the environment in which I was working in Okmulgee and McIntosh Counties and then move on to the COURT REPORTER MURDER case.

As I learned over time various individuals were engaged in illegal activities. I never saw much prostitution, but someone seemed to run that business. Someone else was selling drugs. Another guy would not commit burglaries, but he would get someone to commit them, and then he would send a rental truck to California each week to sell stolen property at flea markets. The attitude of those in these activities seemed to be, don't tell on me and I won't tell on you.

When I took over as District Attorney there was an open gambling establishment on Main Street, and it had been there for years. I had had no complaints about the establishment by any citizen. No-one seemed to object to its presence.

I had established a reputation as a prosecutor who enforced the law. I had made some enemies.

The law was that if gambling was going on in the county, presumably the D.A. knew about it and could be removed from office if he were not actively prosecuting the gambling, whether he actually knew about the gambling or not. That meant to keep one of my enemies from getting me removed from office I had to prosecute the open gambling business on Main Street. I went to the Chief of Police who didn't want to get involved; he liked his job and didn't want to lose it. Drew Diamond was a police officer in Tulsa before he became Chief of Police there. I brought him down to run the operation and left it in his hands.

One day the Okmulgee Chief of Police called and asked me to come to the Police Station. I walked to his office and was ushered into a room with several police officers sitting around; the door was locked behind us. One of the officers said "One phone call right now would be worth $3,000.00". As it turned out they were gathered to make a raid on the open gambling establishment. We were all locked in to be sure there were no leaks.

We walked over to the gambling establishment, and the officers arrested the gamblers and the operator. As I recall City Council members were gambling and were arrested. The gamblers were charged in City Court, posted bond and left.

I filed felony gambling charges against the operator. When the case went to trial, I called the gamblers as witnesses; they couldn't remember even being there, until we pulled out the documents showing that they had been arrested and posted bond. As I recall, the operator was convicted of felony gambling charges.

I had demonstrated that I vigorously prosecuted gambling, and no efforts were made to remove me from office for not enforcing that law.

OKMULGEE AND MCINTOSH COUNTIES AS INTRODUCED TO ME

Okmulgee became the capital of the Creek Nation at the western end of the Trail of Tears after the Creek Indians were forced to leave their rich farms and nice homes in the east. There were arguments among three groups of Creek Indians, those who came before the Trail of Tears, those who came on the Trail of Tears and those who held out and came later. The Trail of Tears was a very hard journey; many died along the way.

Bell Star was a famous early day outlaw. She was revered by young people when I arrived in McIntosh County, which was included in the territory of the Creek Nation. Archaeological sites in McIntosh County date back to 6,000 B.C. and there is evidence of indigenous people who predated any of the plains Indians and the tribes that settled in the territory in the 1830's following Indian Removal from the American Southeast. In addition:

- Coal miners moved into the area to ply their trade, and later oil boomed.
- Glass workers manufactured bottles and plate glass.
- Covington Aircraft continues to rebuild radial aircraft engines.
- In earlier days there was a law school in Okmulgee.

There was a bad race riot in Tulsa, Okla., in 1921. Many black people left Tulsa, and a good number settled in Okmulgee.

Robert P. Crotty was a podiatrist who could work wonders. I could walk in with a sprained ankle and walk out without hobbling. Another podiatrist said that Dr. Crotty didn't know what he did but, it worked. It was like magic.

Lake Eufaula in McIntosh County provides lake income. The shore line has been said to be about 600 miles. When I arrived the best duck hunting in the U.S. was at Lake Eufaula. There were also people who would provide any game at any time in any quantity despite laws to the contrary. Okmulgee Technical College was established after World War II to train returning G.I.'s in civilian trades. It is a quality institution where training includes automotive technology, diesel technology, heating, ventilation, air conditioning, refrigeration and other subjects in demand. Oklahoma State Technical Institute is part of Oklahoma State University. I taught two classes during one trimester, One was business law to accounting students, who were very bright and had a lot on the ball. The other class was in general business principles. I had some very bright students, and some who were only able to learn to wipe tables; I never was able to keep more than a third of the class awake on any given day, a tough assignment.

The oil man, Waite Phillips lived in Okmulgee and played a card game that didn't suite him, so he moved to Tulsa to build the Phillips Petroleum Company instead of building this company in Okmulgee.

Putty Gilmer invented the parking meter; he had one beside his driveway on 8th street in Okmulgee.

Another fellow developed many plants. He also showed me where the early Indians would herd the buffalo over the edge of a steep creek bank breaking their legs and killing the animals. There were many early Indian arrow heads to be found there. However, the creek bed has been reworked, and I suspect it is hard to find any today after all that dirt work.

Lawyers are not usually allowed to serve on juries. However, I was told about a time when a lot of cases were backed up. They needed to be tried, but there was no money to pay jurors, so all the lawyers in the county served as the jury panel to get through the backlog of unheard cases.

Assistant District Attorney

The first day I reported for duty as Assistant D.A. I was introduced to a number of men who all seemed to be prominent in the City of Okmulgee. They explained that they did not want wives working; it was OK for them to earn a little hair money but no significant work. In that gathering I was asked if I wanted to pay no taxes or pay a little tax; I responded that I would rather pay a little tax.

That same day there was a hotly contested election contest going on in the large courtroom. The small courtroom was packed with people who had been charged with driving under the influence or public drunkenness at Lake Okmulgee over the Labor Day holiday. I had studied criminal law at the Oklahoma City University School of Law, but my greatest interest had been in business and health insurance. I followed the First Assistant District Attorney to the large courtroom expecting to follow him around for a week or so and learn what an Assistant District Attorney was expected to do. The election contest went on and on. Finally, Charley Pugsley, the First Assistant D.A., handed me a pile of files over a foot high and said, "The courtroom is over there," pointing in the direction of the small court room. When I walked in, there was standing room only. I had a good law education including criminal law, but I had no idea what initial appearance was; it was so simple I just didn't remember it even being mentioned. I walked up to the bench and asked Judge Cyrus, "What do I do?" He said, just read the Information (the charge) to each defendant, explain that they have a right to an attorney and ask if they understood the charge, and on misdemeanors how they plead. I never forgot that experience, and from time to time over the years I had the opportunity to assist some new lawyer on procedure.

A day or so later I walked a couple of blocks to lunch, and on the way back an older gentleman stepped out the door of an office across the street from the courthouse and said, "Come here." I walked in and saw a man and a woman there wanting to be married. He asked the man, "Do you want to marry this woman?" and got a positive response. Then he asked the woman if she wanted to marry this man, and she too gave a positive response. Then he said, "You're married". He was a Justice of the Peace whose jurisdiction had been reduced so that he could hear cases where no more than 50 cents was at issue, if I recall correctly, but he could still perform marriages. The new office of Special Judge now performed all the work of an examining magistrate, work previously done by a Justice of the Peace.

The first week while serving as Assistant D.A. I was in the law library and met Jack Scott, a lawyer who had previously been County Attorney. He asked me if I knew what bigamy was. I told him what I had learned in law school. He said he thought he knew what bigamy was when he filed a case in which a man lived in the house with one wife, and another wife lived in a tent in the back yard. The case went to the Criminal Court of Appeals, as it was named then. Jack reached up and pulled down a reporter in which the decision was published. It held that this was not bigamy. Not too long after that some appeal judges went to prison.

Shortly after I became Assistant D.A. a petition arrived in our office roughly printed on yellow tablet paper with poor spelling. What the petition boiled down to was that the petitioner had been in prison about 20 years, was still there, and he had never entered a guilty plea, nor been found guilty. Therefore he should not be there. I went to the court records and found an entry that showed his appearance and a lawyer entering a guilty plea for him. Everything looked regular. The lawyer who had entered the guilty plea was still alive, so I went to visit him and showed him the petition. His response was that the petition was absolutely true. He explained that the black petitioner had been charged with the rape of a white woman, and there was a mob getting ready to lynch him, so he jumped up and entered the guilty plea for the defendant and saved his life. The Duty of the District Attorney is to See That Justice Is Done, and I believe it was, albeit somewhat late. Or is it ever too late if a life is saved?

A misdemeanor jury term had been called to try D.U.I. and other offenses. I walked into the jury room and found the jury panel assembled with Harry Pitchfork sitting there telling interesting stores. I suspected that his intent was to curry favor with the jury and get them to like him, thus giving him a better chance to win his case. I enjoyed his stories until the trial judge came in and opened court.

The jury was impaneled, the evidence heard, and we moved into closing arguments to the jury. I told the jury that Harry had lots of very interesting stories, but his stories had nothing to do with the guilt or innocence of his client; I won a conviction. Harry had been an American civilian lawyer who was involved in the Nuremberg Trials after World War II, when top Nazi officers were tried for war crimes. I was told that Harry had been considered for appointment as U.S. Attorney General. The Nuremberg judges were from Great Britain, France, the Soviet Union and the United States. Twelve prominent Nazi criminals were sentenced to death. Harry had also been County Attorney for Sequoyah County, Okla., and had been active in Democratic politics.

Special Judge

Our Special Judge announced that he was resigning from his position as he was going to work for a major drug house. Ray Courtemanche was Court Reporter for one of the judges in our courthouse but worked for whomever needed a record. Ray came to me and asked if I would like to be the new Special Judge. I was flattered but told him I didn't feel I had enough experience to be a judge. He told me that if I did not take the job a young lawyer who was about to be graduated from law school would get the job. He also said that he liked how I did my work in court. I accepted the job. It was years later that I heard of the deal Ray had made to deliver Okmulgee County to the Governor Hall camp in exchange for getting to appoint all the judges.

My duty as Special Judge was to hear all preliminary hearings, conduct all misdemeanor trials, hear and decide small claims and conduct civil marriages. The work load was such that I could do my own docketing, and I learned a great deal.

I performed a lot of marriages. One comes to mind when the lady came right into my office, and the guy seemed to drag a bit but got in. They both said all the right words, but I suspect that the bride's dad was outside with a shotgun.

Another time a lady brought candelabras and flowers and made it a fine wedding.

Still another time my family and I went to the movie. We were outside in line to buy tickets when a couple in greasy jeans and chains walked toward us. My wife grabbed our daughter and retreated because she didn't know if I was going to get beaten up, stabbed or what. The man said, "You married us, and we just wanted to let you know that it worked." I was glad to hear that.

Shortly after I was appointed as Special Judge the case of Betty Elain Vassor came before me for a Preliminary Hearing. She had been charged with manslaughter after the death of her husband. She and her husband were involved in a divorce. No restraining order had been issued. Mr. Vassor came to the house to try to talk his wife out of the divorce. Before he could leave he was shot and killed.

Usually, it is the duty of the Examining Magistrate to determine if a crime has been committed, if there is probable cause that the defendant committed the crime, and if so to issue an order sending the case to trial. There the burden of proof is guilt beyond a reasonable doubt.

I listened carefully to the evidence, and it became clear that a crime had been committed, and there was probable cause that Betty Elain Vassor had committed the crime. However, it also became clear that the crime committed was not manslaughter, as charged, but murder. I issued an order binding Betty Elain over for trial on the charge of murder.

The prosecution and the defense were both hopping mad at me. The case was appealed to the Court of Criminal Appeals, where I was treated like dirt – as though I didn't know enough to come in out of the rain. The bind-over order was reversed to the charge of manslaughter. Betty Elain Vassor was tried on the charge of Manslaughter and convicted. An appeal was sent to the Court of Criminal Appeals. In their decision, they commented that she was very lucky that she had been charged with manslaughter rather than murder. Without saying so the court had come to realize that I was correct that the proper charge was murder.

The next time I went to the State Capital I ate lunch at El Charito Mexican Restaurant. I didn't see any of the judges from the Court of Criminal Appeals, but they saw me and invited me to come join them for lunch. It is more fun when the judges realize that you are correct.

State v. District Court of the 24th Judicial Dist., 323 P2d 993 was filed by Harry Pitchfork when he was County Attorney of Okmulgee County. The Oklahoma Court of Criminal Appeals by its decision of April 2, 1958, agreed that the Honorable Jess I. Miracle, District Judge, had exceeded his authority in directing the County Attorney in how to do his work. The Court of Criminal Appeals set out in the case that the County Attorney not only directs under what conditions a criminal action shall be commenced but from the time it begins until it ends his supervision and control is complete, limited only by legal restrictions. No judge can be expected to know all the law. Lawyers advise the court as to what the law holds. I don't recall any lawyer citing this case to me or requesting that I change my decision. I subsequently tried cases before Judge Miracle and found him to be a fair and honest judge.

I was a member of the Rotary Club in Okmulgee. While I was Special Judge I was elected to the club's Board of Directors. At our organization meeting the president said we needed a project. Over a very short period of time Okmulgee had lost about a third of our doctors. I suggested that we set up a Doctor Procurement Committee. The president said, "You are Chairman." I knew that I could not solve the problem; nor could our committee solve the problem. But I knew that people in Okmulgee had worked all over the world in the oil business and had lots of contacts. We met with every organization in Okmulgee to spread the word and help us find doctors.

Don Reynolds owned the Okmulgee Daily Times newspaper and as I recall about 50 other small-town newspapers, as well as billboards in Nevada and across the nation. He helped us a great deal with advertising. It probably didn't hurt that I had handled the claims for Don-Ray Media, which he owned, while I worked for the American Fidelity Assurance Company while attending law school at night. We received applications from as far away as Germany.

Our local Hospital Administrator interviewed the applicants. We learned that old doctors who wanted to move their practice too often had questions of drug problems or had had too many patients die. Young doctors would look at our new hospital and were eager to establish their practice in Okmulgee. However, while the doctors were looking at our new hospital their wives were looking at our schools. The new grade school had been built about 1923! The average age in Okmulgee was about 55, and school bonds always went down in defeat because the old people didn't want to pay for schools. So we told the old people that if we younger people needed doctors, we could drive to Tulsa, but if they wanted doctors in Okmulgee, they would have to vote for school bonds. This time school bonds passed at election time. We got schools and doctors.

I am a Mason. One day one of my lodge brothers came before me on a charge of Public drunkenness. If I remember correctly, his wife had divorced him, and it really tore him up. He went out and got drunk. Being brought before me was more than enough punishment for that offense. I never heard of him ever being involved in any other offense.

I had never been with any law enforcement agency before going to Okmulgee. While I was Special Judge there was a sweep of arrests of the children of main street business owners in Henryetta on drug charges involving baggie quantities of marijuana. My duty as Special Judge was to determine if there had been a crime and if there was probable cause that each of these defendants had committed the charged crimes. The evidence was clear, and the cases proceeded to trial, where I believe all of the defendants were sentenced to prison. I felt this was overkill. Because there had been violations of the law there should be some punishment, but not the state penitentiary.

After I ran for the office of Associate District Judge and Pete Richardson beat me, I opened a private law office in Okmulgee. I did real estate title work, collections, divorces and had a general practice.

Some lawyers, if they knew that one of the really well qualified title lawyers had examined a title, would check it only after his examination. One day as usual I did a complete examination of a title that one of the expert title lawyers had examined, and I found a problem. We corrected it, and my stature went up.

Another day a lady who had just moved from California came to see me. She had bought a new car just before leaving California, and it was a lemon, which was not a totally unusual problem at the time. I thought there was no way to get any recovery without filing a legal action and bringing the car company to the table in Okmulgee County. I told the lady I would write one letter, and if the problem didn't get solved that I would file suit. THEY GAVE HER A NEW CAR. I charged her $25.00 for the letter; I didn't charge her enough!

Another time I was court appointed on a juvenile case. The child had been declared delinquent and had been turned over to the custody of the Department of Institutions, Social and Rehabilitative Services (Department). After the child had been in training school about a month the family came to me complaining that their son was asleep on the top bunk when the house parent pulled him out of his bunk on his head. This almost sounded farfetched. However, as a lawyer I had a duty to investigate. I got to talk with every boy who had been present in the unit at the time; every one of them told the same story.

I asked the local trial judge to remove the child from the training school. The Department had a lawyer at the hearing before Judge John Maley. Lloyd E Raider was a respected expert in the area of public welfare. He had been very successful in managing his budget and because of that the legislature had broadened his operations. He assisted U.S. Senator Robert S. Kerr in developing the Kerr-Mills bill, which amended the Social Security Act and set the stage for Medicare. President John F. Kennedy placed him on the President's Panel on Mental Retardation. Lloyd Raider was considered by many to be the most powerful individual in Oklahoma politics.

Mr. Raider had secured passage by the Oklahoma legislature of an act that provided in part, "The court may commit the child to the custody of the Department; provided, any order adjudicating a child to be delinquent and committing the child to the Department shall be for an indeterminate period of time.

"Any decree or order made under the provisions of this Act may be modified by the court at any time; provided, however, that an order … committing a child to be delinquent to the Department, may not be modified."

I filed action to remove the boy from the department and was met with strong opposition by the department and a denial of my request in the Court of Criminal Appeals. I challenged Lloyd E Raider, the local District Court, and the Court of Criminal Appeals in the Oklahoma Supreme Court. The decision of the Court of Criminal Appeals was set aside and vacated, judged to have been rendered in excess of that Court's jurisdiction.

I did my duty for my client and the community. Again it was more fun to win.

DISTRICT ATTORNEY

George Inglish was a respected lawyer and also part-time Bankruptcy Judge. I was at the point in my practice to consider getting a better office and an expanded library. All would mean more investment. He asked what was wrong with the District Attorney's Job. After running for that office and serving a four-year term I could have answered that question with a lot more understanding.

During the campaign my signs kept being torn down. There was one on the corner of 8th and Alabama, I believe it was, that would be down. I would get out of my car and put it up, drive around the block and find it back on the ground. Finally, I wore that person out, whoever it was. I had a sign in front of a salvage business north of town that was getting run over constantly; I stopped that when I drove nails facing out toward any oncoming tire.

The day before the election I caught a couple of thugs tearing down my signs on a busy street with other people in the area. I got out of my car and told them in a loud voice that if they tore down another one of my signs, I was going to put them in prison because I was going to win the election. They apparently believed me because no more of my signs were torn down.

This kind of thing is why they call an election a campaign.

While I was still a new D.A. a man came to visit me. As our visit ended, he said he would help me with anything other than a bank robbery. I asked why he would not help with bank robberies, and he told me that the famous bank robber Pretty Boy Floyd had eaten at their table many times during the depression when times were really hard, and when he left there was always money under the plate. Years later after my visitor had died, I was told that Pretty Boy Floyd was one of his family members.

While I was still a new D.A. another fellow came to visit. After we had visited several minutes, he said that some D.A.'s would take $300.00 a month to call and tip off gamblers before a raid. Then he asked, "Are you that kind of D.A.?" I responded, "No, I am not that kind of man." After visiting a few more minutes he asked if I were the kind of man who would call and tip off gamblers for $400.00 a month. Again, I replied that I was not that kind of D.A. After more visiting, he asked if I were the kind of D.A. who would take $500.00 a month to tip off gamblers and I gave the same reply. This question was repeated several times until he finally reached, I believe it was $4,000.00 a month, and I gave the same reply. He did not actually offer me a bribe, but I felt sure that if I had said yes money would have arrived each month. Even if he had directly offered me a bribe, I did not have a recording of the conversation so it would have been just my word against his; undoubtedly if I had filed a criminal charge, he would have walked off because of the words said, not a direct offer. I told a city detective about the conversations, and he said the guy was an old un-indicted hit man.

BUDGET

When I took over as D.A. my budget was controlled by the County Commissioners. Former District Attorney Odie Webb's last six months in office were funded by the first six months of the budget year. My first six months as D.A. were funded by the last half of the budget year. When I took office, I found that Odie had spent more than his half of the budget. I went to the County Commissioners and told them that I would get by until budget time, but I would need an increase with the new budget. When the new budget year started, I found that the County Commissioners had cut my budget!

One of the local newspapers reported that about one fifth of the employees in the Okmulgee County Courthouse had been fired on orders of the county commissioners because of a money crisis. Special Judge Anne Moroney was reported as saying she would not be able to hear any new small claims.

Henryetta Dailey Free-Lance reported on May 28, 1980, that Sheriff Gene Rice and his deputies were behind in receiving payments for travel. The last gas reimbursement checks that Okmulgee County deputies received were paid on April 21 for travel claims filed from January 24 thru February 24th. A deputy's maximum monthly salary was $688.00 and each had to finance his own patrol car and insurance.

The Dailey McAlester News-Capital & Democrat reported on April 4, 1980, "Prime rates (those charged favored customers) are up to 20 percent in New York and larger Oklahoma banks are charging slightly above that figure."

I took pictures of the fancy County barns with new equipment and air conditioning and pictures of court records stored in the basement because of lack of space and clearly showing damage because these records had been flooded. I filed an action in Tax Court on the basis that the District Attorney was a constitutional officer. Constitutional offices had first claim on county funds. Offices created by statute had second claim on county money. Finally, the third area allowing the expenditure of County funds was for discretionary items, such as the County Fair. The County Commissioners seemed to believe they needed to spend the most money on roads and the County Fair. I lost in Tax Court in what seemed to be a political decision. The County Commissioners had hired a lawyer to defend them in Tax Court; he came to me after the decision in that court and told me in a friendly way that if he ever made me mad to be sure to let him know and we would work out the problem; he clearly knew that I should have won in Tax Court. Even though I lost in Tax Court there was a great deal of publicity as to what happened. It wasn't long until the U.S. Attorney had filed charges against virtually all County Commissioners in Oklahoma. As I understood it these charges alleged that kickbacks had been taken on contracts. There are 77 counties in Oklahoma, and each county has three County Commissioners. The Oklahoman, the largest daily newspaper in the state, reported on March 2, 1984, that there had been 230 convictions or guilty pleas as a result of the case. I was told that all but three County Commissioners in Oklahoma were sent to prison. I have often wondered if any of them would have gone to prison if the Okmulgee County Commissioners had just been fair with me and my budget needs; then there would not have been a Tax Court action nor publicity.

Marian Opala was a law student in Poland when the Germans moved into his country during World War II. He became a freedom fighter. After the war Gene Warr, who created the Warr Acres addition to Oklahoma City, got Marian to Oklahoma City where he completed his law education. Early Marian was defending a man on a charge of murder. The deceased died more than a year and a day after the injury. Marian brought out the fact that under old common law it was not murder if the deceased did not die within a year and a day, and he won his case. He was a real legal scholar. Later Marian was the first Court Administrator for the State of Oklahoma, served a short time on the Worker's Comp Court and was appointed to and served the rest of his life on the Oklahoma Supreme Court. He was one of my law school instructors. Marian taught me to read and analyze the law. While I was Special Judge and he was Court Administrator he saw to it that I was able to attend the National College of the State Judiciary four-week course for judges of unlimited jurisdiction in Reno, Nev., where I learned a great deal.

When I first arrived at the courthouse in Eufaula I was impressed by the size of a large copper still sitting outside. It had been confiscated from some bootlegger.

The McIntosh County lawyers didn't like the idea that an out-of-county lawyer was the Chief Law Officer for their county.

One time I went to Checotah in McIntosh County to talk with a woman to find out what she knew about a particular crime. One of the police officers saw me and joined me; I didn't really mind until he started interfering by saying to the woman as I asked a question "if you know," strongly suggesting that she keep her mouth shut and not answer my questions. I quickly and strongly told the officer that if he did that again I would put him in jail; he stammered and stuttered, and by that time he had insured that my witness would not say anything. After all she lived in that small town!

Not long after I took office as D.A. Judge Layden from McAlester started putting together the "Docket from Hell" for McIntosh County. I saw him personally list every case that appeared in the books that had never gone to trial for whatever reason. He was going to show me up as a poor lawyer not able to take care of the business of the office. I walked downstairs to my office and told my assistant and my secretary to hold all traffic tickets and I would personally take care of them later. A few days later the Court Clerk asked my secretary where the traffic tickets were and she told her that she would have to talk with me. When the Court Clerk asked me about the traffic tickets, I told her that Judge Layden was preparing such a large docket that I didn't have time to take care of traffic tickets. Of course, my real reason for not signing the traffic tickets was they couldn't be filed or any money collected on them until I had approved their filing. Traffic tickets provided the money to pay jurors and hold court. Without them being signed and filed there could be no term of court. Judge Layden's "Docket from Hell" disappeared and reasonable dockets prevailed. Professor Quinlan at O.C.U. Law School had taught us to find the levers of power and flip them.

One time I appeared before Judge Layden who was taking a plea from a traffic offender. He explained to the offender that some people are safe driving 100 mph, but other people are not safe driving over 40 mph, so the 65-mph speed limit was a compromise so we would all be driving about the same speed and hopefully avoid accidents. I thought he did a good job of explaining this to the offender.

Shortly thereafter Judge Layden scheduled a reasonable docket of cases for trial. Odie decided he would show me up in a case. These are the facts of that case: A man worked for the Federal Aviation Administration, the F.A.A., in Oklahoma City, and had bought a lot on Lake Eufaula in McIntosh County and was in the process of building a house there on weekends. On the particular weekend involved the man had brought his young grandson and granddaughter to help him; they had done a lot so he was going to take them swimming in the lake. A guy who had a relative in the neighborhood showed up wanting to see what had been done in the house. The grandfather didn't like the guy, but he didn't want to upset him because he had been in and out of prison and had a bad reputation; at the same time if you made the wrong person angry in this area your house was likely to burn to the ground. So, he invited him in and showed him the house. The guy ended up tying the grandfather to a pole in the basement. He raped the little girl upstairs and committed sodomy on the little boy. In the meantime, the grandfather got loose and went to another house, where he called the police. The guy realized the grandfather had escaped so he stole a car and left. The law enforcement officers caught him before he had gotten very far. At trial because the outlaw had former felony convictions, he was charged A.F.C., or after former conviction of felonies. That meant that if he were convicted punishment could be 20 years minimum on each count. The usual way to prove A.F.C. was to call the Court Clerk to read the documents that showed the convictions. Odie would say anything he felt like, and when he got a conviction reversed, he would argue that he convicted outlaws and the Court of Criminal Appeals let them go. Odie was not careful with what he said, and he opened the door for me to do more than just have the clerk read a dry document showing the convictions. In fact, he opened the door so wide that I was allowed to call a woman this outlaw had committed a crime against in another county. The essential elements of that case were that he had escaped from confinement. The lady lived in a trailer house Southeast of Oklahoma City just north of I-40 near Anderson Road. The lady had been sick and was on valium when her neighbor called to tell her to be careful because there was a manhunt in their area. She told her neighbor that she would tell her husband when he got home. The neighbor who had called knew that she did not have a husband, so she called the law. In the meantime, this guy demanded that she fix him breakfast. Because of the valium she was moving too slowly for the guy, so he picked up a butcher knife and tried to cut thru the collar of her bathrobe; because it was too thick, he failed to cut her throat. Law enforcement arrived and arrested him. She got to tell this entire story to the jury in Eufaula. It was an easy case to argue. And when it came to argue punishment, I told the jury they could give him 1,000 years on each count if they wanted to. I also told them that he didn't get far with the car and didn't hurt the car and we didn't want anyone to think he was being punished because of passion so only give him the 20-year minimum on that count. At times it seemed that the Court of Criminal Appeals would reduce punishment if they felt punishment was too harsh and had been set because of passion.

Judge Maley in Okmulgee told me one time that Odie would say anything to get a conviction, but when I convicted someone they were convicted.

About that time a note from former Judge Bell was found in the D.A.'s office addressed to former County Attorney Odie Webb. It directed him to meet Judge Bell after the trial ended that day so they could figure out what they needed to do. This didn't sound like even-handed justice.

Gene Stipe was a lawyer and state Senator from McAlester, the next county south of McIntosh County. If a defendant wanted to win a not guilty verdict in a criminal case, he would usually hire Senator Stipe, who seemed to have a lot of power because of his position in the State Senate. There was a case where cattle had been stolen from a local rancher and the owner wanted to be certain that the jury convicted the outlaw so he hired Senator Stipe to sit at the prosecution table with me during the case so that everyone on the jury would know which way they should vote. I was convinced that the defendant was guilty, so I went along with the plan and we won another guilty verdict.

At a meeting of all the District Attorneys in the state there was a lot of talk about being underfunded. It was decided that we should each write to our state legislators and plead our case for more operating money. I wrote to Senator Stipe, and nothing was ever said, but I could feel that I had made a mistake and had lost support from him. Stipe was controversial and sometimes noise could be heard of corruption. Stipe eventually pleaded guilty to federal campaign violations and perjury in 2003 and was given probation and fined more than $735,000. He was considered to be the Dean of the Oklahoma Senate. Former Governor George Nigh said, "If there was a man of the people, it's Gene Stipe." Only Georgia Senator Hugh Gillis who had 56 years in legislative service eclipsed the legislative service of Gene Stipe. It is a small world, George Nigh's wife and I went to grade school together; who would have ever thought either of us would have ended up in life where we did.

Richard Pyle, who had been U.S. Attorney for the Eastern District of Oklahoma, was a good lawyer and had returned to private law practice in McIntosh County where he represented a criminal defendant. We had had a preliminary hearing and heard from all the witnesses. All but the last one were pillars of the community and there was nothing to question regarding their testimonies. The last witness had some characteristics that a defense lawyer could challenge. At trial the plan was for me to examine all of the witness except the last one, and my assistant, Val Pitman, would question that witness. I had finished my questions, just following the Preliminary Hearing transcript virtually word for word, and Val started to stand when I touched him on the arm and announced that the State Rested. Pyle had not asked a single question! He had focused on the one witness who could be challenged so we just kept him from asking any questions. Of course, he could have called the witness as his witness, but that would have lost the impact he was hoping for. Again, justice was served, and we won a conviction.

Val had an interesting background. He had been a Class A welder, had worked as an experimental engineer on production and modification of aircraft. He served in the Second Armored Division known as "Hell on Wheels," in Germany during World War II. After the war he returned to Hollis, Okla., where he started his own auto sales and service business before attending law school at the University of Oklahoma and Oklahoma City University School of Law. He served three terms in the State House of Representatives. He practiced criminal law. As Val told me he knew all the tricks and had made up most of them. One of the things I noticed while he was First Assistant D.A. was that when we had a jury term he would come to court in a nice-looking suit with every hair in place; before we would walk in to be seen by the jury, he would pull some hair down on his forehead; his theory was that the gals would notice this and want to reach out and put it back in place and would lean toward whatever he said, this seemed to work. While I was in law school, he spoke to our criminal law class one night. I remember there was an effort to require lawyers to keep hours for billing purposes; Val was strongly against such practice because as he said he was working on the case when he was in the shower; when he took on a criminal case to defend, he said to the client: "Give me some money" and when he ran low on money, he would tell the client to give him some more money. Because he was somewhat controversial, before I hired him, I talked with every lawyer and judge I could find who had had experience with him. One of the Oklahoma County judges said he had heard the noise but had real doubts there was any substance to any wrongdoing. I found him to always be honest and a good lawyer.

One time early in my term as D.A. someone told me about a large marijuana field in McIntosh County. I passed this information to the Oklahoma Bureau of Narcotics. I felt they thought I was too new to have any significant information. But they flew a helicopter apparently from Oklahoma City to near the Arkansas line on some business and on the way back they flew to the field I had pointed out to them and they found a major field of sinsemilla marijuana. They called for help in confiscating the field. It was not long before sunset, but they flew to Okmulgee and flew me to see the field myself. Then they returned me to Okmulgee. The plan was that I would drive down the next morning and assist with securing a search warrant for a building near the field. I drove to the field the next morning and found the field swarming with law enforcement officers. The officers found a rattlesnake in a gunny sack in a trail to help keep unwanted visitors out of the field. They also found trip guns under construction which when completed would have been placed to aim a 12-gage shotgun at the trails. I started working on the search warrant when a report came in that there was a dead body in the adjacent Deep Fork River. I assumed that the guard had failed in protecting the field and had been shot. Vegetation was dense, and the Deep Fork was full of fallen trees and reportedly stolen safes etc. The report of the dead body had come from two commercial fishermen who made their living catching fish and knew the river well. I got in their boat to go see the dead body as no Medical Examiner was available in our area who would be expected to travel into such rough country. Also, the only people authorized to move a dead body in Oklahoma when there is an unattended death is a Medical Examiner or the District Attorney. An Oklahoma Highway Patrol Lieutenant stood and watched as I got in the boat and departed up stream with the two fishermen. They had a second boat secured to the side of the boat we were riding in. I had taken hold of the side of the boat for stability when one of the fishermen cautioned me to keep my fingers inside the boat to keep from having a finger cut off in case the boats came together. When we got to the body it was obvious that it had been caught there on a snag for probably a couple of weeks and had nothing to do with the marijuana field. We returned to the field and the O.H.P. lieutenant was still standing there. After I got out of the boat he said, "I feared for your life when you got in that boat! These are the guys we know killed a game officer, but we haven't been able to prove it." I had told the fishermen while we were on our trip that if they would file a claim with my office, I would authorize payment for their expenses; they were reluctant and never did show up to file a claim. I have often wondered what I didn't see at the marijuana field while I was diverted to see the body. The value of the harvest was estimated at about $25 million. I always felt that the great majority of law enforcement officers I worked with were honest, but occasionally there would be a question about a throw-away knife to drop if an unarmed person were killed. Law officers are people, but my experience has been that they are actually trying to protect the public. One Okmulgee officer was convicted of some crime after my term ended; I know him, had worked with him and was shocked that he had been convicted of any crime. He was a nice soft-spoken guy. One day early in my term he brought a thug to my office to hear what he had to say; I was shocked at how roughly he spoke to the guy. Later I asked him why he spoke that way to the guy, and he explained that it was necessary to speak in language the guy understood. That is the way it sometimes works in the real world.

Before this I had set up a Child Support Enforcement Office staffed by a lawyer, secretaries and an investigator. Don Pope was the Assistant District Attorney in charge of the Child Support division; he and his staff did a good job. The investigator was Art Hackney, a retired Oklahoma Highway Patrol Trooper and former Okmulgee County sheriff. This unit would collect back child support. A small percent of what was collected became available for official expenses of my office. This would have been the source of any funds paid to the fishermen if they had filed a claim. A front-page article in the Henryetta Daily Free-Lance dated October 22, 1980, reported that our Okmulgee-McIntosh County Child Support office had consistently led the state in the percentage of cases in which it was able to collect child support. At the time of the article the D.A.'s office had been able to purchase a couple of tape recorders, a camera and other needed equipment.

Another time an airplane landed at Okmulgee and ran off of the runway into the mud. It was noted that the fuselage of the plane had been extended, and it was found to be full of dope. We forfeited the aircraft to the City of Okmulgee. That air field is an alternate for the Tulsa airport and was used for training during World War II.

Val Pitman, my First Assistant, whose office was in Eufaula called me one evening and told me that the Sheriff was going to arrest him. I called for two Oklahoma Highway Patrol officers to meet Val and me in my office in the Courthouse in Eufaula. The Sheriff never did come to arrest Val; however, it was reported to me that the next morning that he had resigned as Sheriff and became the Chief of Police in Checotah.

Later it was reported to me that the City of Checotah was confining people in their city jail for such crimes as rape and burglary. At that time the law was that there were two types of City Courts in Oklahoma, those "OF RECORD" and those "NOT OF RECORD." The only city courts OF RECORD in Oklahoma at that time were in Oklahoma City, the state capitol, and Tulsa, which was still known as "THE OIL CAPITOL OF THE WORLD" These courts of record were authorized to put people in jail and assess larger fines. Courts Not of Record were limited to assessing only smaller fines and not putting anyone in jail. I had my hands full and didn't have resources to get into this issue, and I knew that surely some private attorney would sue the City of Checotah and make some money and solve the problem. I never did hear of that happening.

None of this surprised me because I had previously been in a meeting with some Checotah officers when the question came up about some activity the local police wanted to pursue. I explained to them that such activity was unconstitutional; the response to me was, "We don't follow that here! "

One of the new car dealers in my district encouraged me to go after the dope dealers. But he wanted me to wait to take any action until after the local marijuana crop had been harvested and those growers had bought new pickups. If I had followed that advice a new crop of marijuana would have made its way into the community. Freedom is not free. If we are to be free from drugs in our community, we just might have to forgo the sale of a few new pickups.

Somewhere along the way there was an attempted assassination in Tennessee. An alert neighbor wrote down the tag number of an old pickup which seemed to be parked in the wrong place. The assassin shot the local man thru and thru with a .45 caliber gun. That would have been expected to kill him, but it didn't seem to do the job.

Immediately a manhunt started.

That night the little town of Dewar in Okmulgee County had one police officer who was on duty. Nothing was going on.

A pickup drove by with a flickering tail light. Since the officer had nothing to do, he stopped the pickup and issued a warning. Because he still had nothing to do, he ran the tag number and learned that this was the pickup wanted for the Tennessee shooting. The officer knew the direction the pickup had gone and knew where it had turned. He went after it and saw a garage door being pulled down to conceal the pickup.

The officer arrested the driver and one passenger.

Legal action was started to extradite these two men back to Tennessee. They were represented by high dollar out-of-the-area lawyers. Quickly the legal action moved to the Court of Criminal Appeals in Oklahoma City, where a hearing was held in the afternoon on the Habeas Corpus action to deliver the bodies of the defendants from confinement. Instead of announcing their decision the Judges adjourned the hearing until the following morning. The following morning, I drove back to Oklahoma City for the hearing. Overnight the prisoners were spirited over the state line and were no longer in Oklahoma. I announced this to the court and immediately the case was dismissed because there was no body within our jurisdiction to bring before the court.

I was later told that the driver was a flunky, but the other guy was a national hit man. I was also told that bail bond for the hit man was set at $25 million in cash, which was posted. He walked off and apparently was never seen again.

I was told that the lawyers were Mafia lawyers and the $25 million cash bond forfeited was just part of the cost of doing business.

One time a black lady from Tulsa came to Okmulgee to spend the weekend with her black girlfriend. She slept on the couch. It was summer and the windows were open. A man came in and raped her. I filed rape charges and took the defendant to trial. Ed Boatman was the trial judge. We put on a good case for the prosecution. Then the Defense attorney as always entered his Demur to the Evidence (He was saying to the court that even if everything put on were true it was not enough to justify a conviction) fully expecting to have it overruled and to move on with the trial. Judge Boatman sustained the demur to the evidence ending the trial and freeing the defendant who could not be further prosecuted for this crime because he had been put in jeopardy in front of a jury. I went to Judge Boatman and asked him why he did that. He said, "It was nothing but a nigger rape case." I appealed the case to the Court of Criminal Appeals where it was found that Judge Boatman should not have sustained the demur to the evidence. At least I got on the record that he was wrong.

Operating Procedures for My District Attorney District

I had an operating procedure that called for me or one of my Assistant District Attorneys to be notified whenever something serious happened. One morning I opened my front door and picked up my morning newspaper; the headlines told of a downtown seven-story building burning and collapsing in the street crushing one of our firetrucks. The Chief of Police told me they had just been too busy to call that night. From the look of things that seemed to be the case.

THE COURT REPORTER MURDER

Shortly before time to close the office for the day on Feb. 3, 1981, I was sitting in my Okmulgee District Attorney's office working on upcoming trial matters when Assistant District Attorney Roy Powell called and said: "Jim! you had better come out! Ray has been shot!"

Ray Courtemanche was undoubtedly the most politically powerful person in Okmulgee County, and his influence extended to the State Capitol and apparently even to Washington, D.C.

In that call Roy informed me that Ray had been shot at his home on Mission. I immediately drove to Ray's house. A number of officers were already there. I looked into the crime scene and saw Ray lying on the floor in a pool of blood. I saw what I needed to see to know the questions I would need to address during trial. I left the detailed investigation work to the investigating officers.

One of the first officers on the scene was an Okmulgee police officer who took a written statement from our only witness, the lady who lived next door. This statement taken at that time was vitally important to the trial of this case.

Remember we had no cell phones then, only land lines. There was so much telephone traffic that the entire Okmulgee telephone system collapsed under the load, and it was some time before service was restored. Apparently, many people were calling everybody they could think of to say that they had not committed the killing. Criminal enterprises and political groups were anxious that they not be blamed for the killing of Ray Courtemanche. That evening it looked like a hundred law enforcement officers were scurrying around to locate the killer. The Okmulgee Police department was there, as was the Okmulgee County Sheriff and agents from the Oklahoma State Bureau of Investigation. I thought I even saw federal agents there, but O.S.B.I. was the primary investigative agency as the investigation got under way. The number of officers was undoubtedly far lower than the initial activity made it appear.

INVESTIGATION

Ray was shot about 4:15 p.m. on Feb. 3, 1981.

The lady who lived next door to the south had observed Ray drive into his drive on her side of his house.

She had earlier placed her trash can near the street on his property. She put her baby down and started to explain why she had her trash can on his property when she saw that he had already moved his trash can from the front of his house.

She heard a noise and walked out into her front yard and saw a man running across the Courtemanche yard to a red car with black trim parked on the drive in front of Ray's house. The man saw her and turned his head away trying to pull a red ski-mask over his head. He pointed a gun in his right hand toward the lady and drove off to the south on Mission Street at a fast clip. She did not recognize the man but later after the case had developed when she was told that Dexter Bailey was the suspect, she became frightened, so frightened that I was told that she and her family moved a couple of hundred miles away.

The lady ran to the back door of Ray's house yelling "Ray" and found him lying on the floor. She went inside and touched him to see if he had any pulse, then saw the wound and left. She went home and called an ambulance and her husband and then ran outside screaming.

A man was driving on Highway 75 when he turned east onto 36th street. He met a red car coming from the east driving fast. He pulled to the shoulder and saw that the driver was a white man with medium length brown hair. Later he was shown a composite picture of the suspect and was shown a photo lineup but was unable to identify the driver.

Still another man had gotten off work and went to visit a friend who lived at a mobile home park on Mission. He left the friend's and drove north on Mission and saw a red car with black trim pull out from one of the houses on Mission and traveled south. The car got the man's attention because it was traveling fast and seemed to be fishtailing and was in his lane for a short time. He saw the driver and described him as a white male in his early 30s, clean shaven, with medium length brown hair. He said that the car was clean with no decals, and the driver had something red in his hand and appeared ready to toss it into the back seat. He saw a woman out in the front yard crying and thought they had had a fight, so he didn't think much about it.

A law enforcement officer showed this man a photo lineup, but he picked out a photo of someone other than the defendant charged in this case. A local attorney, went to the home of this man and tried to get a signed statement from him. The man was very uncomfortable and apparently mixed up the story he had previously given O.S.B.I. and refused to sign the statement.

On the morning of Feb. 4, 1981, a man was driving from his residence west of Okmulgee on his way to work in town. He crossed a bridge over the Deep Fork River and saw a gun lying on the bridge. He stopped and picked up the gun, a .38 caliber Colt Detective Special, by putting a pencil thru the trigger guard and lifting it. The gun was delivered to law enforcement officers.

Law enforcement officers interviewed a student at Oklahoma State Tech who drove a red 1980 Ford Mustang with a Wyoming tag. He worked part-time for K.D. Bailey on the Bailey Ranch, which was managed by Mr. Bailey's son, Kenneth Dexter Bailey. It came out that the student's red Mustang was driven by Kenneth Dexter Bailey about the time of the Courtemanche murder. Reportedly Dexter had asked to borrow the car because he was going to try to collect money from some guy who would run off if he saw his vehicle. He had supper with Dexter and his wife, and then as he started to leave, he had to change a flat on the front left wheel of his car.

The A.T.F. traced the ownership of the .38 Colt and found that it had been sold to a man living in California in 1960. This man subsequently moved to Luther, Okla., and about 10 years before the murder he had given the gun to his daughter who pawned it at the Golden Pawn Shop in Tulsa, Okla., about four years before Ray was killed.

This gun was traced as having been purchased at the Golden Pawn Shop in Tulsa by Brett Richard Bailey, the brother of Kenneth Dexter Bailey. When O.S.B.I. and A.T.F. agents contacted Brett Richard Bailey and showed him the Tulsa Police department form showing the purchase by him, he called his father, K.D. Bailey, the attorney father of Kenneth Dexter Bailey, who had advised him not to make a statement.

When Ray's wife was interviewed, she said that she had no idea who would want to hurt her husband and that the composite drawing being circulated by O.S.B.I. didn't look like anyone she knew. She also said that she did not know all of her husband's business or political contacts. She did tell the sheriff that Dexter was at their home the day before the murder and when she arrived, he suddenly left. She understood that Dexter was asking about Ray helping him get a job but she thought that was strange since his own father knew enough people to get his own son a job.

Ed Boatman had been County Attorney for Okmulgee County in the early 1950's and by the time of Ray's murder had been appointed to one of two District Judge positions in Okmulgee County. It seemed likely to me that Ed Boatman would make an effort to be involved in the development of the investigation. This seems consistent with the case of State ExRel. Boatman v. Payne, 257 P2d 842 filed while he was County Attorney wherein he attempted to use a writ of mandamus to force a judge to render a decision he felt should be imposed. The Criminal Court of Appeals of Oklahoma cited State v. Valdez, 59 P2d 328. "It is clearly apparent that the trial court had jurisdiction herein to refuse the application for revocation of the suspended sentence herein involved, and relief against the court's action would not lie through the writ of mandamus." The court refused to grant the writ of mandamus that Mr. Boatman had requested.

As District Attorney I had the duty to decide if any charge should be filed against any individual and if so what charge. I was the Chief Law Officer for the counties in my District, Okmulgee and McIntosh Counties. I was not the Chief Law Enforcement officer, that was the Sheriff in each county. As the Chief Law officer I had the responsibility to decide whom to charge and on what charges. Therefore, I made an effort to keep up with this significantly developing case.

Unbeknown to me but not surprisingly the O.S.B.I. interviewed Ed Boatman shortly after the murder. He undoubtedly described his long relationship with Ray including some business connections along the way. I feel sure that he would have described Ray's involvement in elections and pointed out who he believed were Ray's enemies. A defamation suit had been filed by Ray and Kenneth Butler against a newspaper, a business and a couple of individuals.

I was later informed that Ed Boatman encouraged the O.S.B.I. to hypnotize my only witness very shortly after the murder, and as I was to learn it was performed in a non-neutral setting, running the risk of contamination of the memory of my witness. This was done without my knowledge. At that time, I was already certified by the Law Enforcement Hypnosis Institute as a Forensic Hypnotist, trained to retrieve lost memories. Hypnosis should be used only as a last resort. Even then if it involves legal matters, it must be done very carefully, hopefully with a good video record of exactly what transpires. In this case we had the interview by the Okmulgee officer before our only witness was hypnotized setting out what she saw and this did not materially differ from her post-hypnosis rendition. Even though it showed consistency and the lack of contamination of her memory the fact that she had been hypnotized created questions of doubt about this mysterious process called hypnosis and its impact on people involved in the case. A jury can convict only when it finds evidence of guilt beyond a reasonable doubt. Hypnosis as done in this case created some doubt.

As the investigation continued, one of the Okmulgee detectives mentioned to me that Ray had had an affair with a local woman some time before the murder. He knew that I knew the lady, who was attractive. He said that he was not comfortable interviewing her and he asked me to interview her. I called her to my office. She denied any affair with Ray, but even if it had happened, I was satisfied that there was no connection to the murder. I suspect the detective was poking a little fun at me even though there was never any improper contact between her and me. There has to be a little levity even when things are deadly serious.

Kenneth Butler had been the Assistant District Attorney just before I arrived to take the position he had vacated. In those early days we would try two full D.U.I. jury trials each day until after a couple of court terms he was worn out and we cut down the load. That did help him be recognized as an experienced criminal lawyer.

Kenneth Butler had been a business partner with Ray Courtemanche. They were involved in convenience stores and some real estate, and they shared an office. K.D. Bailey had been the State Senator, but Kenneth Butler defeated him and became the State Senator. K.D. Bailey had owned real estate, which was rented for state offices, but after the election Butler and Ray Courtemanche rented property for state offices to occupy. That reduced money coming in to K.D. Bailey and increased money coming to Courtemanche and Butler.

After law enforcement officers had connected the dots leading from the murder to Kenneth Dexter Bailey they visited their prime suspect. He claimed to have been at his father's law office about the time of the murder taking care of a race horse bill. He described buying a newspaper and pastry at a local bakery. He indicated that he had used his employee's red car because it was at the ranch and had gas in it. Also, his pickup would be needed by his wife to pick up his son after school. He then related having worked with some cattle and taking a shower and shaving his mustache before going to the Moose Lodge, where he played poker into the evening.

Dexter said he went to Ray the day before the murder to see if he would help him get into court reporter school. As I understand it K.D., Dexter's dad, had encouraged his son to quit the rodeo circuit and get a real job.

The day before the murder he was at Ray's home talking with Ray. He indicated that when Ray's wife came in, he realized that it was getting late and he was to take his son somewhere.

Dexter did admit having guns, including a .38 revolver Colt Detective; he didn't know when he last fired it. He said he won the revolver in a poker game out of state. The officers asked to search his home which he refused until he called his father who agreed and came to the house and told the officers that his son had cooperated enough. Dexter's father refused to allow a picture to be taken of his son. Later that day Dexter went to the Police department and allowed a picture to be taken and explained further that the reason for taking the shower was that when he got home the afternoon of the murder he had diarrhea and messed his clothes.

Potential witnesses to the newspaper purchase and the pastry purchase were unable to confirm Dexter's story.

There was a report that prior to the murder Dexter had asked about purchasing a silencer for his gun.

There was a witness who reported hearing gunshots and seeing Dexter with a gun in his hand in the area between his house and the house of a hired hand early the morning of the murder.

A hired hand ran an errand, and when he returned he found that Dexter had used his car. After supper with Dexter and his wife, as he started to leave, he found that he had a flat tire that he had to change. He said that Dexter was wearing a blue goose down jacket, lace up boots, and a cowboy hat.

A woman said that Dexter's wife was upset with Dexter because he had burned up all the newspapers she was going to use to house break a young puppy. It was my understanding that while law enforcement officers were on their property Dexter's wife told a lady who was present and had observed Dexter shooting a gun in the area of the trash cans not to mention this fact to the officers.

Obviously, there were other interviews by law enforcement and lots of discussions with law enforcement officers to be certain that all the dots were connected leading from the murder to the prime suspect, Kenneth Dexter Bailey, when I filed a charge against him for the crime of the murder of Ray Courtemanche.

LAW ENFORCEMENT OFFICERS

PRESENTED THE RESULTS OF THEIR INVESTIGATION TO THE DISTRICT ATTORNEY

Law enforcement officers presented the results of their investigation to District Attorney James D. Jordan. Their investigation essentially showed:

Ray Courtemanche was shot in the back of his head about 4:15 PM on Feb. 3, 1981, while entering the back door of his home on South Mission, in the City of Okmulgee, County of Okmulgee, Oklahoma.

A neighbor, a lady, heard the shot and saw a man run from the back of the Courtemanche home carrying a gun in his right hand; he pulled on a red ski-mask and pointed the gun at her. The man got in a red car with black trim parked on the circle drive in front of the Courtemanche home and drove south on Mission at a fast clip swerving at times.

At least two drivers saw the red car driving South on Mission then West on 36th Street. The red car was driving too fast for the road conditions.

On Feb. 4, 1981, a man was driving from his home west of Okmulgee when he drove over a bridge crossing the Deep Fork River where he saw a gun lying on the bridge. He retrieved the gun and turned it in to law enforcement.

Law enforcement interviewed a student attending Oklahoma State Tech, a post-secondary vocational school in Okmulgee. The student drove a red 1980 Ford Mustang with a Wyoming tag. He worked part time for K.D. Bailey on the Bailey Ranch, which was managed by Kenneth Dexter Bailey. The red car was driven by Kenneth Dexter Bailey about the time of the murder of Ray Courtemanche. The student had to change a flat tire on the front left wheel of his car before he could drive home.

The A.T.F. traced the gun picked up from the bridge as having been purchased by Brett Richard Bailey, the brother of Kenneth Dexter Bailey at the Golden Pawn Shop in Tulsa, Okla.

On Feb. 4, 1981, three .38 caliber bullet casings were found in a trash can located outside the fence around the residence of Kenneth Dexter Bailey and outside the fence around the residence of a hired hand.

Consent to search was given, and a red ski-mask was taken from the house occupied by Kenneth Dexter Bailey on Feb. 8, 1981. A burnt zipper was removed from a trash can.

A search warrant was issued on Feb. 20, 1981, for the area behind Kenneth Dexter Bailey's house. Three projectiles and several casings were found and submitted to the O.S.B.I. laboratory.

On Feb. 26, 1981, the Firearms and Tool Mark Examiner for the O.S.B.I. determined that the revolver found on the Deep Fork bridge had fired the death projectile and that the three spent .38 cartridges found in the trash can behind Kenneth Dexter Bailey's house had been fired by the murder weapon.

Law enforcement had connected the dots from the murder to Kenneth Dexter Bailey, and there was no evidence suggesting that any other person was responsible for the murder.

Kenneth Dexter Bailey, Jr was charged with First Degree Murder on March 2, 1981, in the District Court of Okmulgee County. Kenneth Dexter Bailey was released on $100,000 bond.

Two witnesses were arrested on Material Witness Warrants and released on their own recognizance.

PRECURSOR TO PRELIMINARY HEARING

As an Assistant District Attorney, Judge and District Attorney, I have been involved in a good number of preliminary hearings. Most are rather short, an hour or so. Some go longer, but I suspect if we checked we would find that most would be no longer than two or three hours. The Young brothers from Sapulpa, Okla., were interesting lawyers. One brother was the District Attorney for his district. The other brother was the State Senator for his district and engaged in the practice of criminal law. The Senator would come to Okmulgee to defend various people charged with crimes. He always called me the smiling judge. When it came to Preliminary Hearings, he would always have one more question; it was always slightly different so that exact question had never been asked. He would go so long while I was Special Judge hearing these matters I would frequently have to cut him off and stop the hearing to get all the cases heard. That left him in a position from which he could argue that he had not been allowed to have a full and fair hearing, but there was usually no real delay in getting cases to trial.

The suggestion had been made that I withdraw from prosecuting Dexter Bailey. Some people may have thought I could not win such a politically charged case. Maybe some people felt that I would favor one side over the other. There may have been those who thought that no matter how the trial came out – win or lose – I could not be reelected if I conducted it. I felt that it was important to put on a full and fair trial. I knew that out of area attorneys could not know the inner working of the county; I didn't know them all, but I did know many. Because it was as significant a case as it was, I did secure assistance. I was the only District Attorney that I knew of who was trained in investigative forensic hypnosis, which was an important part of this case. I devoted my full time to the preparation of the case letting my assistants conduct all the remaining matters. When information was leaking out of my office, I moved all of my preparation involving the case to my house with brick walls and thick drapes and never discovered any additional information leaks.

PRELIMINARY HEARING

The state capital was and still is in Oklahoma City, which is in Oklahoma County. Oklahoma City is the largest city in the state. Consequently, the District Attorney there has more lawyers serving as Assistant District Attorneys than we had in my district. Bob Macy, the District Attorney for Oklahoma County sent three Assistant District Attorneys to assist with this case. Because a defense attorney, Ed Parks, had subpoenaed the head of the O.S.B.I. to come testify in our Preliminary Hearing the Attorney General sent an Assistant Attorney General. The Okmulgee City Attorney was present to watch out for the interest of the Okmulgee Police department . Of course, I was much involved.

Ed Parks, who was from Tulsa, appeared at the Preliminary Hearing wearing a cape, top hat and carrying a cane – a colorful person.

The defendant was represented by Boyd and Parks with both Ed Parks and Charles Dunn appearing, as well as by K.D. Bailey and Dennis Seacat of the firm Bailey, Romine & Seacat.

The Preliminary Hearing started on Monday June 15 and ended on June 24, 1981, an exceptionally long preliminary hearing.

The Attorney General moved to quash the Subpoena Duce Tecum requiring the head of the O.S.B.I. to appear in this Preliminary Hearing. Mr. Parks was asking for photographs, tape recordings, records of payments to informants, etc. The argument was made that this request was overly broad and cited statutory authority, as well as U.S. vs Nixon, 41 Lawyers Edition 2nd 1058, which held that the request had to be relevant, not otherwise producible in advance of trial; the defendant cannot be properly prepared for trial without inspection ahead of time, and it must be a good faith request and not a fishing expedition. Ed Parks argued that he had been in cases where the O.S.B.I. was involved where on examining an O.S.B.I. agent he would be told that that agent did not have the item. Rather it was in the possession of some other agent; Mr. Parks stated that if he requested the top guy there would be no passing the buck and he would get to see all the evidence. There was also argument that the Okmulgee Police department was delaying in the submission of evidence; the City Attorney argued against the release of information. The case of Stafford vs District Court of Oklahoma County, 595 P2d 797, 1979, was cited to support the proposition that the prosecution was under no duty to provide exculpatory evidence prior to the preliminary hearing, that discovery was to take place subsequent to preliminary hearing. The Judge quashed the subpoena for O.S.B.I. records and records of the Okmulgee Police department and advised defense attorneys that subsequent to the preliminary hearing all exculpatory evidence, all technical reports, all signed sworn statements, any conviction records of any witnesses and records used to refresh memory should be available the them.

Then there was another conference with all the lawyers and the judge on the admissibility of testimony by Jean Dugger, the next-door neighbor who the state intended to put on as a witness. The defense objected because she had been hypnotized. A tape was made of the hypnotic session, and a copy of the tape had been provided to Mr. Parks. He had heard the tape but there was further discussion about the quality of the tape. It was agreed that the original tape would be made available for review by the defense.

Mr. Parks argued further that the case had received wide publicity in the news media, which could taint the selection of a fair and impartial jury. He argued that what evidence is kept out should not be disclosed in the news media.

Mr. Bailey argued that his request amounted to a request of the court to hear the Motion to Suppress prior to the admission of the evidence. He contended that damage would be done if the court's ruling came after the news media had published the evidence.

The Court reasoned that really had to do with a jury that had been impaneled, and the judge did not believe that he could keep the entire community from hearing evidence or the prosecution from hearing evidence. The court further said that the motion to suppress would be taken up as each witness testified. The judge noted that there were 50 to 60 witnesses, seven witnesses would be held to testify and the others would be on call.

TESTIMONY AT THE PRELIMINARY HEARING

The state called Billie Jean Dugger who lived next door south of Ray Courtemanche on the date he was killed. She had known him since she and her husband had purchased their house about a year and a half before the killing. By her account on Feb. 3, 1981, at approximately 4:20 p.m. she was in her living room in the front of the house when she heard and recognized the sound of Ray's car. She saw him pull up to the mail box to get the mail as always. Her child cried in another room, so she went to check on the child. She intended to catch Ray and explain why her trash can was on his property. She saw Ray walk to get his trash can. She checked the child, walked out the door and started down the front steps when she heard a loud noise; at that instant she did not know what the noise was. She saw a person running from the back of Ray's house toward the front of Ray's house. The person turned, glanced at her, seemed startled, and turned back around. She estimated that he was approximately 30 to 40 feet from her. She continued to walk and they got closer. He turned and pulled a red ski mask down over his face. He turned away and continued to run to a vehicle. She got within about 10 feet of the man. He jumped off the upper level, proceeding very quickly. Before he got into the car, he turned wearing the ski mask and raised a gun in her direction. She heard his car speed away very quickly and turned back. She ran to the lower part of the drive intending to get the tag number, but the car was too far away. He slowed and looked back at her. She thought he might intend to return; she turned back toward her house. He sped away quickly.

She ran to Ray's back door on the east side of his house where she saw Ray through his storm door lying in his doorway. She opened the door intending to touch him and saw the wound and realized that he was dead. She ran home, called an ambulance and then her husband. She went back to Ray's back door where she saw that Ray had not moved.

She went to the front of her drive and screamed to the golf course across the street; apparently no-one heard her. She saw the vehicle of Jim Newport, an employee at the drug store, approaching; she stopped him. Both she and Jim went to check Ray; Jim checked for a pulse but found none and he waited with her for the ambulance.

She described the man who ran as being in his 30's and estimated his height at six feet. He had dark hair. He was in motion and his hair caught in the wind. He had an athletic build, and she estimated his weight at 170-175pounds. She said that he was wearing dark clothes like blue jeans or slacks and a jacket if she were not mistaken. His hair was not long; it was not over his ears. He had dark eyes and no glasses. She didn't remember any facial hair. He had an item in his right hand; she realized it was a gun when he raised his arms to pull the ski mask down and she saw the gun clearly. She described the car as having the body style of a Mercury Capri, red with black trim around the windows and bumper. She saw no bumper stickers. She saw the tag on the rear of the car with a light background and dark letters, but it was too far to read it clearly.

She saw similarities between the defendant, Kenneth Dexter Bailey, and the man she saw that day, but she said she couldn't positively identify him.

The defense attorney, Ed Parks, wanted to hear the hypnosis tape and reserve cross examination of Billie Jean Dugger until Tuesday afternoon.

The next witness was the forensic medical examiner who testified to his qualifications and experience and testified that Ray was shot in the back of his head while alive. He further testified that in his opinion Ray was shot from three feet or less, and the evidence did not suggest that it was high-powered ammunition. He did not find the bullet. He also testified about the chain of custody of various pieces of evidence and procedures.

The next witness was Richard Powell. About 4:15 p.m. he had been driving north on Mission, the street in front of Ray's home. He saw a small red car come out of a drive and swerve toward him going south on Mission. He didn't see the driver, but did see something red in his hand wadded up as though he were going to throw it in the back seat. Mr. Powell had to pull onto the shoulder. He described the driver of the red car as having brown hair of medium length. He said that the red car seemed to be either a Capri or a Mustang, fairly new, bright red with black molding around the bottom. He also saw a lady with brown hair wearing glasses down by the road going to her house. He saw no glasses, ear rings or hat on the driver. He had seen pictures of the defendant, Kenneth Dexter Bailey, in the newspaper and had seen a composite drawing. "I don't know if it was Dexter or not," he said. He did say that the composite was fairly close but he saw the driver only from the side, hair was half way to the ear and he saw no beard or mustache. The O.S.B.I. had shown him a picture line-up consisting of probably 10 pictures, but he did not see the driver well enough to pick out any picture. He testified that he had not been hypnotized. He did see Dexter's picture on TV, but the hair of the driver was longer.

The next witness was Hadley Crook, a National Guard Technician. He testified that at about 4:00 p.m. he turned onto 36th street and he met a car driving at a high rate of speed coming over a hill; he had to pull off onto the side. He described the car as a red compact, not a foreign car, American as far as he knew. It was a late model. The driver was Caucasian. He said he didn't know if the driver was a man or a woman, but he thought a man. Hair was straight down over his eyes, ear length. The composite drawing looked similar, but the hair was fluffy, not slicked down.

The next witness was Raymond Caudill who testified that he lived west of Okmulgee. On Feb. 4, 1981, he was on his way to work, and as he crossed the Deep Fork river bridge, he saw a pistol lying on the bridge. He used a pencil to pick up the pistol and locked it in his pickup. He had heard a report of the shooting on the 7:30 morning news. He told his boss about finding the pistol, and his boss called the police.

The next witness was Paul Rose, owner of the Golden Pawn Shop in Tulsa. On Jan. 20, 1978, he sold a Colt detective special revolver, number 750207, to Brett Richard Bailey. He identified the gun as the same one identified as State's Exhibit # 16. He also testified that Brett Bailey had talked with him about three or four months before the Preliminary Hearing about the gun. He also testified about another individual who had worked for him and had stolen the gun, but said that he had recovered the gun. Mr. Rose did tell Brett Bailey that there had been inquiries about the gun.

There was further discussion about the defense motion to suppress evidence.

The next witness was Mike Stacy. He testified that on Feb. 3, 1981, that he lived on the Bailey Ranch and worked there as a ranch hand. He testified that the house where he lived was about 15 yards from the house occupied by Dexter Bailey. He said that he had made a trip to Oklahoma City with Dexter on Jan. 30, 1981, and there was some discussion about silencers, but Dexter did not ask where he could get one. On Feb. 3, 1981, he heard shots, looked between the houses, saw Dexter with something in his hand and asked if he got what he shot at. Mrs. Stacy heard shots about 10:00 to 10:30. Mr. Stacy saw Dexter during the morning hours of Feb. 3, and Dexter had his mustache. About 3:30 that afternoon he did not see Dexter but later he saw him without his mustache; Dexter commented on shaving it because of ringworm. Dexter borrowed the red Mustang belonging to another ranch hand and returned to the ranch about 4:00 or 4:30 p.m. Law officers asked about guns and which house he lived in and what parts of the property he had access to. Officers returned and talked with Mike Stacy who gave them permission to walk over property to which he had access. There was what appeared to be a fresh bullet hole in a trash can. Officers searched under the authority of permission given. They had a search warrant and recovered ballistic evidence.

Billie Jean Dugger was recalled to the stand and testified that she had attended night law school a little over three years. She was an intelligent alert witness and at one point responded to questioning by saying, "You have reversed the events." She was questioned several times on the day of the murder. She was immediately taken to the Okmulgee Police department and gave a statement that was reduced to writing; She read and signed it. She testified that the details were as appeared in her statement. While on the trip to the police department with the officers they drove past a local car dealership, and she showed them the body style of the red car that had left the scene of the killing. She testified that the man leaving Ray's house raised the gun in her direction but did not aim at her. The officer just listened and typed; THIS WAS EXTREMELY IMPORTANT. The O.S.B.I. was considering hypnosis as an aid to getting complete information to find the killer. The next morning, she went to the police department , and the O.S.B.I. wanted to perform hypnosis that morning. The large courtroom in the courthouse was available so they had Mrs. Dugger sit in the judge's chair while she was being hypnotized. The O.S.B.I. agent conducting the session and an O.S.B.I. artist were the only other people in the room at the time; Mrs. Dugger faced a wall during the session, and the artist sat behind her, out of her view and said nothing. Mrs. Dugger said that prior to the session she was apprehensive, and the O.S.B.I. agent who was to perform the session explained: "This hypnosis is not what you expect. We will in no way be in control of you. You will be totally coherent. You will be alert to what is going on around you ..." Mrs. Dugger said that she had never previously been hypnotized, nor had she been hypnotized since. Hypnosis was to be an aid in relaxation and thinking about the events of the prior day. She left the courthouse about 1 1/2 hours later. After the hypnosis she worked with the O.S.B.I. artist who was trying to put together a composite drawing of the man who left the murder scene. The hypnotist and the artist were in a rush to get to Weatherford for another case. The composite drawing was shown to her and she was not completely happy with the results. The defense attorney, Ed Parks, had listened to the tape of the hypnotic session. Mrs. Dugger said her memories were also sketchy under hypnosis. She was searching her mind, just as she would have been relaxed in any other state. Someone apparently told Mr. Dugger that they had caught a man and his car was white and he was blond; your wife was wrong. That turned out to be an entirely unrelated matter, but it illustrates some of the frenzied confusion going on at the time. She was not able to make a positive identification from a photo lineup.

Richard Coleman was the next witness. He worked on the Bailey Ranch until sometime in March, riding colts to break them in, until he worked himself out of a job. He owned a 1980 Mustang with a 1980 Wyoming tag, and he still owned it on Feb. 3, 1981. The car was a three-door sedan, sports package, 4-speed red with a bit of black trim. Dexter asked if he could borrow the car because he was trying to catch a guy to collect money who would run if he recognized his car. It was a cool day, and Dexter was wearing a navy-blue goose down jacket with fur collar and jeans. He testified that he had talked with the defense attorney, Ed Parks, and most of the people around the defense table and told them what he had told the police and what his testimony was to be. They did not ask him to change it. Dexter borrowed the car about 3:15 to 3:30 in the afternoon. Mr. Coleman left the feed room about 4:30 to 5:00 p.m. and turned out calves for roping a little after 5:00. Mr. Coleman discovered that his right front tire was flat. He had supper with Dexter and his family. He went to the car wash because he had just returned from Wyoming, where the car had picked up road chloride.

A local lawyer, Dale Rainey, was called to testify but there was an in-camera hearing to see if his testimony should be allowed. He knew Ray Courtemanche in a professional way since Ray arrived in Okmulgee in the early 1950's. He had known Kenneth Dexter Bailey since he was a kid. On Dec. 2, 1980, Dale Rainey went to Ray's office on business. Ray told him that he had been threatened and he just wanted someone to know about it. Who threatened you? Bailey. It wasn't K.D.; it was one of the young ones. What did he threaten you about? He's demanding that I get him a position and told me that if I didn't, he would blow me away. At this point the defense attorney, Ed Parks, brought out that Dale Rainey had said, "They are trying to blackmail you into getting them a position. Is that what you are saying?" he replied, "That's it." Mr. Parks presented the judge a brief prepared on the question of hearsay and double hearsay. I, the district attorney, pointed out that the defense brief presented to the court and read by the judge appeared rather long and said, "We have never been supplied with a copy, don't know what it says, do not know how to respond." Mr. Dunn advised the court that they did not wish to wave any work product privilege because the brief is in the form of a memorandum from myself to Mr. Parks.

The court asked if that limitation was waved and received a positive response. Then the judge noted, "When you gave it to me you certainly did". The court allowed the testimony of Dale Rainey for purposes of the Preliminary Hearing over the objection of the defense.

The judge announced that he had been handed a copy of a Motion To Quash Subpoena on behalf of Brett Bailey, the brother of the defendant Kenneth Dexter Bailey. It was announced that Brett was in the hospital with foot surgery. The motion was confessed, granted and held for naught.

Examination of D.F. Rainey resumed. Mr. Rainey pointed out Kenneth Dexter Bailey. He had had no social relationship with Ray Courtemanche. Mr. Rainey had been a judge in Okmulgee County in 1966, having been appointed by Governor

Henry Bellmon. He was asked if one of Ray Courtemanche's sons had appeared before him on a second-degree burglary charge; he said it was possible but he had no memory of it. Mr. Rainey testified that he had not repeated Ray's conversation to Mrs. Rainey. He did testify that he ran into a local bail bondsman who indicated that he was doing some work on this case, and Mr. Rainey told him about Ray's conversation. Then I, District Attorney James D. Jordan, came to his office and talked with him about it. Mr. Rainey testified that he and K.D. Bailey had some important cases on opposite sides. In one case one of his clients came to him dissatisfied, and he gave her the file, which she took to K.D. Bailey. Mr. Rainey testified that he had not discussed his testimony with Mrs. Courtemanche. He did recall that an evidence man had come to his home.

The next witness called was Helen Courtemanche, the window of the deceased. She testified that she was the Secretary of the Okmulgee County Election Board. She returned home on Feb. 2, 1981, about 5:00 or 5:15 pm. Dexter Bailey was there, and he immediately jumped up as if she had startled him. Ray said to her "This is Dexter, you remember him, he is looking for a job." She testified that his hair was loose, not plastered down against his head like today. Ray said he would help him find a job if he could. Mrs. Courtemanche testified that she and Ray had been married 30 years in August. He adopted her two sons. They moved to Okmulgee in 1956 when Ray was looking for a job and worked for Judge Barnes until Judge Barnes was appointed to the Oklahoma Supreme court. Their son had ridden and played with Kenneth Dexter Bailey. Dexter and his family did not come to their house, and she couldn't remember being in the Bailey house. Mickey McElroy had been Secretary of the County Election Board while she was assistant. When Mickey resigned, she was appointed as Secretary. She testified that Dexter's hair is different today. Ray was employed by Judge Woodliff until he resigned and then worked for Judge Boatman. Ray was very interested in the affairs of the community and offering to help Dexter was no different from his help for other people. In addition to his work as a court reporter Ray was involved in several other business affairs. Eddie Evans and Kenneth Butler were business associates. He had bought lots in Henryetta with an attorney who practiced there. Ray owned buildings with David Jones and Kenneth Butler. The Welfare Office, the Tag Agency and the Parole office rented space in these buildings. Ray worked as a court reporter and reported all of American Airline's hearings. Ray with Kenneth Butler and Eddie Evans owned two convenience stores. Ray was a director on the Board of the First National Bank in Henryetta, and he owned stock in that bank. Helen could not remember Ray ever telling her he had a terrible dislike for anyone; he was well liked and had good feelings for people in the community. A bail bondsman, Mack Kelly, was a good friend and had been in their home many times.

Ray was an ardent supporter of Kenneth Butler, who defeated K.D. Bailey for the office of state Senator. She knew the elected county officials. She was asked about writing a letter to me, District Attorney James D. Jordan, suggesting I disqualify myself or seek outside help, because I had a backlog of cases and she understood that I was not sure that I would have all the time needed to take care of the case properly. She responded that I, the District Attorney, agreed to seek help and would welcome help. She said that the letter followed conversation and was not at the suggestion of attorney friends. She had talked with her family and an attorney, Dick Gibbon, about what happened. Immediately after the shooting she was take to the home of Mack Kelly where she talked with O.S.B.I. agents (not in the presence of Mack Kelly or his wife) and spent the night. A Henryetta attorney, Richard Hutton, took care of the probate; she was the sole beneficiary. Ray owned one rental house. She was asked if Ray had any connections in Dallas or Detroit, Mich.; this was apparently an effort to learn of any organized crime connections that Ray may have had, but none ever came to light or were even suspected.

Dennis Grable, a member of the Okmulgee Police department , was dispatched to the Courtemanche home at 4:20 and arrived at 4:21. He saw the body, called the detective and returned to his duty when the detective got there.

Lt. Roy Fields was the next witness. He received the call about 4:20 and went to the Courtemanche home where he spent about four hours. He worked with Chief of Police Chester Hodge. Thirty to forty general information interviews were conducted. The only person ever really considered to be a suspect was the defendant. He asked the ambulance crew if he was signal 30, that is, was he dead? Yes. He told them to pack up and leave. He stationed Officer Fry at the door to see that no-one entered or left. He searched the house to see if there were any other victims. He made photos of the crime scene and area. (Assistant District Attorney Roy Powell arrived and saw what had happened and called me, District Attorney James D. Jordan, and advised me that Ray had been shot and that I had better come out.) Helen Courtemanche was arriving with Mack Kelly. She was getting out of the car and had to be put back into the car. He worked with Rodger Chrisco of the O.S.B.I. processing the scene. Evidence was bagged. The storm door was dusted for fingerprints. The O.S.B.I. took finger prints, and a bullet was picked up off the floor. The officers returned to the police department to discuss what they knew, but that night they had no suspect. A section was cut from the curb where a car tire had scrapped it. As the case developed, they talked with Dexter, and he consented to his house being searched. During that time Detective Fields watched TV and visited with Dexter. Detective Fields didn't see any officers remove anything from Dexter's house. They did take a gun or guns. There was more than one search, and the officers found a burned zipper in a trash can, a red ski cap, a ski mask, a gun and ammo.

Chester Hodge, who had been Chief of Police for Okmulgee since 1979, arrived at approximately 4:30 pm. O.S.B.I. agent Chrisco arrived about 5:30. Detective Fields was conducting the investigation, and the chief usually did not make suggestions to him in the course of investigations. Fields did not discuss with Chief Hodge the testimony he had given the day before. Chrisco spotted a spent bullet on the floor. Officer Fry was stationed to keep anyone from entering or leaving the house. The Chief returned to the Police Station. At that point they had no suspect. A number of people were interviewed, perhaps as many as 60. Chief Hodge was asked if he had worked with Agent Chrisco on a load of dope at the airport. But that was the following day, and the O.S.B.I. was not involved; it was handled by the Drug Enforcement Agency out of Oklahoma City.

With everything going on one of the local bankers called his wife and told her to stay inside and keep the doors locked. Gloria Hollis told me "I was scared". There was a lot of fright in the community – so much that people were calling each other to the point that the telephone system collapsed. It took some time to get service restored.

O.S.B.I. agent Rodger Chrisco made sure the utility room where Ray was murdered was secure, then processed the scene. A lead projectile was lying 1 foot and 5 inches northwest of the victim's head on the utility room floor. It was photographed then retrieved. Further investigation revealed that the day of the murder Dexter had borrowed the red car of one of the ranch hands. Dexter claimed he had bought a newspaper and a creampuff and had gone to his father's business. He said he had shaved his mustache because of ringworm. Dexter came to the police station at the request of officers and the D.A. This time he claimed that after borrowing the red car that he ran to the house and found the door locked, was delayed and had an accident in his pants. He said that was the reason he took the shower. Dexter's name first came up on Feb. 4th; he became a suspect when it was learned that he was in a car that matched the description of the getaway car. Defense Attorney Parks asked the O.S.B.I. agent if he was armed and when he received a positive response, he asked the judge if he allowed that. The judge indicated that he had not even thought about it. Interestingly the defense had had arms in the courtroom previous to this. Mr. Parks brought out that no electronic surveillance had been used, witnesses had not been tape recorded, Ray's premises had not been vacuumed and there were no footprints but just outside the door there was a small piece of blue fabric. Officers dropped in to visit with Dexter when he did not know they were coming. They did not serve a search warrant on Dexter but with his permission they took a .38 Special Colt detective and a red ski mask. The officers had secured a search warrant issued by Judge Anne Maroney. The officers decided to go talk with the man. If he let them search, good. If not, they would serve it. Dexter was not under arrest and no Miranda warning was given.

There was a Motion to Quash the third subpoena for Brett Bailey because he was in a hospital in Tulsa, and his doctor was in Grove. The matter was continued until 10:00 the next morning for either the doctor to appear or to review an affidavit from the doctor.

Chain of custody of each item of evidence was carefully laid out throughout this hearing.

Detective Captain Harry Ledbetter of the Okmulgee Police department testified that he carefully picked up the pistol recovered from the bridge, attempting to preserve fingerprints, and kept it under lock and key until he delivered it to an O.SB.I. agent to deliver to the O.S.B.I. lab.

Robin Estes was the O.S.B.I. agent hypnotist. She testified that on Feb. 4, 1981, she picked up a projectile from agent Crisco at the Okmulgee Police department and delivered it to the O.S.B.I. lab in Oklahoma City. She also picked up a gun in a sealed envelope from Okmulgee Detective Ledbetter and delivered it to the O.S.B.I. lab in Oklahoma City. She was at the lab probably three or four hours, left about 1:00 or 2:00 p.m. and returned to Okmulgee about 4:30 or 5:00 p.m.; she brought the gun back and redelivered it to Detective Ledbetter. She remained with these items of evidence while in Oklahoma City where she delivered the projectile to Tom Jordan, who test fired the gun before she took it back to Okmulgee as directed by agent Roger Chrisco. She first took the gun to be tested for trace evidence by the chemist, who looked for fiber, blood, hair etc. on the gun. Then she took it to be checked for fingerprints and then took it to Tom Jordan.

James Pratt had been an O.S.B.I. agent 3 1/2 years. He and agent Powell went to the Bailey ranch on Feb. 4, 1981, to visit with Dexter, but he was not there. Mike Stacy, who was there in front of the frame shop, said he thought Dexter would be back the following weekend, out on the rodeo circuit. Stacy was asked about the red car, and he said Coleman routinely drove a red Mustang and he usually got to the ranch about 10:00 after class and that he had been at the ranch on the 3rd. He was shown the composite drawing. He said he thought it resembled Dexter, but the hair was too long. The day of the murder Stacy had gone to Morris about 3:15 or 3:30. When he returned Bailey was gone with Coleman's car. He estimated that it was close to 5:00 when Dexter returned to the ranch. He knew that Bailey owned some firearms and had been practicing with a hand gun south of the house area. He said to Dexter, "Did you hit it?" or "did you get it?" and Dexter said, "I was just practicing". "If it had been a .22," he said, he probably would not have heard it as clearly as he did from the distance. Stacy invited the officers into the frame shop because it was extremely cold. The agents asked if Stacy was allowed into the shop and he said yes, and he had a key.

A Polaroid picture was taken of a picture of Dexter displayed there; Stacy said Dexter had shaved his mustache off on the 3rd. Pratt next returned to the ranch on the 5th with Powell. Stacy was present when they arrived around 11:30 or noon. Stacy had called and asked them to come out. Dexter's son had told Stacy that Dexter had a .38 pistol. Stacy had a right to go anywhere on the ranch and they didn't need a search warrant and it was OK to search. There was a 55-gallon trash can and an aluminum trash can in the area. Pratt advised Stacy that he had an absolute right to refuse to let them search and request a search warrant; Stacy had said "Anything to help."

Pratt saw a caved in hole in the 55-gallon drum and a caved-out hole on the other side of the drum and noticed that the hole was not rusted. He held a bullet next to the hole to judge its size. Powell noticed a cartridge casing inside the drum, then a second and then a third were found. Before removing these items from the drum, they called Regional Inspector Joe Collins who said to sack them up. So, they put the items in a sack, sealed it and marked the sack for identification. He had held a sack for the shirt the night before at the crime scene. He went with Sheriff Gene Rice to investigate another disturbance in Okmulgee where a gun had been fired near a warehouse by a man who was driving a red Pinto. Pratt was assigned to locate Kenneth Butler and interview him. Pratt believed this was at Mack Kelly's residence and he talked with him about a half hour while agent Estes was present. He did not interview Mr. Kelly at that time.

On the way back to the police department they stopped and interviewed Betty Reynolds, an employee at the Handi-Mart located at 6th Street and Wood. They arrived at the police department about 9:30 or 10:00, then went home to Tulsa. He returned to Okmulgee the next day with Estes because his car was still in the shop. He initially went with Okmulgee detectives Fields and Ledbetter to interview Mr. Caudell at the auto repair shop where he worked. They drove to the bridge where Mr. Caudell had found the gun, and he pointed out the location where he found it. After returning to the police department he was assigned to interview people at the courthouse; agent Crisco wanted him to interview two judges concerning background, Ed Boatman and Anne Moroney. He first interviewed Judge Boatman alone.

Then with agent Powell he interviewed Judge Moroney. He completed the interviews and was back at the police department about 11:00 or 11:15. Then he was assigned to interview Dexter. He was aware that Mrs. Dugger was being under hypnosis and a copy of the composite was given to him just before he left; he had to wait for it to be completed. On the 3rd he went to the ranch and saw only Mike Stacy. He was told Dexter would probably be back that weekend. Dexter had left on the morning of the 4th.

Standing outside Stacy said, "It's cold out here. Do you want to go inside here?" Stacy seemed very relaxed talking with them. At that time Dexter was not a suspect. He said he didn't believe they asked to look around at all that day. They were there about 45 minutes and talked about activities on the 3rd and the vehicle that Coleman drove and the fact that Dexter had left in Coleman's vehicle on the 3rd about 3:30 and returned about 5:00. They spoke with Agent Chrisco and Detective Fields and watched to see if Coleman came to work that day. He didn't, so they went to Oklahoma State Tech where he was a student and asked if he owned a vehicle of the description they were looking for. Yes. He said he was on the Bailey ranch on Feb. 3, 1981, from 3:00 to 6:00 p.m.; he said Dexter had borrowed his car shortly after he arrived and returned about 4:30. He said Dexter said he needed to borrow his car to catch a guy who owed him a gambling debt who would run if he saw his car. He said Dexter had shaved off his mustache on the 3rd. Coleman left the ranch about 7:00 and had to change a flat, then went to a car wash. Coleman gave permission for his car to be inspected and photographed. Mrs. Dugger was brought down to look at the car, which she said looked the same except for the front left tire. She couldn't remember anything about the tag either while under hypnosis or when not hypnotized. Pratt testified that somewhere along the way they went out to the airfield because there was an airplane out there full of marijuana. "We were more in the way than assistance; the Oklahoma Highway Patrol had that matter under good control." They only stayed about five minutes. Then they went to the police department, home and back to the police department the next morning. We were asked to re-contact Mr. Stacy who said Mrs. Stacy had been in the kitchen on the 3rd and heard three or four shots. She saw Dexter firing the gun, open it and fired another and left the area. He said Mrs. Stacy said that she had talked with Dexter's wife who was upset because Dexter had burned some newspapers she was using to train a new puppy in the trash can and they were threatened their trash service would be cut off. Stacy had some question about his relationship with someone on the Okmulgee police department, so when he called, he used the code name Remington. Stacy thought the composite drawing resembled Dexter but younger, and the hair was shorter. Pratt confirmed that there had been no electronic surveillance of any kind. He went to the courthouse to interview Judges Boatman and Moroney just for general information; Judge Moroney had last seen Ray at lunch on the 3rd, and Ray had transcribed a hearing about 3:00 or 3:30. That was the last Judge Boatman had seen of Ray. Judge Moroney was a friend of Ray's wife. Judge Boatman said Ray was very politically active and mentioned K.D. as in the group opposed to Ray's group. It became apparent that there was a discrepancy as to time; it was Pratt's initial impression that Stacy was at the ranch when Coleman arrived, but Coleman had arrived ahead of him. Stacy occupied the rental house and had access to the ranch. Agent Powell had secured a search warrant. The draft search warrant was approved by the D.A. and the judge. However, the search was conducted with permission rather than by executing the search warrant. They found three spent casings, which they put in envelopes and marked. Powell had seen the first casing. Tom Jordan had identified the round found at the murder scene as having been a reload round, rounds in the trash can were three different manufacturers, crimped and at least one was split, indicative of reload ammo. The trash can with the burned contents disclosed remnants of burnt newspapers and a chunk of metal, a zipper. Stacy asked "Why don't you take it?" Also, as the casings were examined Stacy asked "Why don't you take them?" We marked the evidence about 12:15 and left about 12:30 to the police department and to lunch.

Dexter gave permission for the search in his house, so the search warrant was not used, so there was no return of the search warrant.

There was discussion about the filing of the affidavit for the search warrant and defense attorney Parks was informed that it would be filed miscellaneous. The Judge gave him the number.

There was further discussion regarding the search warrant and a great deal of rehash of what had been testified to previously.

The casings had been discovered in the bottom of the trash can one at a time; one was seen and when one was lifted from the bottom of the container residue came with it disclosing another.

O.S.B.I. agent Bob Powell testified that he was hired July 1, 1979, and that previous to that he had worked as a civilian with Naval Intelligence for two years and been in the Air force four years in the Office of Special Investigations. He taught school. His training included 11 weeks at the O.S.B.I. Academy, 12 weeks training with the Air Force Office of Special Investigations in Washington, and three weeks of advanced criminal investigation in the Philippine Islands when he worked there. The instructors were F.B.I. agents, Army C.I.D. instructors, other Air Force instructors, anyone who would be involved in investigations. He did not know Ray before he was murdered. He arrived in Okmulgee on Feb. 4, 1981, about 10:00 A.M. after the inspector had called and told him the night before that he might be needed. At the briefing there was no suspect. He was not focusing on the car but on interviews. He remembered the interview with Judge Moroney, which lasted 30 or 40 minutes, but not with Judge Boatman. He returned to the police department for a briefing. Agent Chrisco told us that he would like for us to return to the Bailey ranch to interview Dexter, who had been to the Courtemanche house the day before. Our firearms examiner had determined that the death projectile was a reload rather than a factory load. We were more concerned with interviewing than with physical evidence at that time. Mike Stacy was glad to talk with us; it was cold and windy so he took us into the frame shop, which was used as a part-time office. He came and went and had a key. Powell did not make any notes but went over Mr. Pratt's notes and said they were accurate. Mr. Pratt asked if there were any pictures of Dexter in the frame shop, and Mike found an older photograph. Pratt also asked the description of Coleman's vehicle, and was told it was small, red with black trim and was a late model. When Mike arrived the previous day, Coleman was there but his vehicle and Dexter were gone. Most of the conversation involved locating the car and determining where it was the previous day. Powell couldn't recall specific questions or answers given. Mr. Pratt took a picture of a picture of Dexter in the frame shop. They talked to Mr. Stacy about a pistol, but Powell wasn't sure if that was on the 4th or 5th. They learned that Bailey did have a pistol and fired it behind the building. A question was asked about a red ski mask; he said his boy, I assume Dexter's son, had one. We weren't accusing anyone of anything at that time. Dexter's name came up, and he had been at Ray's home the day before the shooting. Stacy wanted his name kept out of things as long as possible; there was someone with the local police department with whom he had some issue. Stacy said there was discussion about a silencer – where Dexter could get one; Stacy said he didn't know anything about silencers but that he had heard that a potato placed over the end would work. Powell testified in response to a question: "Well, Sir, it's my understanding that any time you conduct an investigation, that - - especially of this magnitude, you want to make sure the individual you're talking to understands…" This confirms that the O.S.B.I. considered this a significant case. There was additional discussion regarding where Dexter was standing when shooting the gun, search of the premises and the collection of evidence, including a zipper. They returned to the police department about 2:30 or 3:00 when Mr. Chrisco said to give the evidence to Mr. Ottwell to take to Oklahoma City. The evidence was flown to Oklahoma City and delivered to Tom Jordan, again being very careful about chain of custody.

Then there was discussion about subpoena dodges having been run into before. Request was made to have the doctor appear. The doctor was in his office this morning when his signature was secured. Monday morning it was discovered that the Tulsa County Sheriff's office had made a notation "Moved, not found." Further discussion concerned second and third subpoenas and the witness' good faith of not being there because of serious surgery as a result of fracturing two toes. The court ordered Dexter's brother to appear in court on Monday morning at 9:30.

There was a comment that it was unusual for Coleman to lend out his car. Coleman told us that Dexter returned his car approximately 4:30 p.m. Coleman usually went home about 5:00 and was getting concerned about getting it back in time to go home. Then he had to change a flat tire and took his car to the car wash to wash off road film. He didn't know what caused the flat.

O.S.B.I. agent Powell holds a private pilot license and flew an airplane provided by the O.S.B.I.. There were further questions about searching with metal detectors, shovels and screens and finding three .38 short cartridges and two barrels which he transported to Oklahoma City. Mr. Powell made two trips to Oklahoma City, the first with a projectile and the other with projectiles and casings, which he delivered to tool mark examiners Jordan and Looney.

Assistant District Attorney Elliott objected in the name of weariness to cut off the fishing expedition at some point, saying now that we have passed this witness' relevance to our Motions to Suppress, we have passed him through the chain with the items to be litigated in this preliminary hearing. The Court sustained the objection and the defense had no more questions at that time.

O.S.B.I. agent Ottwell received items of evidence from agents Pratt and Powell and Detective Ledbetter and transported them to the lab in Oklahoma City. He testified that he was age 25 and had been with the O.S.B.I. at that time about three or four months. Prior to that he had been employed by the F.B.I. as a secure teletype operator from October 1977 through 1980; prior to that he had been a United Parcel Service employee and loaded trucks while in college. He saw the revolver found on the road in the possession of Detective Ledbetter and never examined it or handled it himself. He transported it from Ledbetter to Powell at the Okmulgee City airport on the 24th; it was in a bag. His assigned area was Okmulgee, Muskogee and Waggoner Counties; he had been talking to an Oklahoma Highway Patrol trooper when he learned of the shooting and he drove to Okmulgee, arriving approximately 8:00 p.m. Officers, press and various news channels were already there; he recalled Channel 8. He was instructed to interview the neighbor lady, Billie Jean Dugger, at her home. Agent Estes and Detective Ledbetter were with him. A vague description of the individual was secured as well as a description of the car. Mrs. Dugger was not evasive. Estes took notes while he took none. Time spent with Mrs. Dugger and her husband was about half an hour. Then they interviewed neighbors south of the Dugger residence; some other residents of the area were not home. Mrs. Dugger had heard a loud report; it startled her and she stopped. She walked thru the steps with him down her steps. She showed him exactly where she stood when she saw the individual and where she stopped. He didn't remember discussing what Mrs. Dugger said to him with either Agent Estes or Detective Ledbetter. His last discussion with counsel for the state was this morning in the D.A.'s office. He testified that he interviewed Mr. Hamilton and others he didn't remember. He was accompanied by the D.A., Mr.

Jordan, and then went to the police department where there was discussion by Okmulgee officers, O.S.B.I. agents and the D.A. as to the course of events and establishing a game plan for continuing the investigation. He returned the next morning. There were a lot of people who needed to be interviewed and he was given instructions by his supervisors to interview Randy Joslin (another court reporter), various people at the courthouse including Judge Maley. No appreciable leads were developed. Defense attorney Parks asked who else he was to interview; Assistant D.A. Elliott objected to getting into work product and pointed out that we have gone a week without objecting; the Court sustained the objection. Agent Mr. Ottwell further testified that during this case that he was called off to work on another case about three weeks after this shooting. He also testified about being at Dexter's premises. Defense Attorney Parks covered a lot of what had already been covered. Mr. Ottwell did testify that on one occasion that Attorneys Seacat and Romine appeared and asked them to leave the premises; nothing was taken from the property at that time.

Tom Jordan appeared to testify. The Court announced that he would allow his testimony to be put on and allow all objections to be brought up on the Motion to Suppress. Tom Jordan testified about his extensive qualifications and experience and that he was firearms and tool mark examiner with the O.S.B.I. and had been for 7 1/2 years. He had worked in this field 8 1/2 years, the first year with the F.B.I. in Washington, D.C., where he underwent 500 hours of classroom instruction in that field. With the O.S.B.I. he worked under training and supervision of Ray Lambert who had over 26 years working in this field. He had an additional 80 hours of training from the F.B.I. Academy, 124 hours from World Wide Association of Firearms and Tool Mark Examiners, 80 hours with Smith & Wesson, 120 hours from the National Rifle Association, another 40 hours with the Chicago Police department. He said he was a member of several professional organizations, read publications and attended workshops and seminars, as well as taking any other type of training that became available. He explained how his work is done. He had made thousands of examinations over the proceeding 8 1/2 years. He carefully explained when and where he had seen this weapon and carefully explained the chain of custody. He also testified about a projectile that had been fired in this firearm, the same firearm that had been used to shoot Ray. He first saw the firearm when it was delivered to him by agent Robin Estes. In reply to questions, he explained that all ammunition is not made the same way or made from the same materials; they are all lead, but some have jackets etc. He explained how a dual microscope is used to compare a test projectile against the submitted projectile. He explained that projectiles shot into sand are sandblasted and the markings are damaged. The envelope containing suspect projectiles are sealed in envelopes and marked for identification.

Larry Mullins, an O.S.B.I. Crime Scene Specialist was put on out of time. There were no fingerprints of value. He also testified that a latent print of value is not obtained very often from a handgun. The only fingerprints he compared were those of the victim and Dexter Bailey.

Mr. Parks mentioned how tired he was and the court pointed out that the prosecution was resting subject to the Defense Motion To Suppress and the appearance of Brett Bailey. Mr. Parks suggested that Brett Bailey be scheduled for Monday and at the conclusion of the state's testimony to let the defense put on their evidence if any in further support of his Motion To Suppress. Mr. Parks talked about needing to spend the weekend to review what else he needed to do. K.D. Bailey commented that what they were talking about was not repetitious. Mr. Parks wanted to be able to put on evidence of ownership of the property where the projectiles were recovered. Mr. Elliott pointed out that legal argument needed to be made and notwithstanding the case in question the evidence should be admitted. Mr. Elliott further pointed out that the state was not relying solely on the consent of Mr. Stacy for the admissibility of the casings. The judge commented that he learned something new every day. Mr. Parks said that Mr. Elliott wanted him to worry all weekend, and the Court pointed out that he wanted him to study all weekend. The Judge then announced that it would be taken up on Monday.

On Monday the District Attorney's office appeared by James D. Jordan, the District Attorney, and Assistant District Attorneys Tom Elliott and David Hardwick. The Defense appeared by Boyd and Parks, including Ed Parks and Charles Dunn, and also by Bailey, Romine and Seacat, including K.D. Bailey and Dennis Seacat.

Brett Bailey appeared and testified that he lived in Tulsa and Defendant Dexter was his brother. He also testified that he was familiar with a pawn shop in Tulsa by the name of Golden Pawn and knew Paul Rose. He bought a .38 Colt blue steal gun from Paul Rose, which was similar to the death weapon. After the O.S.B.I. came to his house he went to the Golden Pawn and ask Paul Rose about the serial number on the gun he had purchased. He last saw the gun in about 1978 when he sold it. He previously had an antique store and then had a booth at a flea market. He had discontinued the antique store and had gone to work for the Ford Motor Company but kept the flea market booth on the side. He had no records regarding the sale of the gun. He remembered O.S.B.I. agents coming to his home to visit with him. He got home and the agents were there. The house was locked and he entered a window. His dog ran out, and he said, "Don't shoot my dog, he won't bite you." The agents wanted to talk about the gun. He told them he would first have to talk to his dad. After he talked with his dad he said to the agents, "I have no comment to make to you gentlemen." His dog was a small miniature boxer. He stepped outside to visit with the agents and showed them his driver's license as requested. He remembered that his dad and the attorney, Mr. Seacat, who was with his father's firm were on the line, but he couldn't remember what was said. At the time of the interview, he owned one weapon, a .25 automatic. He didn't remember how many weapons he had owned; he had sold one or two. He never had a license to sell guns. Mr. Parks on cross examination learned that the men crossed the street and identified themselves and at that time he thinks they showed their badges and asked if they could go inside.

At this point the court pointed out that the state had rested subject to the introduction of the three shell casings, and Assistant District Attorney Elliott stated "That is correct." The court asked, "Mr. Hardwick, do you have any argument you want to make as to the admissibility other than a consent search?"

Mr. Parks asked if they could call one more witness before they made such an argument, that witness being Mrs. Stacy.

There was discussion regarding an affidavit which Mrs. Stacy read and said was still true. She then testified that they had lived on the Bailey ranch nine days before Feb. 3, 1981, and had not previously been on this ranch. Mike had worked there about three weeks, and she had been there one time to see what the house looked like and to see what to get rid of or to buy. She was on the ranch on Feb. 4th and had left a short time to go to Gibson's for groceries and other items. She didn't remember the exact time, but she did remember that it was dark while they were at Gibson's. Assistant District Attorney Elliott asked, what kind of garbage removal service did you enjoy and do you enjoy at the Bailey Ranch? Her response was that she no longer lived there; they had lived there from about Feb. 3rd or 4th to May 1981. The first week or so they would pick up the trash twice a week. There were big containers that serviced two or three houses. Then the service went to one time a week. There was a 55-gallon drum directly behind their house, outside the fence. A truck would pull into the loop drive and pick up their garbage and then go to the stables.

The court then asked, "Are there any more witnesses you would like to call, Mr. Parks?" The reply, "No, No sir".

The court then asked Mr. Hardwick if there was any argument regarding admissibility of shell casings. Mr. Hardwick replied by asking if the court would allow any argument on factual issues as well as legal issues and the court responded in the affirmative.

Then argument was presented regarding consent to search jointly occupied property being valid. Curtilage was discussed, that is the enclosed ground and buildings immediately surrounding a dwelling house. The area of discussion was south of the curtilage fence, off the defendant's curtilage property in plain view and the issue of admissibility should turn on the totality of the evidence. Mr. Stacy had invited the agents out, had a key and invited them in out of the cold; the agents expressly advised him that he had a right to refuse to let them in and to require them to secure a search warrant. Mr. Stacy reaffirmed his permission to look around and actually lead them around the property. Consent was valid and sufficient to allow access to the agents. It was pointed out that Article II, Section 30 of the Oklahoma Constitution does not prohibit all seizures but only unreasonable seizures. The agents were in a place where they had a right to be, they observed fresh bullet holes in the garbage can, which was an inadvertent discovery.

The most persuasive argument was that the evidence had been abandoned and the U.S. Supreme Court had held that there was no reasonable expectation of privacy regarding items that had been deposited in trash containers. Twelve cases were pointed out as supporting this conclusion. It was pointed out that guilt or innocence of the defendant should be the central concern and exclusionary rules were to deter unlawful police activities. If such rules were applied indiscriminately, the opposite effect of generating disrespect for law and the administration of justice would result. It was pointed out that good faith of law enforcement agents was required and, in this case, there was no oppressive police misconduct. There was discussion of just how careful the officers had been to make every effort not to violate the defendant's rights. A 1979 case was pointed out to the court, but it was also pointed out that this case had been overruled. There was no hint that the officers knew there were going to be three expended cartridges in the garbage can. Agent Pratt was a 1976 graduate of the University of Oklahoma School of Law. Great care was taken, and there was no oppressive police conduct to deter. The agents were on the ranch at the invitation of Stacy, who had a key and had given consent. The casings were in the trash can and had been abandoned and were in plain sight. Exhibits were admitted.

There was an off-the-record discussion.

Testimony was given that the flat tire from Mr. Coleman's red car was brought to the police station. A section of curb was cut out where a tire had hit leaving the victim's house leaving black residue. Perry Harkrider, an officer with the Okmulgee Police Department, did some background interviews but never interviewed the defendant, Mr. Coleman, or the Staceys.

Gene Rice was the Sheriff and had been since 1977. He heard about the shooting on his police radio, had jumped in his unit and proceeded south on the Okmulgee Beeline then on the Southern Mansion Road and then toward the town of Morris looking for a red Ford car. The information he had was that the car was being driven by a white man. Officer Bryant from the Sheriff's office was with him and he is now the dispatcher. He went to the Courtemanche home and saw Ray lying there. Ray was one of his supporters, and he knew his wife. He did not go into the room where Ray was lying but he did help load Ray, who was one of his good friends, into the ambulance. Ray had not told him of any threats. Then he went to his office and bawled his eyes out. He went to the Bailey Ranch when they had a search warrant; he did very little. He talked to Dexter about the rodeo he had been to, but did not go into the house. Dexter was a suspect at this time. He went into the frame shop; Dexter's wife was there. Sheriff Rice was there to assist if needed.

Mr. Parks called a lake patrol officer who heard the broadcast on his radio and went to Ray's house. He stayed in the driveway and kept the news reporters and anybody else who came along out of the yard. City detective Roy Fields let him borrow a walkie-talkie. He told the Okmulgee Chief of Police that he was on the scene, and he stayed there until the hearse left. He went to the Bailey residence twice, on the 17th and 18th after the officers had a search warrant. He didn't read the search warrant. There were probably 6 officers there on the 17th and 18th. The first time he was there about two hours. He was looking for projectiles. He dug up a projectile that looked like a .38 or .357; he initialed the end and gave it to agent Mr. Ottwell. Oklahoma Highway Patrol trooper Leon Hudson was there. He heard the radio dispatch somewhere between 4 and 4:30. He saw 3 or 4 Oklahoma Highway Patrol units. The Sheriff arrived about 5 to 5:30.

Leo Albros testified that he had been with the O.S.B.I. for 15 years. He came to Okmulgee on February 4th and was dispatched to the State Medical Examiner in Tulsa. His job was to collect evidence. He observed wounds and collected hair samples, nail clippings, blood samples and any projectiles. He did everything but collect the projectile. He submitted evidence to the O.S.B.I. lab in Tahlequah where the analysis would be made. He turned his evidence over to Bob Powell at the lab. The Medical Examiner investigator in his presence looked for loose hair on the victim's hands etc. Alsip found black gloves along the side of a road and gave them to Mr. Albros and he delivered them to James Powell. He was back in Okmulgee on February 25th, he believed, to help the Oklahoma Highway Patrol search a creek out west of town. No weapon was found while he was there but a .38 cartridge case was found. The Oklahoma Highway Patrol with three skin-divers with metal detectors searched about four or five hours. O.S.B.I. agent Chrisco was in charge. Mr. Albros did not work on this case between the 5th and the 25th of February. On February 12th he had traveled to Eastern State mental hospital to check the description of a man who had checked himself in and that day and was pretty well satisfied the man had nothing to do with the murder. He did see the red car on February 4th at Oklahoma State Technical College after dark. The story was that the red car had been lent to Mr. Bailey and he had washed it before he drove it to the campus. Mr. Albros noticed no broken fingernails etc.

Patty Harris was called. She testified that she was the dispatcher at the Okmulgee Police Station and had been for 11 months. She had received a call from E.M.S. (ambulance service) at 4:32 in the afternoon. Mr. Dugger from M&D Star Drug called at 4:32. The clock was right above the radio and she logs everything. There were no electronic recordings. There was an offense report by Captain Rade. When the log contains calls that are important we send a unit out, she said. The log contained the description of the suspect vehicle, a red Mercury Capri driven by a white male with a ski mask. If the chief advises that a suspect has been booked, we can give out his name. Unit 5 arrived at Ray's house at 4:37.

The court asked if we had a Xerox machine in the District Attorney office and D.A. Jordan answered NO, but we can make copies in the Court Clerk's office.

Jackie Roberts was called. She is an O.S.B.I. Special Agent. She works in the Special Projects Section and is trained in hypnosis. She described her training and the books she had read and talked about having to demonstrate the ability to hypnotize various individuals. She had training with difficult subjects such as deaf people. She described various tests to determine if a person is actually under hypnosis. She described pre-hypnosis where the subject is put at ease and evaluated for any medical problems. She said she had found that everybody has misconceptions and fears of hypnosis, about loss of control and not coming out of hypnosis. She explained that when a person witnesses or is a victim of a crime that person becomes traumatized and often will block information as to what they have seen or heard, but not in every case. She testified that she had four questions she uses, falling, elevators, heights and she could not remember the fourth one, which caused concern about her qualifications or experience. If she describes an elevator in her induction technique and the person is afraid of elevators, she has found that that person will not go into a hypnotic state. She described three states of hypnosis, light, medium, and heavy and testified that if a person is in a heavy state, that person will not be responsive. She explained that the person is always awake during hypnosis and will hear what is said by someone other than the hypnotist. She testified that often people think of hypnosis as spooky. She testified that it is possible to give inaccurate information while under hypnosis and even do it willingly. That is why everything has to be corroborated. She brings a person out of hypnosis by counting with the person's breathing; the faster the person breathes the faster he comes out of hypnosis. A person can bring himself out of hypnosis on his own. At times if the subject is breathing slowly, he may want to stay in a hypnotic state because he enjoyed it. Agent Roberts testified that she does not make any effort to evaluate the accuracy of what is said; she leaves that to other agents to confirm. She tries to get the person relaxed so that they have no anxiety. She makes notes of what the other agents have told her before the hypnotic session.

Agent Robert's notes were given to defense attorney Parks. Prior to the hypnotic session at the Okmulgee Police Department she was given the approximate time of the homicide, the fact that the driver of the getaway car was described as a white male, about 30 with dark hair and that a red ski mask had been seen. And she was given a description of the vehicle. She described the level of hypnosis Mrs. Dugger was under, between light and medium but this did not remain constant during the hypnotic session. She responded that the session took place in a courtroom with Mrs. Dugger sitting in the judge's chair facing the wall. The only person in the courtroom besides Mrs. Dugger and the hypnotist was the O.S.B.I. artist who was sitting out of Mrs. Dugger's sight and was listening to the description of the suspect so he could draw a picture of the suspect. The hypnosis session started at 11:15 a.m. on February 4th. Agent Roberts had met Mrs. Dugger at the Okmulgee Police Station and then came to the courthouse because space was available there. Agent Roberts had not had any prior conversation with Mrs. Dugger. No questions were asked about the hypnotic session on the short ride from the police department to the Courthouse about three blocks away.

When Agent Roberts arrived at the police department, she advised that she needed a quiet room free from distractions and someone else arranged for the courtroom. Once in the courtroom she spoke with Mrs. Dugger explaining what to expect. She said that she would not have control over her mind and that Mrs. Dugger would not do or say anything that she did not want to do or say. She asked about possible health problems, such as heart problems, epilepsy, high blood pressure or diabetes. She asked where she lived, her date of birth, and her phone number. That was all. She pointed out that this get-acquainted information was not being recorded, but she made notes. When she arrived at the police department, she had been advised that they needed hypnosis in order to get a composite picture of the suspect. She did not question Mrs. Dugger except when she was under hypnosis. She explained that she did not attempt to confirm the accuracy of what came out under hypnosis as that would be checked by other agents.

She had listened to part of the tape of the hypnotic session on Tuesday and the entire tape on Friday before court time and confirmed that the tape was accurate. She listened to the original tape, which was admitted into evidence. Everything Mrs. Dugger said under hypnosis was recorded. When Mrs. Dugger was narrating seeing Ray on the floor she was breathing deeply. Mrs. Dugger was under hypnosis 50 minutes. Agent Roberts suggested three or four face shapes when asking the shape of the face of the suspect, round, square, oval, oblong. Subjects under hypnosis usually select one of these types. Agent Pratt, the artist, was taking his own notes. When the information had been given by agent Chrisco agent Pratt was present but she didn't know where Mrs. Dugger was, outside in the reception area; she had not yet met Mrs. Dugger. She had filled out a form about background, which Mr. Park asked for, but an objection was raised because she had not referred to it. The court sustained the objection. Mrs. Dugger related details about the auto and the suspect. Agent Roberts testified that she could only be concerned with what was brought out under hypnosis and not what might have been in the subject's mind. Mrs. Roberts explained that hypnosis would enhance recall. All of the subject's efforts are focused at that point on one event; a lot of things are in our subconscious that we cannot recall and thru hypnosis we are able to reach a few of them. Agent Roberts testified that she had never had anyone try to change anything they had said under hypnosis. She had never had anyone say, "That is not what I meant." Agent Roberts concluded that people under hypnosis clarify descriptions of suspects and vehicles. Agent Roberts stated that she never recorded pre-hypnosis sessions. Mr. Parks asked if Mrs. Dugger heard the facts discussed by officers if that might influence what she said. Agent Roberts stated that she could not tell if a subject had been influenced by something that she heard said. She did acknowledge that in some of the sources she had studied the possibility of contamination had come out and that it was possible for people to confabulate. She again pointed out that it is up to other agents to confirm what comes out under hypnosis. Mr. Pratt was able to hear what Mrs. Dugger said while under hypnosis. The question was asked if there was conversation after being returned to the here and now and Agent Roberts said she might have asked Mrs. Dugger if she wanted a Coke or something to drink and she said yes. Agent Roberts was asked if she had hypnotized other people and she said yes but none having to do the Courtemanche homicide. It was further brought out that Agent Roberts usually would not keep a person under hypnosis over an hour, because people might need to go to the restroom or get something to drink. She stated that people under hypnosis tend to get a dry mouth. When asked why, she responded that the blood pressure is lower with a slower heart beat rate and people tend to not swallow. When asked Agent Roberts said she had never had a follow-up session and she did not believe that an additional session with Mrs. Dugger would be of any value.

Assistant District Attorney Elliott objected because a medical report had been supplied to the defense, but testimony was heard from the O.S.B.I. Regional lab. All the hairs recovered during the examination were consistent with the hair of Ray Courtemanche except item 27, which was a cow hair. There was discussion about how their work was done.

Then the comment was made that Mr. Stubbs would be traveling out of the country starting the next day. Mr. Parks complained that for seven day he had no opportunity to call any witnesses.

Agent Harvey Pratt was called as a witness. He testified that he was sitting quite a distance from Mrs. Dugger, but the session was recorded. He allowed the witness to view the Identikit Mark II, which contained maybe 100 eyes, and other facial features. He did his first drawing in 1968. He is a member of the O.S.B.I., an Inspector. The witness was watching his work all the time and told him when to quit. A white male was all he knew.

Amos Dixon was called as a witness. He was an employee of the Department of Transportation. He saw Ray about 4:10 on Feb. 3, 1981. He looked at his watch while standing in the door at Handi-Mart. Ray was driving a little gray car. He saw a red car immediately behind him and turned east on highway 62.

Then Cara James, age 17, was called as a witness. She worked at Peoples Bakery on Feb. 3, 1981 but no longer works there. She knew Dexter Bailey after he introduced himself. She could not remember if she had seen Dexter in the bakery on Feb. 3. Someone else came in, perhaps one of his lawyers? She talked with the agents only three times. Her father is a police officer in Okmulgee. Her answers were that she couldn't remember. The shop was open until 5:30.

Cheryl Womble was called as a witness. She was employed by Kenneth Butler. Ray never told her of any threats on his life. Ray and Mr. Butler owned two stores together. She was strictly a private secretary. She did not handle any work to do with Quik Trip or rental property. Ray was on the Board of Directors at the First National Bank in Henryetta. She knew that Dexter had been at Ray's house the day before the shooting because it had been reported in the newspaper, and she had heard people make comments. It was common knowledge. She had only one visit by law enforcement and Mr. Farish, who served a subpoena. Yes, she knew the lawyer, Mr. Rainey; she remembered that he was not in Ray's office Dec. 3, 1980.

Joel Anderson, Medical Examiner for Okmulgee County, was called as a witness. He said that the Okmulgee police department had called him to Ray's house on Feb. 3, 1981. He arrived about 5:00 p.m. He took his camera. The projectile was under Ray and was discovered after the examination and the body had been moved. It was approximately a .38. It could have been a .45, he said, but he doubted it because a .45 would have made a larger hole. It was larger than a .22. He just made an examination and referred for autopsy. He said it appeared that Ray had been shot as he entered his home, rather than after entering, and the gunshot wound came from behind. He heard that neighbors had heard and seen the suspect. Dr. Anderson was at the scene approximately 30 minutes. It was announced that it was not expected that Dr. Anderson would be called at trial or at any other hearings.

Then there was testimony from Toxicology that blood tests and stomach contents were as stated in his report.

There was discussion regarding other witnesses who would be called only in regard to chain of custody.

Discussion remained regarding nine more witnesses.

There was discussion about calling Officer Rade, but the court pointed out that it did not appear that he had been subpoenaed and said that it was going to have to stop somewhere.

Duane Woodliff, a lawyer, appeared on behalf of the First National Bank. There had been a motion to quash the admission of various records because of state law, the National Banking Act, questions regarding relevance and obligations to other customers who might have been in a business relationship with Ray Courtemanche. It was argued that Mr. Woodliff could not make a finding of relevance, only the court could. Loans from the bank to Ray could be relevant, and it was argued that there should be the opportunity to look at relationships of other people, especially outside the county, who might have a financial motive to have committed the crime. The court asked about relevance. Mr. Parks argued that they should be allowed to look at mortgages, contracts, co-signed notes or loans, records having to do with the organizations of which Ray was an owner or officer, director or shareholder. The court quashed the subpoena except as to mortgages, and cosigned notes or loans. The court noted that exceptions are automatic and just need to be noted in any appeal. When you object, that protects your record. If you do not object, then the objections are not preserved.

W.R. Stubbs was called as a witness. He was the President and Chairman of the Board of Directors for the First National Bank, Henryetta, Okla. Ray Courtemanche was on the board of directors. He had been a charter member and shareholder. Mr. Stubbs did not come on until 1974. New members were needed with diversification and a lot of good friends and connections. A person had to have 100 shares to qualify to serve on the board. Ray helped get business for the bank and spent most of his life trying to help other people. Mr. Stubbs noted that he and Ray didn't always vote the same way. Mr. Stubbs was a personal friend of Ray's but had never been in his home, nor had Ray been in his home. There were nine members of the board and one advisory director who lived part time in Oklahoma and part time in Minnesota. None of the directors served on any other bank board of directors to his knowledge. Ray and Eddie Evans started with a $10,000.00 loan with the present balance $431.00 due monthly and secured by real estate. Ray and his wife had a loan of $13,304.00 secured by two lots in Stubbs Estates in Henryetta not yet due. Ray and his wife had another loan of $21,992.00 on March 10, 1980, secured by real estate with a balance of $19,992.00 secured by a second mortgage. Ray took out another loan of $6,474.28 on Nov. 20, 1980, with a balance of $5,214.28 not due until Nov. 20, 1981, secured by a $10,000.00 CD. Ray, Eddie

Evans and Kenneth Butler made another loan on Dec. 1, 1980, for $100,010.00 due Sept. 1,1981, on real estate and equipment. Ray and Kenneth Butler had a $23,000.00 unsecured loan. Eddie Evans, Kenneth Butler and Ray had a $15,279.06 loan securing equipment. There was also a $15,419.30 loan with Eddie Evans and Kenneth Butler for equipment having to do with the convenience store in Preston. There were no loans secured by any type of life insurance on Ray's life. The First National Bank in Henryetta did business with Fidelity Bank in Oklahoma City as a correspondence bank to handle overlines of credit and various other matters. Ray had no loans with the correspondence bank that Mr. Stubbs knew of. Since Ray's death no loans had been paid off except a loan to Ray and his wife Helen had been reworked with a new due date of Jan. 24, 1982, with a balance of $11,954.00. A note with a due date of April 10, 1981, with a balance due of $19,792.00 had been paid off.

Betty Reynolds, an employee at Handi-Mart located at 6th Street and Wood Drive testified that she saw Ray about 4 or 4:30. Larry Maddox, the manager, told her about Ray being shot about 6:30. She came on duty at 3:00 and went off duty at 11:00. Her conversation with Ray had to do with the identity of a man wearing a red baseball cap in the store; he was writing down prices. He asked how much were cigarettes and was told 80 cents, said thank you and left. Ray did mention that he had a meeting to attend. Ray and the clerk didn't know him. She received a call from Kenneth Butler who asked if she had seen Eddie Evans or Larry Maddox and told her that Ray had been shot and the O.S.B.I. would be coming in. Ray owned interests in various real estate including property occupied by the Tag Agent, Court Related Community Services and Parole Office.

Eddie Evans was called as a witness and testified regarding ownership of business interests with Ray. He also testified that there were no reciprocal life insurance policies on each other's lives and that notes were not secured by life insurance. That evening he talked with law enforcement officers going through things on Ray's desk.

Vic Fry, an auxiliary police officer, arrived at Ray's house around 4:20 to 4:30. He always put on his cap and jacket for identification. Small red car was the only description he heard with one male occupant. The Chief and Detective Fields were outside Ray's back door. He was assigned to guard that door, protect the crime scene, and not let anyone in or out. He was there until 9:00 when he left to go to work. He went home, took a bath and went to work. He confirmed the description as a white male with a ski mask.

Mack Kelly was a licensed bail bondsman. He had known Ray probably 10 years. He had not done any business with Ray. He saw Ray in the lobby of the courthouse. Ray never evidenced any fear for his life to him. Mr. Kelly did not remember a conversation. He did not see Ray later in the day. He received a call telling him that Ray had been shot. He went to the courthouse to pick up Mrs. Courtemanche. They arrived at the Courtemanches' house about 5:00. Officers told Mack to take Mrs. Courtemanche away from the scene. He took her to his house. Mack had several conversations with law officers several days after the shooting. He was asked if he was ever asked to do any investigating and he said no. Did he report to anyone what the lawyer, Mr. Rainey, had told him? He said yes, he had reported it to me, Jim Jordan, the D.A. Mack said that he had told me that Ray said his life had been threatened, and indeed he had. He had never before related to Mack any fears for his life or family. Mack told his wife, Mrs. Courtemanche and his son about this conversation with Jim Jordan. He didn't remember if he related this conversation to Mr. Butler or Mr. Evans. A defense attorney asked, "Have you, at any time, at any place, or at any hour, and if so, tell me when and where and the hour, have you met with other members of the community, particularly Mr. Butler or Mr. Evans, and discussed the facts of this case?" Assistant D.A. Elliott said, "Judge, I object. That is totally irrelevant." The Court said, "I completely agree. I will sustain that objection."

Jim Newport testified that he was part owner of Star Drug and Gibson Pharmacy, that he knew Jeannie Dugger, and that her husband was part owner. He is no longer associated with that organization and he lived a half mile south of the Duggers' home. He saw her in her driveway on his way home for lunch about 4:30 or 4:40. She was running down the drive waving her arms and said, "Ray has been shot." He checked for a heartbeat and found that he was dead. He went outside and told her that he was dead and she burst into tears. He asked if she had called an ambulance, her husband and the police.

She said, "I didn't get the tag number" two or three times. And "I don't know if I could recognize him or not… white…hair short…not crew cut…heard a loud noise…saw someone coming out of the back with a gun in one hand and a ski mask in the other. He was with her 15 to 20 minutes. Before he left the ambulance, police cars and sheriff car were there. He had visited with her two or three times. She didn't really know the kind of car. She didn't discuss the case at all. Ray was an acquaintance, but he didn't really know him. He knew Dexter.

Kenneth Butler was called and testified. Ray was a good friend. He had an office in my building, and we had business investments together. Ray kept the office there about two years, as long as I had been there. He had been in partnership in two convenience stores and a couple of small real estate investments, but he had sold those holdings sometime before. We had attempted three or four oil ventures with others and part ownership of some downtown rental property in Okmulgee. Ray never shown fear for his life. He had been invited to a meeting to decide whom to support for a city council race. I did not see Ray after I left my office about 2:30. I learned of his death when I returned to the office about 4:30 and received a call and was told that he had been killed. I stayed at the office. I did see Mrs. Courtemanche that evening at the residence of Mack Kelly. I did not ask people about their activities the evening Ray was killed; nor was I asked to investigate. I was questioned by O.S.B.I. agents Pratt and Estes at the residence of Mr. Mack, the bail bondsman.

Tom Jordan used different magnifications to examine ballistic evidence. He said there is sometimes confusion between class characteristics (caliber, consistent with evidence) and individual characteristics (unique to that gun). He did not wash Exhibit #14. He described sand blast effect when a bullet is fired into sand. He described firing pen impressions and breach face markings. His comparisons are not digital but he simply uses a comparison microscope and they do not use numbers as are used with fingerprints. He testified that a .38 can be fired in a .357 but not the other way. He discussed reloading and indicated that a reload press was not necessary, a case loading kit not absolutely necessary but reload scale was very important. He discussed reloaded cartridges when the exact amount used was not known.

An O.S.B.I. chemist was called and testified that after testing the tire submitted to him it did not make the marking on the section of curb submitted to him.

A brief discussion was held with the judge and it was announced that the state would not call Francis McCain nor use her at trial. Defense attorney Parks intended to call Doug Rade whose name came out that week. He was said to be the first person on the scene. There was discussion regarding six other witnesses whom the defense desired to call the next day. The court commented that all that is being done is fishing. The defense also wanted to call all CETA (a government program) employees hired thru Ray Courtemanche by David Jones. The court asked if we could enter some stipulations. I, as the D.A., responded no because there were things we did not know, and if we were not careful, we could stipulate our case away. The court asked about Doug Rade and I said that he was shift captain and it was not believed that he was the first person on the scene. Mr. Dunn said that he thought that the report said that Rade was the first person on the scene. I replied as D.A. that I didn't believe that was true.

There was more discussion about what witnesses should be called. Regarding Cindy Thomas, Assistant D.A. Elliott said she didn't see Dexter. Defense attorney Bailey said he didn't think she would be able to identify Dexter Bailey as the man who bought the newspaper about 3:30 or 4:00 in the afternoon or in that neighborhood and said just keep the nickel. I as D.A. said I thought we should hear her. It was pointed out that she was subpoenaed for the next morning. The court said, "let's get her here."

Defense attorney Parks offered to stipulate that the testimony of Ken Courtemanche that transferring the welfare department from a Bailey building to a Courtemanche building would make K.D. really mad and got a response that yes, I guess so with no death threats mentioned. Assistant D.A. Elliott so stipulated.

Concerning other potential witnesses, the court commented that Ron Forman who worked for the Creek Nation Housing Authority was present and Cindy Thomas, who worked for the Okmulgee County News, was on her way. But the court sustained objections to Mr. Jones and Ms. Womble because they were too peripheral. Ms. Thomas said that a man came in between 3 p.m. and 5 p.m. – I can't say it was him – and asked for change for a dollar. Then he returned and asked for change for a quarter. She had two dimes but not a nickel. He said keep the nickel. She said she never got a tip until then.

Mr. Forman said he had known Dexter about nine years. Dexter had not made a work application with the Creek Nation Housing Authority to his knowledge; he assumed that he had made it with the Creek Nation. He had received a call from Ray asking if Dexter had gone to work for the Creek Nation and responded not to his knowledge - he didn't do the hiring but would find out. Chief Cox said no he had not hired Dexter, but an application had arrived in response to an ad for a job at Dustin. Ray didn't ask to help or block the application; it could have been a year before.

Defense attorney Parks moved to exclude the testimony of Mr. Rainey. The court observed that his statement had no bearing on his ruling in the preliminary hearing.

Defense attorney Bailey demurred to the Information. (This is simply a statement to the court that it is his position that if everything in the Information (the charge) was true that there just wasn't enough to proceed). He renewed various motions and moved the court to dismiss the Information. The court overruled the demure and other motions. The court found that the crime of First-Degree Murder had been committed and that there was probable cause to believe that Dexter Bailey had committed the crime, and the court bound him over for trial. However, the court lifted travel restrictions on Dexter and allowed him to remain free on his bond.

TRANSCRIPT AVAILABILITY

The Tulsa Tribune newspaper carried an article on page one of section D "Methods Vary in Distribution of Transcripts," July 8, 1981, which disclosed that Don Shaw, District Attorney for McCurtain, Choctaw and Pushmataha Counties often asked Court Reporters to delay making a third copy of court transcripts until he could pay his share. Muskogee County District Attorney Mike Turpen said that he routinely received a "free" copy of transcripts ordered and paid for by defense attorneys. I, Okmulgee District Attorney James Jordan, often "did without" transcripts that my office could not afford, but asked that the court fund my office's share of the $3,500.00 transcript of the preliminary hearing for Dexter Bailey, who was charged with murder in the first degree in the slaying of long-time court reporter Ray Courtemanche. District Judge John Maley said he could order that the court fund pay for transcripts only when a defendant is declared indigent. "I don't think the district attorney is declared indigent." Instead Judge Maley ruled that Mr. Bailey's attorneys must provide Mr. Jordan with a copy of the transcripts they ordered and paid for. He also ordered Mr. Jordan to provide Mr. Bailey's attorneys with a copy of a portion of the transcript he ordered and paid for. District Attorney Mike Turpen, Mr. Bailey and state court administrator Marvin Emerson said they believed the law clearly required the party ordering the transcript to pay the reporter $2.00 per page to transcribe the court proceedings. For that fee, set by law, the reporter is required to produce an original and two copies of the transcript, they agree. The law is less clear on the distribution of the copies.

SUBSEQUENT TO THE PRELIMINARY HEARING

Subsequent to the preliminary hearing a proposal was made to District Attorney James D. Jordan that a District Attorney from a larger district take this case to trial and that D.A. Jordan withdraw. As District Attorney I did not reject this suggestion without giving it considered thought.

I considered Ray Courtemanche a friend and wanted to be sure he got the best representation possible. This was above and beyond my duty to faithfully protect the citizens of Okmulgee and McIntosh Counties.

Hypnosis

At this time there was a lot of interest in the admissibility of the testimony of previously hypnotized witnesses in courts across the nation. The Law Enforcement Hypnosis Institute working with the Los Angeles Police department had had considerable success using hypnosis to apprehend and convict criminals. One of the important cases involved the kidnapping of a bus load of school children and burying the bus with the kids still inside in a pre-dug ditch. The bus was found and the kids recovered, but they were so traumatized that they could not tell the officers anything about the perpetrators. Thru the careful use of hypnosis law enforcement was able to get enough information to find the perpetrators, arrest them and convict them; this was such a noteworthy case that a movie was made relating the incident. In another case a low-level drug dealer used the drugs with his girlfriend and didn't pay his supplier who came and killed him while his girlfriend was there but so stoned out of her mind that she did not even know her boyfriend had been killed. Again, through the careful use of hypnosis law enforcement was able to get enough information from the girlfriend, which she did not even know she had, to find and convict the killer. It was obvious that the prosecutor who got a conviction in the Courtemanche case and did it so that it withstood appeal would have made a name for himself on the national stage.

To my knowledge I was the only Oklahoma District Attorney trained and certified as a forensic hypnotist. Many people can induce hypnosis, but special training and care are required to perform the task without contaminating the evidence and ending up with a botched case. Medical doctors have used hypnosis to perform surgery, but some legal cases have been messed up by medical doctors. One case that comes to mind involved a medical doctor who hypnotized a person who was a witness to a crime. The doctor got the person under hypnosis and appeared to get the person's attention directed to the proper bedroom and then asked the person what he saw in the mirror. The problem with this question was that the doctor did not let the subject simply tell what he saw but asked what he saw in the mirror. The subject gave a response. However, this could have been the result of confabulation; in other words, there may not have been a mirror in the room but because it was suggested the mirror may have appeared in the mind of the subject who may have confabulated and told what he saw even if there were no mirror! It is absolutely critical to be extremely careful and ask questions that do not suggest anything to the subject. Hypnosis should never be used in a criminal case until all other avenues have been exhausted. This is the last resort.

I was trained at the Law Enforcement Hypnosis Institute July 26 - 29, 1979, in Los Angeles, Calif., and hold certificate number 835. Interestingly medical doctors who are trained in the use of hypnosis have been required to attend shorter sessions and do not get training involving the forensic use of hypnosis.

The O.S.B.I. in this case snapped up my only witness without my knowledge and hypnotized her in a rush session. The agents were in a rush to put together a composite drawing of the perpetrator and rush to another case in far western Oklahoma. Our only witness was not happy with the drawing. Everything did not seem to be properly recorded, preferably with video or at least voice; it is important to record and preserve fully all of the contact the hypnotist has with the subject or everything that has anything to do with the hypnotic session.

As the years passed I would occasionally cross paths with the O.S.B.I. hypnotist who always seemed to want to say something. She never said anything until one day she and I were the only passengers ridding up the elevator to the Oklahoma City jail when she said, “I wish I had had the training you had.” I said nothing but thought “I also wish you had had the training I had.” The blame for not following the best practices was not on the O.S.B.I. agent. She had been trained as someone else dictated, and she followed the orders given. But, as she testified, often people think hypnosis is spooky. Lack of full corroboration of careful practices can be enough to taint a case.

As this case developed certain confidential information was slipping out of my office. I was never sure if someone was dirty, or if there was a listening device in my office.

I knew the case inside and out and was probably the best qualified person available to handle this case tainted by “spooky” hypnosis.

There was also the fact that any out of area prosecutor could not know the local people and situation as well as I did; I knew that there were things I did not know, but I knew that I would know more about the local situation than they would.

Years later I was working in Tulsa as a United States Administrative Law Judge and went to Luby’s Cafeteria for lunch. As I started to leave two ladies sitting at a table I was passing asked if I was Mr. Jordan who had been the prosecutor in Okmulgee and I acknowledged that I was. They asked if I remembered them. I didn’t, so they reminded me that they had been on one of my juries in Okmulgee County in which I was prosecuting a man for stealing cattle. They then asked if I knew that the Sheriff was related to the defendant; no, I didn't know that, but I had noticed that the testimony just didn't fit together neatly. This is just the kind of thing where out of area prosecutors would be at a disadvantage.

I moved the preparation of this case to my house, which had brick walls and heavy drapes to block any eves dropping. I shared my preparation with no one, so that there could be no leaks. I did all of my own trial preparation there and controlled the case by myself.

CHANGING HORSES

Gotcher, Gotcher and Taylor, Attorneys from McAlester, Okla., entered the case on behalf of the defendant. One of the firm's attorneys, Steven W. Taylor, filed MOTION TO EXCLUDE TESTIMONY OF BILLIE JEAN DUGGER. He also filed BRIEF IN SUPPORT OF MOTION TO EXCLUDE TESTIMONY OF BILLIE JEAN DUGGER. He stated in his brief that Billie Jean Dugger, the only witness at the scene of the alleged murder of Ray Courtemanche, underwent police questioning while hypnotized and after the hypnotic session was allowed to testify at a Preliminary Hearing and gave critical information. He also stated that the use of hypnosis on witnesses for the state in criminal cases was coming under fire throughout this land. He argued that the clear trend was to exclude evidence where the witness's testimony had been enhanced by hypnosis. He then cited the then recent pronouncement of the Arizona Supreme Court (In Banc), State vs. Mena, No. 5026-PR (Ariz Feb. 3, 1981), reported at 28 CrL 2518 (Mar 11, 1981):

"It is generally agreed that hypnosis is a state of altered consciousness and heightened suggestibility in which the subject is prone to experience distortions of reality, false memories, fantasies and confabulation (the 'filling in of memory gaps with false memories or inaccurate bits of information'). (Cites omitted) In the context of pretrial interrogation under hypnosis, these distortions, delusions and confabulations are apparently aggravated by the tendency of a subject to respond in a way he believes are desirable to the hypnotist. This may happen even without any intent or awareness on the part of the hypnotist or subject …

"The determination of the guilt or innocence of an accused should not depend on the unknown consequences of a procedure concededly used for the purpose of changing in some way a witness' memory. Therefore, until hypnosis gains general acceptance in the field of medicine and psychiatry as a method by which memories are accurately improved without undue danger of distortion, delusion or fantasy, we feel that testimony of witnesses which has been tainted by hypnosis should be excluded in criminal cases."

Taylor also cited State vs Mack, 292 NW 2nd 764 (Minn. 1980), People vs Tait,

297 NW 2nd 893 (Mich. App 1980) and People vs Bicknell, Cal. Ct App 1st Dist, Jan 16, 1981), reported at 28 CrL 2484 (Feb 25, 1981).

Taylor also pointed out that the Oklahoma Court of Criminal Appeals had rejected evidence due to a lack of acceptance in the scientific community of the procedures used to obtain it. Fulton vs State, 541 P2d 871 (Okl Cr 1975); State vs Cook, 574 P2nd 1073 (Okl Cr 1978).

It should be mentioned that State vs Mack points out that the experts agreed that hypnosis is capable of releasing emotional memory blocks.

It also needs to be pointed out that all people are subject to suggestion.

Importantly it must be noted that Dugger gave the same description to a police officer shortly after the event and before hypnosis, so her testimony was not enhanced.

People v Tait, 297 NW 2d 853 (Mich. App 1980) cites State vs McQueen and points out "…the use of hypnosis bears upon credibility, not admissibility."

Fulton v State 541 P 2d 871 (Okla. Cr 1975) pointed out that the results of polygraph examination had been admitted over the objection of the defendant when the law was that the results of polygraph could only be admitted by stipulation.

State v Cook 574 P2d 1073, (Okla. Cr 1978) was tried by a judge who suggested polygraph. Defendant's willingness to take the polygraph test, not new information gained, was properly considered by the trial judge.

The court allowed the out-of-state deposition of Dr. Diamond in the case against the defendant, Kenneth Dexter Bailey. The lawyers also agreed to take the deposition of Dr. Reiser that same afternoon.

DEPOSITION OF BERNARD L. DIAMOND

October 12, 1981

I understand that there are two types of court reporters, those who are so totally focused on typing what is being said that they really are not following the testimony, and a second group that listens to and follows the testimony, which they then type. This may be a subtle difference, but it seems that those who just type are faster and more accurate. We had a world class reporter in each of these depositions, yet they both became so engrossed in the testimony that they lost their typing and were just listening in one instance each.

This deposition of Bernard L. Diamond was taken starting at 10:04 on Monday morning in Corte Madera, Calif.

James D. Jordan, Esquire, District Attorney, Okmulgee County, Okla., appeared as counsel on behalf of the Plaintiff; and Steven W. Taylor, Esquire, Gotcher, Gotcher & Taylor, Attorneys at Law from McAlester, Okla., appeared as counsel on behalf of the Defendant, Kenneth Dexter Bailey, Jr.

Testimony in this transcript took up approximately 101 pages plus five pages of curriculum vita and bibliography of writings, symposia, film and an interview with Sirhan B. Sirhan, who was convicted of having assassinated Senator Robert F. Kennedy, reported in Psychology Today, vol 3, no 4, pp 48-55, Sept 1969, by Dr. Diamond. This material disclosed that Dr. Diamond earned his M.D. degree and had worked as an intern and resident at the Neuropsychiatric Institute at the University of Michigan, that he held various certificates and had engaged in considerable work in the area of psychiatry, and that he had written more than 50 articles and book chapters on forensic psychiatry, criminal behavior and related issues. He also used hypnosis on soldiers returning from severely traumatic combat during World War II. Seemingly the purpose of that hypnosis was to release bad memories and allow the soldiers to live more normal lives. It was clear that he had been extremely involved in psychiatry and criminal law.

EXAMINATION BY MR. TAYLOR

Mr. Taylor asked what documents Dr. Diamond had reviewed regarding this case. His response was: ...newspaper clippings from Oklahoma on March 3, 1981, a composite sketch made by a police artist from descriptions of Mrs. Dugger, the transcript of the direct examination of Harvey Pratt, the police artist, a copy of the Motion to Exclude the Testimony of Billie Jean Dugger, a transcript of the testimony in the preliminary hearing of Mrs. Jackie Roberts, who was the hypnotist in this case, one of the direct and one of the cross-examination of the preliminary hearing testimony of Billie Jean Dugger.

Special note: This did not include the written statement given by Mrs. Dugger shortly after the commission of the crime and before being hypnotized. That statement shows that her testimony was not enhanced.

Dr. Diamond also testified that he listened to a partial tape recording of the hypnotic session. It was of very poor quality, he said. Most of the time he could understand what Mrs. Dugger said, but he could understand only about half of what the hypnotist said. The tape ended abruptly, he added, so he had no information regarding what happened or if the subject awoke or what.

There was nothing on the tape regarding pre-induction or post-induction. Dr. Diamond testified that at a minimum there should be a transcript of everything that transpired between the hypnotist and the subject from the time the hypnotist was introduced to the subject and all interchange after the hypnotic session.

Dr. Diamond testified that there was some scientific experimental reason to believe that the previous interrogation of the defendant and post-hypnotic interrogation by either the hypnotist or by other people could become psychologically consolidated into the hypnotic experience so that when the subject eventually testifies in court, the subject may not be able to keep the various interrogations straight; the suggestibility that is induced by the hypnotist might spill over into pre-hypnotic experiences both backwards and forwards and into subsequent interrogations.

Dr. Diamond testified that it was his opinion that one of the essential elements of any hypnotic state...is suggestibility, that hypnosis is a state of heightened suggestibility.

Dr. Diamond proceeded with his testimony saying that there were many different forms of suggestion that are given under hypnosis. He further stated that he thought that most investigative hypnotists tried to avoid direct or rather crude suggestions or leading questions. He further stated that it had been his experience that the context of the hypnotic session was of vital importance. The purpose of hypnosis, the subject's understanding and concept of what is expected of her are very important, and the physical surroundings are very important. In this case, the hypnotist was introduced to the subject at the police station, and the actual hypnosis was conducted in a courtroom in which the subject was seated in the judge's chair on the bench. He said that he couldn't think of any physical context that would be more suggestive toward production of law enforcement's point of view than this context.

Dr. Diamond further testified that there was reason to believe that persons in a state of hypnosis have an abnormal desire to please the hypnotist, so they will bring up from their own memories and memories of other experiences and other contexts. They will tend to mix them all up and try as much as possible to produce the desired result, that which they imagine or anticipate will please the hypnotist.

Mr. Taylor, one of the attorneys, asked if there were anything in the record of the tape recording or the testimony of Mrs. Dugger or Miss Roberts that indicated that we knew what Billie Jean Dugger's expectations or instructions under hypnosis were. Dr. Diamond responded that there was no record, so he could only make presumptions.

Mr. Taylor, the attorney, asked if after completing the hypnosis a subject could distinguish which of his thoughts and recollections and experiences are a product of his own memory and which were a product from the hypnosis itself. Dr. Diamond responded that he believe, based on his own clinical experience and on scientific research in this field, that it was impossible for a subject to make an actual differentiation between what was factual and true, what the subject remembered or reported as a valid or true memory and what might have been a contaminated memory introduced by the context or induced by the hypnotist or introduced into their own memory by their own confabulation.

Mr. Taylor asked could a witness who was previously hypnotized restrict his or her memory to actual facts free of any fantasy or confabulation? Dr. Diamond stated that in his opinion once a witness was hypnotized that witness's memory was irrevocably contaminated insofar as distinguishing between the effect of hypnosis and actual memories if not hypnotized.

Attorney Taylor asked if distortions of hypnosis would disappear. Dr. Diamond stated that they would persist, many of them indefinitely.

Then Mr. Taylor asked if there were independent corroboration of the hypnotically enhanced memories would that ensure that all or most of the subject's memories were reliable. Dr. Diamond responded that no corroboration independently gave such assurance. If the hypnotic enhanced memory is corroborated in some details, it tells you nothing about the other details, he said.

Special note: Mrs. Dugger's memories were not enhanced by hypnosis. As set out before, she gave a statement to an Okmulgee police officer immediately after the killing and before hypnosis, and it was clear that her memory was the same before and after hypnosis. There was no enhancement or contamination. In fact, it is not at all certain that she was ever actually put into a hypnotic state.

Dr. Diamond continued to testify about the hypnotized subject having false confidence in the correctness of his testimony. He further stated that hypnotic experience tended to freeze a person's memory from that point on. The fixation of the memory at this stage of hypnosis can seriously interfere with cross-examination, he said, and might change a witness who might have been hesitant or uncertain to become unshakable. He further stated that juries and other people tend in judging an individual's truthfulness not only by what they are saying but also by such cues as nervousness, contradictions, inconsistencies, hesitation, lack of eye contact, mannerisms and the like. Consequently a witness who was once hypnotized could come across as very convincing. Dr. Diamond said he felt that the effects of hypnotism amounted to the destruction of evidence. Dr. Diamond stated, "... my position is that whatever usefulness hypnosis may have in a criminal investigation, and undoubtedly under some circumstances it does seem to have usefulness, at least the police feel so, they must recognize that in using this as an investigative tool they have destroyed some of the evidence".

Special note: Dr. Diamond is acknowledging that under some circumstances hypnosis is useful in criminal investigations. This is consistent with the training I, District Attorney Jordan, received at the Law Enforcement Hypnosis Institute.

Dr. Diamond proceeded with his deposition by saying that assuming the hypnotist is honest and is doing a good job, neither the subject not the hypnotist is fully aware of what factors within the environment played a part, what factors within the subject's expectations, and what factors within the memories and previous experiences of the subject served to contaminate the evidence. Even the hypnotist may be unaware of how he or she may have inadvertently led the subject into certain directions in terms of what the hypnotist hears about the matter, Dr. Diamond said. He drew a parallel between a blood alcohol test that had been contaminated with some other substance; he pointed out that while the original blood was still there with the original alcohol the sample had been contaminated by some other substance, so the sample was no longer of any value in determining what the blood alcohol level was. He contended that once a witness had been hypnotized it was impossible to determine the value of his post-hypnotic testimony because of the unknown and unknowable impact on the witness having been hypnotized.

Mr. Taylor asked Dr. Diamond about a California Law Review Article that he wrote in 1979 and was published in 1980.

Dr. Diamond testified that hypnosis was very easily learned. He further said he could teach someone to hypnotize somebody in a very skillful way in one day. He pointed out that it was a very simple technique. Dr. Diamond further testified that what was needed was a knowledge of the scientific background of hypnosis, what it is to what we know about it, what we don't know about it and all the possible effects of hypnosis. He said that required a thorough background in psychological science, knowledge, but that the usual investigative hypnotist did not have that. He said he did not believe a person could acquire that knowledge in four days, eight days or even a month's course.

The attorney, Mr. Taylor, asked about London Associates. Dr. Diamond was not directly familiar with them other than what was contained in the testimony of Jackie Roberts from the Preliminary Hearing.

Dr. Diamond also testified about two resolutions in the October 1979 issue of the International Journal of Clinical and Experimental Hypnosis. One adopted in October 1978 by the Society of Clinical and Experimental Hypnosis and the other adopted August 1979 by the International Society of Hypnosis. Both opposed the training of police officers as hypnotists and opposed the use of hypnosis by police officers and expressed misgivings about the use of hypnosis in the hypnotic setting.

Dr. Diamond commented on his extensive work in university settings and said that he had had to make extensive use of hypnosis. Dr. Diamond said that he had read most of the books in the field. He pointed out that a number of those books were published by Charles C Thomas Publisher, Ltd., and were specifically targeted toward police and criminologists rather than psychologists and psychiatrists. These books have stimulated a lot of interest in the use of hypnosis in law enforcement, he said, and are relied on heavily in the training process, but in his opinion most of these books are totally unscientific, even to the point of making ridiculous and absurd claims. He further stated that many of them contained highly unethical and illegal suggestions on the use of hypnosis, giving a false impression about hypnosis. He said he was unwilling to acknowledge that these books are part of the scientific literature on the subject.

The attorney, Mr. Taylor, asked about books used by Agent Roberts in her training, specifically the Myron Teitelbaum and Harry Arons text books. Dr. Diamond testified that the Teitelbaum book contained illegal, improper and he thought highly unethical instructions on how to hypnotize a person without allowing the person to know that he or she was being hypnotized, in other words doing it secretly. Dr. Diamond referred to the Leyra case (no cite provided but apparently 347 U.S. 556) in which a psychiatrist went too far with a criminal defendant to secure a confession, and which the United States Supreme Court declared improper. This case stated that the psychiatrist had considerable knowledge of hypnosis; however, it did not expressly find that he actually hypnotized the subject but said that he acted improperly. Dr. Diamond pointed out that Arons went so far as to say that it was not necessary to disclose the fact that the subject had been hypnotized to the trier of fact.

Arons had set out certain safeguards: 1. Hypnosis should be carried out by a psychiatrist or psychologist with special training in its use and 2. All contact by the psychiatrist or psychologist with the individual to be hypnotized should be videotaped from the moment they meet until the entire interaction is complete. Dr. Diamond testified that these safeguards were not met in the Bailey case.

He also stated that the third safeguard was no one other than the psychiatrist or psychologist and the individual to be hypnotized should be present in the room before and during the hypnotic session. Throughout the session the police artist was present during the hypnosis. The reason for this safeguard is that it is entirely too easy for observers to inadvertently communicate to the subject what they expect or what they are disappointed with. The fourth safeguard says that because interactions which have proceeded the hypnotic session may very well have a profound effect on the session itself, recordings of the prior interrogations are important to document that a witness had not been implicitly or expressly cued pertaining to certain information that might then be reported for the first time by the witness during hypnosis. Dr. Diamond explained that previous interrogations might very well be inadvertently introduced into the hypnotic session through leading questions.

There is also the possibility that prior information may have been consolidated into the hypnotic session. This is called source amnesia. Dr. Diamond used as an example that he might ask where the quote "To be or not to be" came from. Certainly, you might respond that it came from Shakespeare's play, Hamlet, but you probably would not remember the original source of this memory. Dr. Diamond says that in hypnosis a subject may think a memory came from personal observation while it may have been introduced by a question or word choice in interrogation. Dr. Diamond acknowledged that similar distortions could occur without hypnosis, but he believed they were more likely to occur under hypnosis.

Dr. Diamond testified that he understood that Arons safeguards had pretty much been adopted by the Supreme Court of New Jersey, but he still felt that a witness who had been previously hypnotized should not be allowed to testify in court.

Dr. Diamond stated that he believed that a number of experts including Arons proposed that the best way of going about investigative hypnosis was for the hypnotist to know nothing whatsoever about the case and to have no briefing. This is absurd because if the hypnotist knows nothing about the case, there is no way of defining hypnotic suggestion or focusing in any way that would make any sense, so it's paradoxically necessary that the hypnotist have at least some reasonable knowledge of what is known about the case, and what kind of information is being sought through hypnosis. Yet the very act of knowing that will to some degree contaminate the hypnotic experience and make it difficult to sort out what was inadvertently suggested to the subject, so I don't think the dilemma is soluble. But if those involved want to insist that the witness testify despite the hypnosis, as a very minimum there would need to be very precise information as to what the hypnotist was told and as to what the hypnotist guessed or knew about the material that is being elicited. Dr. Diamond would like a video of the interchange between the police and the hypnotist of what took place before the hypnosis. Note: With today's use of body cameras this should not be a great burden, and in many cases, the video could be made of the first stop and all interaction with police and the subject. Dr. Diamond did say it would be better to have a memo written before any contact between police and the hypnotist as the only thing given to the hypnotist setting out all of the facts given to the hypnotist if there were no video.

In the Courtemanche murder case Jackie Roberts was briefed orally to which Dr. Diamond strongly objected. Dr. Diamond pointed out that Jackie Roberts counted to five to bring the subject out from under hypnosis but when she counted to five she stopped the tape. Dr. Diamond said he had no knowledge of how or when the subject was ever awakened. He also said that there was some reason to believe that the hypnotic trance to some degree continued after the awakening. That can occur; there can be some degree of suggestibility and at least some of the characteristics of being hypnotized even for days, even though when the signal is given, the subject appears to awaken and be out of the trance. I think it is reasonably possible to demonstrate that the subject may not be out of the trance. This is a very common post-hypnotic phenomenon, and it accounts for the fact that a subject can continue in the after-hypnotic period with the same kind of perceptual distortions and hallucinations of memory that he or she exhibited during hypnosis if the subject has been properly cued by the hypnotist. So I am not satisfied that I know when this subject awakened and when the hypnotic trances terminated, and I think that there is easily the possibility that there were some, or there could have been some distortion of consciousness and memory during the hours following the hypnosis, during which she was being worked with by the police artist who made the composite drawing. The full tape recording is also for the purpose of judging whether the subject was actually hypnotized and evaluating the reality of the experience.

Mr. Taylor, the attorney, asked about the use of the Idento-kit during or immediately after a hypnotic session. Dr. Diamond said … "in terms of my own criminological experience I think the Idento-kit is suspect anyhow as a method in terms of that it in itself can induce and suggest to people mistaken memories, and when this is combined with recent hypnotic experience, I think it enhances the hazards of distortion. "

Mr. Taylor ask Dr. Diamond if he drew any conclusions from Mrs. Dugger using the term vehicle in her preliminary hearing testimony. Dr. Diamond commented that this is a term used by police officers. Dr. Diamond stated that during the examination of Mrs. Dugger she was asked about the word and she became defensive and justified it by saying that she needed to be very legal and very precise. Dr. Diamond said that during the hypnotic session of Mrs. Dugger that this word had been used by Mrs. Roberts and it is his inference that this is an example of a post-hypnotic suggestion. And this is the kind of situation where a subject is not aware in his or her memory that something was suggested to them. So, subjects find it very necessary to vigorously insist to themselves and to others that the use of the word or the suggestion of an idea emanated from their own minds. That's very, very characteristic of post-hypnotic suggestions, and I think that this is the most concrete example that I was able to find in the somewhat insufficient record.

Special note: Mrs. Dugger had completed a good bit of law school and was thinking like a lawyer. It is also important to point out that her testimony did not materially differ from the statement she gave the Okmulgee Police officer shortly after the murder and before being hypnotized.

Dr. Diamond strongly disagreed with the practice used by Agent Roberts who did not record the pre induction and post induction interviews as is normally done. He said that she was naive and not aware of the implications of not making such recordings and concluded that she had little or no knowledge of the impact of this on the evidentiary situation from the criminal process.

Dr. Diamond testified that Mrs. Roberts was asked about the depth of hypnosis and she said that she asks a subject to visualize a yardstick and ask the subject to state the depth of hypnosis. Dr. Diamond argued that this interchange of yardstick was simply pseudo-scientific nonsense. Dr. Diamond said typically subjects can be extremely deeply hypnotized and obviously in a deep trance, insist that they weren't and never were, people can be in the lightest possible trance with some question as to whether they were really hypnotized at all and come away from the experience believing they were deeply hypnotized.

Dr. Diamond went on saying that one thing that is important for our purpose here is the false idea in my opinion as to the scientific nature of memory that forms the basis for much so-called investigative hypnosis. This is based on a theory that the human brain is like a tape recorder or like a motion picture film, that everything that is perceived, whether one pays attention or not, is irrevocably engraved upon the brain in true, vivid form, and can under proper circumstances with proper techniques be retrieved, so that the problem of memory is not in the recording, but is in the retrieval or in the playback. …Now this is a false theory, this is an erroneous theory, and I think modern scientific knowledge, and most researchers and psychologists do not support the idea that there is such a permanently, irrevocably engraved memory. There is reason to believe that what is engraved in the brain is some kind of distorted perception of what did occur, which is strongly influenced by what thoughts are already recorded in the brain, and that this recording is sort of fluid and is subsequently influenced by future experiences, so if I record in my mind this room here, that recording is already mixed up with when I've been in this room before, other circumstances, other memories, other experiences, and then two weeks from now, if you interrogate me as to what I remember about this experience, it may also be contaminated by the fact that next week I'm going to be in this room again because this is an office to which I frequently come, and as a result, to some degree or another, every memory is inaccurate and there are distortions which are very relevant to the criminal justice system. There is reason to believe that whatever distortions are likely to occur without hypnosis are greatly exaggerated and much more likely to occur with hypnosis. … People view their thoughts to check if they are remembering correctly; this is called a power of self-criticism. There is reason to believe that hypnosis to some degree in every instance alters the power of self-criticism. Another necessary element of hypnosis is suspension of critical judgement and the way we hypnotize a person is actually an attempt to suspend their powers of critical judgement, and this suspension of critical judgement leaks over and affects their judgement both during and after the hypnosis, so to some degree, how much I can't say, but to some degree in every case a subject who has been hypnotized has less ability to self-judge …I am not in a position to know how much or whether it happens, all I can say is it almost certainly happens to some degree.

Special note: Dr. Diamond said that it ALMOST CERTAINLY happens. He did not say an absolute certainty. This is the reason it is important to verify and confirm whatever is learned from a hypnotized witness.

Dr. Diamond also said that he thought it helped a great deal to know what the witness knew before the hypnosis to compare what they actually knew before and during the hypnosis.

Special note: We know what Mrs. Dugger said before she was hypnotized.

Mr. Taylor, the attorney, asked if an audio tape of what the witness said prior to hypnosis and then what witness said when hypnotized showed no change in the witness's recollection of the incident, would you still be of the opinion that witness should not be allowed to testify before a court and jury? Dr. Diamond responded "yes, I feel the evidence has still been contaminated."

Mr. Taylor asked Dr. Diamond, "What is your impression and opinion in this particular case where hypnosis – they went straight to hypnosis, there was no attempt to draw a composite before hypnosis, there was no investigation done prior to hypnosis, the fact they went straight to hypnosis – what is your feeling and impression about this?" Dr. Diamond responded "Well, I find this very puzzling, because to my knowledge – well, I really have no specific information as to how strenuous or how persistent were the efforts to obtain information from the witness without hypnotizing her. It is my impression from what I have been told that the witness was not given a line-up before the hypnosis and we have no - or I have not seen any accurate record of what interrogation took place. I understand that the hypnosis was done very soon after the event, I have grave misgivings about this, and I personally regard this as irresponsible actions on the part of the investigators."

Dr. Diamond expressed the very firm opinion that the usefulness of Mrs. Dugger as a witness had been destroyed, that the evidence she might have been able to give had been contaminated to an unknown degree and in unknown ways that made it impossible to determine by any known technique or any known expert or by direct or cross-examination how much of her memories are truly valid and relate to what she actually witnessed and how much has been some kind of inadvertent contamination or confabulation.

Mr. Taylor, the attorney, asked, "Do you think the defendant in this case has been denied his constitutional right to confront and cross-examine witnesses against him if Billie Jean Dugger testified?" Dr. Diamond responded, "Yes, I do. A witness may come up with a certain version which might very well be easily exposed as inaccurate, inconsistent, false, by proper direct or cross-examination. When such a witness then relates essentially the same version under hypnosis, this does not in any way, shape or form indicate that the version is correct, but what happens is that you freeze that memory and then it makes it difficult, if not impossible, to demonstrate that the memory is incorrect."

CROSS EXAMINATION OF DR. DIAMOND

District Attorney James D. Jordan took over examination of the witness, Dr. Diamond, who testified that he taught at both the medical and law schools of the University of California, Berkeley. He joined the university in 1964 and had long been a Clinical Professor of Psychiatry. Since January of the year of the deposition his salary was being paid by the Medical School, where he teaches half-time. In January he would return to teach at the Law School.

Dr. Diamond was originally Professor of Criminology in the School of Criminology and Professor of Law. In 1976 the School of Criminology closed, and from that time on Dr. Diamond was full time at the law school. The law school has two divisions and he is in both. One is a professional program in the law school. The other, which leads to a Ph.D. degree, is called Jurisprudence and Social Policy. That is a research program in law and criminology and other aspects of it. He taught two courses in the professional program of forensic psychiatry and one in what amounts to criminal law in psychiatry; the other was non-criminal law in psychiatry, mental health process commitments and confidentiality. In the School of Criminology, he taught courses in criminal behavior, ideology of crime and also a specialty of his, which had to do with psychological evidence in the criminal justice process so he taught courses on evidence. He also had a number of publications concerning polygraph, hypnosis, interrogation, eye-witness testimony and similar issues. He stated that he often published collaboratively with Professor David Lewis, who Dr. Diamond described as a world-famous expert on evidence.

D.A. Jordan asked if he sometime taught people who were to become law officers. He said, yes, we've taught a good many law officers in the School of Criminology and also in special programs that were specifically designed for law officers. For example, he continued, when drug abuse law enforcement was transferred from the Treasury Department to the Special Bureau of Alcohol, Firearms and Drug Abuse, all the new officers – 100 or more – were sent to Berkeley for their initial training at our school, under Dean Loman and myself. Dr. Diamond said, "I would say a third or more of our students at the School of Criminology were regularly enrolled for their Bachelor's, Master's or Doctor's degrees. Also the police were enrolled." He said he taught both groups. "In the Law School I teach almost entirely the law students and some students who are usually lawyers, most of them from foreign countries, sometimes law officials, District Attorneys who come back for Master's Degrees, sometimes Judges. Those in the JSP Program ranged from undergraduate students to Ph.D. candidates, he said.

D.A. Jordan said, "I'm not really clear on what type of subject matter you are teaching in the Law School itself." Dr. Diamond responded, "in the law school I have the total responsibility for teaching just about everything related to both criminal and criminal aspects of legal psychiatry".

D.A. Jordan asked for examples of some matter he might teach in that course. Dr. Diamond responded, "A great deal of what was concerned with was the criminal responsibility." Dr. Diamond continued that his predecessor at the School of Criminology, Dr. Douglas Kelly, had a course for law enforcement people in the use of polygraph, the use of hypnosis, and whatever other scientific or instrumentation was available. When Dr. Kelly died, Dr. Diamond replaced him and was asked by the university to evaluate that course and also the information in the field as to whether that course should be continued. He concluded in 1964 that it should not be continued, but Dr. Diamond was unwilling to teach hypnosis for that purpose.

Dr. Diamond stated that he was certified in 1946 by the American Board of Psychiatry and Neurology in Psychiatry. He said he was one of the founders of the new board, the American Board of Forensic Psychiatry, and was certified two years ago by that board, and was also on the Board of Directors. He further stated that he was one of the examiners for the American Board of Forensic Psychiatry.

He also said he had taught the use of hypnosis in the medical school and also at the University of Michigan. As the senior resident and later instructor he had the responsibility for teaching people under him. At that time he used hypnosis quite widely, and that was part of the training. Dr. Diamond also said that a specialty of his was the accountability for responsibility and began definitions. Dr. Diamond further said that he did a good bit of research and published articles on it, addressing what it means, current decisions, and how things like diminished capacity arise. What interested him most, he said, was the role of the scientist or psychological scientist in the system, rather than factual information. In other words, Dr. Diamond went on, his job was not to teach courses in psychology or psychiatry, as he did in the medical school. It is hard to define his field, he said, not just psychiatry or just law. Rather, it's the interface between the two.

Dr. Diamond also said, "I confuse people, because I'm not a lawyer. It's a field where I think neither lawyers nor psychiatrists have a great deal of expertise."

Dr. Diamond went on by saying that he had never been an advocate of the use of hypnosis by law enforcement, nor by the investigative people, so he had never been in the true position of an investigative hypnotist, He had participated in it on only one occasion, he said, a predecessor of Dr. Martin Reiser, the Los Angeles Police Department's first staff psychologist who had used hypnosis in his work, Dr. William Joseph Bryan, Jr, was a pioneering hypnotist who had done work for the C.I.A, during the Cold War. Dr. Diamond said that he thought he was the first person to start training programs for investigators and others in the use of hypnosis and its relationship to crime. He was invited to participate in one program.

Dr. Diamond said he had also taught medical students. When asked how long it took to train a doctor in hypnosis, he said it was ridiculously easy. He testified that the actual technique takes less than an hour to explain and to teach, but the theory of hypnosis takes years. Dr. Diamond went on to say that he was no longer involved in teaching hypnosis to either doctors or other people because of his concern about the discrepancy between teaching the technique and teaching what it really is all about. He further stated that the time that is allocated to say psychiatric residents is not sufficient to give them any real appreciation, "so my position is that I refuse to teach anybody the technique unless they will make it possible for me to spend hundreds of hours on the scientific background of the technique and that's never possible."

Dr. Diamond testified that he was the Director of a program called the Doctor of Mental Health Program, part of the School of Psychiatry. It was a five-year program after the Bachelor Degree in which students earned a D.M.H. or Doctor of Mental Health. No time is devoted to hypnosis in that program.

Dr. Diamond also commented that when he taught hypnosis to residents at the Neuro-Psychiatric Institute there was a lot of enthusiasm for hypnosis and they spent hundreds of hours teaching it and using it with patients.

Dr. Diamond added that hypnosis was used by him and others, and he did a great deal of teaching of hypnosis in the military service. "During World War II, a lot of us who were psychiatrists were very shorthanded, we were under very great pressure to treat enormous numbers of patients, and it was not unusual to have a boat load of a thousand or more patients admitted to our hospital at any one time, and I was in charge of the various treatment programs here and overseas, and we used hypnosis a great deal because it seemed like a valuable shortcut, and it worked very effectively, and I used it on hundreds of cases, and I don't know how many hundreds of hours or how many dozens of military psychiatrists I taught the technique.

D.A. Jordan asked, "Now, I believe I am correct in that setting you were not interested in retrieving factual information; is that correct?"

Dr. Diamond responded, "That is correct."

Dr. Diamond was asked what was the purpose of the American Board of Forensic Psychology. He responded, "Those of us who founded that board feel that to be a competent psychiatrist and to be qualified by the regular board is grossly insufficient to qualify one as an expert in court, that there is very little in the training of psychiatrists which in any way prepares them to handle the kind of problems which arise in both civil and criminal litigation." He further explained that a person might be a very highly qualified expert in what is or what is not schizophrenia or what is or is not psychosis and not have the vaguest idea of what rule or responsibility exists, let's say, in California, or what standard should be used or what is the basis for ascribing responsibility in a Worker's Compensation case. D.A. Jordan then asked, "Apparently then this, and perhaps this is an oversimplification, it would be a matter of recognizing what the law is and making some effort to apply your findings to that particular law, would that be a fair statement?" Dr. Diamond responded, "Correct". Dr. Diamond did state that this is not a separate board, as it is an additional requirement and people who are not qualified psychiatrists are not accepted.

D.A. Jordan asked, "Now, so that I'm certain on this, do you feel that once a person has been hypnotized, that that person's memory is so contaminated that he should never be allowed to testify in court; am I correct on this?" Dr. Diamond's response: "Yes, that is my posture, once they have been hypnotized in relationship to the events of what is relevant to the event of what is relevant to the criminal, or the civil for that matter, that they have been rendered incompetent to testify. Obviously, I don't believe that if they were 10 years in some other context that they couldn't ever be a witness."

D.A. Jordan then asked, "All right. Let me ask this: I believe you testified a minute ago that your understanding of memory gets down to the matter that memory is not only what we observe and experience at the time but what is already there. Might then hypnosis ever, if your theory is correct, have some effect on a new memory?" Dr. Diamond responded: "Yes. Yes, it does. In hypnosis there is an increased tendency to confabulate. By that we mean when there are gaps in the memory, the subject in a sense makes up the details and fills them in, and they don't make them up out of whole cloth, they make them up from other memories or other experiences or information that they were told or that they were asked. Now, it is true that not infrequently under - - with hypnosis, the individual is able to remember more of what they could have remembered if they hadn't been hypnotized." D.A. Jordan asked, "That is a true fact you are saying there?" Dr. Diamond went on, "And some of these new memories will turn out to be actual true memories." D.A. Jordan: "Thank you." Then Dr. Diamond testified: "So that it is possible to enhance memories through hypnosis, there is no scientific doubt about that whatsoever." D.A. Jordan, "All right." Dr. Diamond said, "The problem is that the additions given by the hypnosis consist usually, in fact always of some mixture of some additional true memories and additional confabulations, and it's not possible to tell which is which, so you are confronted with a situation that here a person remembers such and such, now they are hypnotized they have a much better memory, it's possible that that new memory is truly valid, it's possible that it is truly invalid, most likely it's a mixture, and in between, and the problem is we don't have any technique at this time to sort out which is which".

Special note: Hypnosis should always be used as the very last resort and whatever is learned must be independently confirmed.

Continuing with the cross-examination of Dr. Diamond, D.A. Jordan asked, "Now, this would also be true of the witness who had never been hypnotized, wouldn't it?" Dr. Diamond responded: "it can be true. The problem of eye-witness testimony is a new field of research, and is one that interests me and I have some knowledge about it, it's an area that concerns me. At this stage in my knowledge, I can't consider myself an expert on eye-witness testimony…

Note: Dr. Diamond testified that he has publications on several subjects including eye-witness testimony; is this a contradiction?

D.A. Jordan asked: "…Would it be true that there are cases where it is obvious that unhypnotized witnesses, eyeball witnesses' testimony is inaccurate?" Dr. Diamond responded: "Beyond a doubt." D.A. Jordan continued, "All right. So, this is true regardless of hypnosis on the patient?" Dr. Diamond responded, "It can be true, yes."

D.A. Jordan asked, "Can you give us a definition of hypnosis?" To which Dr. Diamond responded, "Well, there are many different definitions, and the lack of a general agreement, but I think the definition that I favor is that hypnosis is a state of altered consciousness." D.A. Jordan: "Okay. Does it also involve relaxation and concentration?" Dr. Diamond: "Well I haven't finished". D.A. Jordan:" Excuse me, I didn't mean to interrupt you." Dr. Diamond: "I was hesitating. It is a state of altered consciousness in which there is an artificially focused attention on the hypnotist, or sometimes on one's self, like hypnotizing one's self in a mirror, in which there is a suspension of critical judgment, a state of heightened suggestibility and a restriction in conscious perception the sensory organs, the focus on the hypnotist, but reducing the perception of other stimuli." D.A. Jordan asked: "Okay. Are all of these characteristics always present in every incident of hypnosis?" Dr. Diamond responded: "To some degree, the degree of what varies. For example you can have a very light, a very profound sense of alteration of consciousness and a total focusing of awareness on the hypnotist without any, for example, sensory distortions, hallucinations the like. On the other hand, you may have a very light, a very minimal trance or alteration for which in all practical purposes there doesn't appear to be any alteration, yet there may be total loss of critical judgement or there might be greatly heightened suggestibility. …That varies from subject to subject and from incident to incident.

Dr. Diamond said that he believed that most psychologists and psychiatrists would agree with his definition of hypnosis, except those involved in investigative hypnosis. Dr. Diamond said that he was sure that Dr.Reiser would say that a person can be hypnotized and not increase his suggestibility, but Dr. Diamond thought that was utterly impossible, and that is the difference – the other things he thought they would agree with. Also, Dr. Diamond said that some of them would say it is not necessary that there be a suspension of critical judgement, you can induce it or not induce it. But Dr. Diamond said that was not possible.

D.A. Jordan asked Dr. Diamond if he knew Dr.Reiser, and he said yes, very well. D.A. Jordan asked if he had had occasion to discuss theories with him, and he said yes. D.A. Jordan asked when and where these discussions were held. Dr. Diamond said, "Well, Dr.Reiser has been on the other side of a half dozen cases. We've met and discussed our differences. Dr.Reiser and I are both involved in a project of the American Bar Association concerned with setting standards for psychiatric testimony in Criminal Justice Matters." D.A. Jordan asked, "But you've had actual discussions, face to face meetings?" Dr. Diamond responded, "We've talked, yes." Question by the D.A., "And when and where were these?" Dr. Diamond's response, "Oh, I think every trial we've had, we've had some kind of short conversation. The last one was at the American Bar Association in Washington." Further question by the D.A., "Approximately when are we talking about, it that this year?" Answer "Yes, it was this year in the late spring." The D.A. then asked "That's fine. What was the thrust of that particular discussion?" Response, "Well, I think Dr.Reiser and I have a kind of an intellectual armed truce, I recognize that I am not going to change him and he is quite aware that he is not going to change my mind, so we are - I can't really say this is an interchange." Question, "When you run into that, what type of discussion does take place?" Response, "Well, it's usually about the - "Question: "and I'm specifically limiting that to you and he, you understand." Response by Dr. Diamond, "I would say that Dr.Reiser and I have never had what I would consider a valid scientific intellectual discussion of the issues, because our position is so highly polarized and we know ahead of time that neither can be influenced, so it's more polite than penetrating, I'll put it that way. This is in contrast with the kind of discussions that I have with others'' Question, "Let me ask you this —" Dr. Diamond went on, I don't want to mislead you." Question: "No, I'm asking for information I can understand this. Frequently when we run into the situation where we might have a polite discussion talking about the weather and coffee and this type of thing, is that what you are saying, or are you saying you actually talk about hypnosis but don't pursue the depths of it?" Answer, "No, we have a polite discussion about hypnosis of whatever the case may be, and - but there is no depth to it."

D.A. Jordan asked about what research Dr. Diamond had done confirming his statement that there is no way to tell the difference between true memory and suggested memory. Dr. Diamond responded: "Well, my first use of hypnosis was entirely for hypno-therapy purposes. Both before the war and then very extensively in the military, I used it, and I taught the use of it to colleagues in relationship to combat neuroses, and in the treatment of combat neuroses and also in terms of something which I as well as the Army Medical Department were very much interested in with what were the elements of combat which creates combat neuroses. Now, the typical combat neurosis is somebody who that comes in and he is kind of a nervous wreck, he is jittery, he is startled and he is trembling and he sort of gives a vague idea of what happened, but when you really try to pen him down, you can't get any accurate information, so we used hypnosis for that purposes of getting information and indirectly having a kind of catharsis appearing out of emotions and re-experiencing the situation." Question, "Is that a matter of information, or is that a matter of emotional discharge?" Response, "Well, let me explain- now, when we started, this was not only for therapeutic purposes, but for research purposes for the military as well. … And we somewhat naively assumed that when this poured out of this intentionally emotional reaction of that particular experience of the horrors of that they went through, that this was an accurate picture, and we found, I and others were beginning to make recommendations about combat situations and so forth reduce this. It wasn't long before we discovered that there were discrepancies, that some of the stories, as far as we could figure out, could not have happened, and sometimes we would have information from buddies and others, and it was very quickly apparent that there were discrepancies between this and the fact that the individual intentionally recalled an experience, in short told us that this is what took place, what the individual's distorted perspective thought took placed what he believed took place, and we had some very great concern as to whether this meant that it wasn't therapeutically effective, and then what I think we all discovered, I particularly, was that it didn't matter, that what we were really after was what the individual thought occurred, and that the-" Question by the D.A.: "Now this is for therapeutic purposes of treating the patient?" Dr. Diamond went on: "Therapeutically it didn't make a particle of difference whether it was accurate or valid as long as it came forth, and usually we would get some kind of measure, often of both war combat experiences, intermixed with childhood experiences, which were related, traumatic experiences from childhood, and for therapeutic purposes it was desirable to get the mixture, so we stopped implying in any way that hypno-therapy led to some sort of truthful information." Question by the D.A.: "Did you make any effort to verify the information from time to time; I understand you had comments from buddies and this kind of thing?" In response Dr. Diamond continued, "Originally, we made a lot of effort to do that, because we were sort of daydreaming of the possibility of making alterations in the training of soldiers and combat experiences and preparation for it to reduce the incidents of combat, and we dropped it because we felt it was so unreliable. … Now another phase of the work I did had to do with the use of hypnosis, which is specifically authorized in California, on a Defendant by an expert witness for the purpose of defense, and so in more recent years, up until, oh, about ten or twelve years ago, I not infrequently used hypnosis as part of my psychiatric examination of Defendants. I have been very much associated with the diminished capacity defense, one has to know pretty accurately what the individual thought and felt at the time of the crime and if a Defendant has an amnesia or is unwilling or unable to tell or remember the events. It makes it in my mind impossible for an honest psychiatrist to testify about diminished capacity or even about insanity, so I used hypnosis sometimes Sodium Pentothal hypnosis as a technique for cracking the amnesia, and I did a lot of experimental work with various Defendants, and usually I could eradicate the amnesia, and at first, I was under the similar naive idea that what I was getting was accurate information. I no longer believe that's true, that I was confronted with specific situations where I know for sure the information I was getting was not factually accurate, so that led to my experience." D.A. Jordan asked: "Let me ask you this: Now in hypnotizing a Defendant, would his memory thereby become contaminated just as a State's witness?" Dr. Diamond's answer, "I think so, even though the legal issue at least in California is separate". … "I was just going to say that my original purpose in writing that article had been to write an article on all of the uses of hypnosis, not just enhanced by evidence, but certainly to include its use in investigative purposes and its use in defense purposes. When I planned the article, I had not realized how long just this subject would be, and there are very sharp limitations to the number of pages you can get in the Law Review, since there was doubt about this issue, I dropped the other. I still plan to write an article about the use of hypnosis by defense experts for purposes of defense, although I have done it very widely and I will be most known for that use, I have very serious doubts about it, and I do intend to, as I would say, challenge the legality of it because it's now sort of authorized in California." D.A. Jordan asked, "Let me ask you this: How would a court ever become aware if a defense witness had been hypnotized without his disclosing it?" Dr. Diamond responded: "Well I am not sure they can be aware; I think it is possible to hypnotize a person secretly, I think it's possible to hypnotize a person and conceal it, I think it's possible to hypnotize a person and, in some instances, it just doesn't even occur to anybody that it has happened." D.A. Jordan then posed the following: "And certainly I would suppose there could be a post-hypnotic suggestion to forget the fact of hypnosis?" Dr. Diamond replied, "There can be, yes." D.A. Jordan continued, "Back to the Defendant being hypnotized, does that sometimes or has it in your experience, resulted in undesirable coaching?" The Dr. Diamond continued: "One way of looking at the problem of hypnosis is that it's a mild form of subordination of perjury, it's even more than coaching, because a person who has been coached, they know that they have been coached. The problem with hypnosis is it is a form of coaching in which neither the coach nor the person who is being coached knows or appreciates that they've been coached, so it's this deceptive quality about it that is very disturbing." D.A. Jordan then asked, "So partly your answer goes to your specific experience based on past cases that actually frightened you from your own experiences?" Answer by Dr. Diamond, "Right." Question by D.A. Jordan, "Would it be fair to say you are defense oriented or pro-defense in your approach to hypnosis?" To this Dr. Diamond responded, "Very clearly defense oriented."

Special note: Clearly Dr. Diamond was not an impartial commentator. He had taken sides and had a purpose in his position that hypnosis should never be used in investigative work.

D.A. Jordan asked, "Now, you comment on the purpose of the article, was it not your purpose to convince Judges and Courts to exclude the use of hypnotized witnesses?" Dr. Diamond further replied, "Yes, it was specifically for that purpose, it was written in the Law Review to make sure they would read it rather than the Medical Journal, and the hope was that the Appellate Courts would follow my advice and rule that such witnesses are incompetent and that would directly affect the use of hypnosis for investigative purposes and reduce its wide-spread indiscriminate use."

Special note: Again, Dr. Diamond made it clear that he had taken sides on the issue of the use of previously hypnotized witnesses in court and was not impartial. Certainly, he has pointed out what he believes are problems in using previously hypnotized witnesses to testify in court but he has gone farther than just pointing out the problems for the trier of the facts to consider.

D.A. Jordan then asked, "Have you seen better results from your own experiences approaching Judges and Courts this way rather than going to the Legislature?" Dr. Diamond said," Well, my experience in California is that the Legislature is a very poor route to any kind of reform in relationship to such problems of evidence, and like I testified many times before the Legislature on many issues, both as an advocate of various positions and not infrequently called by the Legislative Committee as an expert. I do have a rather dim view of the process, and looking back on my own sort of 40 years of professional experience, the way I have been most influenced has been in testimony in specific cases that resulted in appeals, so that the Appellate Court would say, yes, Diamond said the right thing or said the wrong thing. Secondly, in publishing articles I learned many years ago that if I expected my articles to be read by Judges and lawyers, I have to publish them in law journals and not medical journals, and so I have for a long time mostly published in law reviews and these articles have been cited many, many times in many, many decisions, so it would seem to me that's the way to go rather than through the Legislature." D.A. Jordan asked, "Let me ask you this: What is your view of the Legislative process as practiced in this country, do you feel it is a valid process, or do you do you feel it should be changed?" Answer by Dr. Diamond, "Well if the Legislature does what it's supposed to do, it would seem to me there would be very little work for the Appellate Courts, and I could really satisfactorily that the position that the Appellate Courts do deal with a strict constitutional type of approach. Unfortunately, it's my experience that Legislatures did not accept that type of proper role in legislation, they leave many gaps and do many things which are not proper, and are inconsistent, so we rightfully or wrongfully are forced into situations where the Courts may take a very accurate role in some of these issues, and there is, of course, always who takes priority here, and when the dispute arises as right now in the diminished capacity issue, I consider it unfortunate that we follow the English system of having a kind of tri-party law, that law can be made by the executive in terms of administrative regulations, it can be made by Judges, it can be made by the Legislature, and hopefully it's an interaction of the three law-making groups, what comes out is the best you can do. That is not always true." D.A. Jordan asked, "But you feel there might be a better way to do it then?" Dr. Diamond commented that he believed the deficiencies of the system tend to be the failure of the legislature.

D.A. Jordan asked, "…what is your evaluation of the jury system as we use it in this country today?" Dr. Diamond's response, "I have great faith in the jury system, I'm one of the very few psychiatrists who feels that the last person who should do this kind of thing are experts. In other words, the kind of decisions which have to be made in the legal process, particularly the criminal process, are the kinds of decisions which must sort of reflect the beliefs of the community, and, well, I am sort of looking into one aspect that I hope someday to research which speaks very much in favor of the jury system. … What I think it is, when people are required to make the same decisions over and over again … they do not necessarily acquire expertise in making that decision, as a matter of fact they may very well have their decision- making powers corrupted, and to me one of the great decision-making things of a jury is they only do it once, so if we had a Board of Experts on the side of criminal offenders, I think those boards could become very corrupt in their ability to make rational decisions, so I'm very much in favor of jurymen." D.A. Jordan asked, "I take it when you are using the word, "corrupt", you don't mean take money or anything like that, but their thought process?" Dr. Diamond's response, "No, their thought processes contaminated by their prior decisions."

Special Note: D.A. Jordan had spent three years as Special Judge for Okmulgee County prior to becoming District Attorney. In that position I heard all jury and non-jury misdemeanor cases and all felony preliminary hearings. I came to realize that I was hearing from the same law enforcement officers frequently, was becoming friends with them and was accepting their version of what had transpired a bit quicker than the version of the defendant so I had to consciously consider this fact as I heard these matters.

D.A. Jordan asked, "Is there any way to make exact measurements in the area of hypnosis or anywhere else in the area of psychiatry?" To which Dr. Diamond replied, "No."

D.A. Jordan asked Dr. Diamond about his article in the California Law Review titled "Inherent Problems in the Use of Pretrial Hypnosis on a Prospective Witness" and went on, "I believe you indicated that you based that on a substantial number of cases in your experience. How many cases have you been involved in in forensic hypnosis?" Dr. Diamond responded, "Well, I'd say it depends on how you define forensic hypnosis. If you define it in just strictly the courtroom legal situation, I would say a dozen; if you define it in terms of use of hypnosis for purposes of determining the truth of memories, you might say investigative purposes but not in a criminal setting, then I've got to include all my military and research cases which would number in the hundreds." D.A. Jordan asked, "Okay. Now, that would not necessarily be in the crucible … of trial".

D.A. Jordan asked, "Now, have you had cases where you have had individuals other than yourself and the subject present at the hypnosis?" Dr. Diamond, "Yes". D.A. Jordan, "And how many cases, forensic cases, have you had that happen in?" Dr. Diamond, "Well, in — I don't know the percentage of them, I would say at least half of the courtroom cases somebody else has been present." D.A. Jordan asked, "And how many of those cases did you video tape or tape record?" I tape recorded all of them, none of them were video-taped." D.A. Jordan asked, "When did you commence the taping and when did you stop the recording?" Dr. Diamond's answer, "Well, I would start the tape and I would have the initial contact long before, I might say when I do forensic work everything that I do is taped, audio taped. Now, I'm video tape more, but in most cases, I used audio tape and the instant a person walked in to the room, I have my tape recorder on, and I tell them on the tape, 'I have this tape recorder going, do I have your permission to use it,' and I leave it going until the last contact, so in every case I have full records of everything." D.A. Jordan asked, "When was the last time you hypnotized a criminal defendant?" Dr. Diamond's response, "The last criminal defendant was Sirhan Sirhan at the time of the Robert Kennedy Trial, which was in 1969, late '68 or '69. I don't remember the exact time."

Special note: Robert Kennedy served as the United States Attorney General and US Senator and was the brother of President Kennedy.

D.A. Jordan asked," ...What difference does it make in the depth of hypnosis for forensic purposes?" Dr. Diamond replied, "Well, I don't think it makes too much difference for the kind of things we are interested in here. If you deeply hypnotize a person, you can do all kinds of tricks, I mean you can do something which, you know, are flagrantly improper and irrelevant for legal purposes, but assuming you are not trying to do that, assuming you are not trying to fake evidence, then it doesn't matter what the depth is. ... In terms of a person who is slightly hypnotized, there may be more contamination than if they are deeply hypnotized. ... There may be more contamination than if they are - in other words, the individual may confabulate just as much in a light hypnosis as they would in a deep hypnosis, and the element of suggestibility can be very strong in a light hypnosis. There is a good deal of variation in this, some people are very suggestible in very light trance, others are not." D.A. Jordan replied, "Are we not all subject to suggestions we don't recognize every day?" Dr. Diamond's answer, "Yes." D.A. Jordan asked, "Are we not all subject to suggestions we don't recognize being subliminal suggestions?" Dr. Diamond's answer, "Yes."

D.A. Jordan then asked, "How many theories are there as to what memory is?" Dr. Diamond's response, "Oh, I think there's as many theories as there are researchers, and there are a great many researchers in this area." D.A. Jordan questioned, "Many theories?" Dr. Diamond continued, "Yes. At the present time, I would say the state of the art of research and memory is that all theories that have been proposed, all have grave defects to them, so we know more about the theories that aren't true than we know as what is true, so I think we can say a great deal of what memory is not and we are not so good at saying what memory is." D.A. Jordan proceeded, "... Is there a sort of consensus among psychiatrists or psychologists as to a theory, apparently there is none." Response by Dr. Diamond, "No."

There was a discussion about certainty and approximating certainty and what makes a scientist and what separates pseudoscientists.

D.A. Jordan asked, "... Now, is it possible for a person with no training to go into a hypnotic state, self-hypnosis, and not to know that it is even the state of hypnosis?" Dr. Diamond's answer, "Yes." D.A. Jordan then asked, "... Would that person's memory be contaminated?" Answer by Dr. Diamond, "It could be, it could be. I think that is what happened with Sirhan Sirhan, who is the perfect example of somebody who induced hypnosis by himself and grossly contaminated his own memory." D.A. Jordan continued, "... Now in that view of that type of situation, would you feel that that person should not be allowed to testify? I'm not thinking specifically of a Defendant now." Dr. Diamond responded, "Well, outside of a Defendant, I've never had first hand confrontation with that issue, and I just don't know what my mind would be if it occurs, I do know that — "D.A. Jordan asked, "You can see the possibilities, do you not?" Dr. Diamond went on, "Yes. I think there are possibilities which might indicate that that person's testimony would be incompetent. I'm just not sure."

D.A. Jordan then asked, "How might a Court ever know or the person himself that he had been hypnotized?" Dr. Diamond responded, "They might not be, it might come out completely inadvertently or be just accidentally discovered. ... I think in certain instances, I've learned to suspect that it may occur." D.A. Jordan went on, "...and I suppose this comes from your years of experience in questioning some of your own work?" Then Dr. Diamond said, "Well, I've been burned by it."

D.A. Jordan continued, "... I believe you testified a bit earlier that the tape recorder theory, and I may be in error on this, but I believe that is the same as the cybernetic theory, I believe, that you testified that that is not an accurate theory of memory." Dr. Diamond agreed, "Yes." D.A. Jordan proceeded, "... What data do you base that on?" Dr. Diamond answered, "Well, that's less on my own data as it is various psychological authorities proved and various alternative theories that have been proved" Question by D.A. Jordan, "Can you be more specific as to who?" To which Dr. Diamond responded, "I would rely very heavily on the research of Elizabeth Loftus, Robert Backhouse of the Brooklyn College of New York, and another man by the name of Yarner in Canada, and these three foremost researchers on the problem of memory of a witness's testimony.

D.A. Jordan then asked, "...Now, you testified, I believe, that non-hypnotized persons may recognize a faulty memory, but almost certainly a person who has been hypnotized will have his memory affected and not recognize it." Dr. Diamond replied, "Not be able to tell, accurately tell." D.A. Jordan then asked if there might be cases where an individual might recognize that to which Dr. Diamond responded, "Yes, I think it is possible."

Moving on D.A. Jordan asked, "...in the incident or the case where we might have a witness observe an event and relate that observation and then subsequently be hypnotized, and during hypnosis relate virtually unchanged the prior relating or account, would you feel that that individual had been, well, had his memory contaminated?" Dr. Diamond, "Yes." D.A. Jordan went on, "...a little more specifically, what do you mean?" Dr. Diamond responding said, "As I described it, the fact that the hypnotically recalled memory is identical to the original memory just means that the hypnosis has fixed or frozen the memory, so that a person has simply reputed the memory. Let's assume for the moment that the original memory was false - and then-" D.A. Jordan asked, "Even before Hypnosis?" Dr. Diamond's response, "Before hypnosis, a mistake or something or other. … Or a misconception, then under hypnosis is recalled and the hypnosis can now give the subject the permanent belief that that memory is valid, and you can very easily do this experimentally. You can tell a person, you know, I want you to think of this imaginary situation, you have witnessed a bank robbery, and you tell the person before he is hypnotized, and just imagine it and then you hypnotize a person and under hypnosis you have them recall that memory as if it's real, you see, then you wake them up. Now they have told the same thing but they have lost the recollection that it was a fake memory, a mistaken memory to begin with. … In other words, what you have altered is not the memory or the sense of competence in the memory."

D.A. Jordan asked, "Now, assuming there was no suggestion on the first observation, would your answer still be the same?" To which Dr. Diamond replied, "Yes, it doesn't have to take place, it may not take place, but it can take place. Not because the hypnotist deliberately tried to falsify the memory, but through the individual's own eagerness to please and the increasing suggestibility due to the expectation of a person, the context in which that occurs, and my main criticism of investigative hypnosis, and it's been true in my experience, the investigative hypnotists that I am familiar with, and I've read a good many transcripts, seem to be very conscientious and very honest and try their best not to contaminate the situation, and it seems apparent to me that the subject is the worst source of contamination rather than the hypnotist." D.A. Jordan then asked, "All right. Have you hypnotized Kenneth Dexter Bailey, Jr, with reference to this case or anyone else with reference to this case?" Dr. Diamond asked, "Have I?" To which D.A. Jordan responded, "Yes." Then Dr. Diamond replied, "No." D.A. Jordan then asked, "Has anyone hypnotized anyone that you are aware of with reference to this case?" Dr. Diamond testified, "I know nothing about it except what is in the papers here." D.A. Jordan then asked, "Dugger, incidentally, is the only part you know about in this case?" Diamond's answer, "The only part other than the clippings."

D.A. Jordan asked, "I took your comment a while ago about the diminished capacity of Dexter as being simplicity involved in this matter." Dr. Diamond went on to explain, "It's just that the state Legislature as of last month repealed the laws dealing with diminished capacity in California, and the diminished capacity law in California is the perfect example of what should have been a Legislative action to begin with. The Legislature failed to get into the diminished capacity concept, and as a result the California Supreme Court in effect legislated diminished capacity, and 30 years later the Legislature ruled it out, which means that it was a direct confrontation with the Supreme Court. This involved me, because I was involved from the very beginning in diminished capacity and have been one of the strong advocates and have written a lot of the articles quoted by the Courts in diminished capacity." Question by D.A. Jordan, "In other words, your theory is even if a person does have diminished capacity and might not be criminally insane that they would not be responsible for their action?" Dr. Diamond continued, "They would be at least partly. My theory is, even though the way diminished capacity is worded they would not, and a diminished capacity defense is more sensible and pragmatic and also a more practical solution to the problem of the mentally ill defendant."

D.A. Jordan asked, "Have you evaluated Kenneth Dexter Bailey, Jr?" Dr. Diamond answered, "I know nothing about him and know nothing about the case except a few facts here, nor do I anticipate being called as an expert witness on that grounds. I would not permit myself to be in both aspects of a case, in other words, I can't be a witness on the hypnosis issue and also a witness on the responsibility issue." D.A. Jordan then asked, "All right. Now, why do you say you could not be on both?" Dr. Diamond continued, "Well, see, I haven't the slightest idea, and I don't want to know and shouldn't know whether everything that Mrs. Dugger told about is the God's truth or everything is totally false as a result of hypnosis, I haven't any idea and can't know and it's not my job to know, all I know is under the circumstances under which she was hypnotized, the probabilities of contamination are very high, and neither I nor anybody can sort it out to find out how much occurred or whether it did occur. That is a roll which is, I think, not compatible with the other issues of the case." D.A. Jordan then asked, "In other words, are you saying that any time an expert witness appears before the Court that that expert should have a demeanor of impartiality?" Dr. Diamond went on, "No. Actually, the reason I feel there is a conflict is it is my feeling that a witness is never impartial." D.A. Jordan, "Okay."

Dr. Diamond said, "One of my articles that have taken a lot of flak is entitled "The Fallacy of the Impartial Expert". I think an expert is never impartial, and also I think an expert becomes part of the system." D.A. Jordan, "When do you feel an expert becomes part of the advocacy?" Dr. Diamond, "As soon as he listens about the case, as soon as he is contacted by a lawyer." D.A. Jordan, "Or the law enforcement official or whoever?" Dr. Diamond, "Yes, so that you see – it is bad enough to be an advocate on one aspect of the case without also getting involved in other aspects of the case."

D.A. Jordan, "Would you distinguish between investigative and clinical hypnosis and also witness preparation?" Dr. Diamond, "Well, in the first place, clinical hypnosis and research hypnosis and investigative hypnosis, I think, are all the same. What is different, I think, are the goals, and the fact the goals are different in no way, shape, or form changes the phenomena itself, I think it's identical. Dr.

Reiser does not believe that, I think that, and I think Dr. Arons believes it, and many others. Now, in terms of preparations for a witness, I think there are things that are done sometimes knowingly or unwittingly in the preparation of a witness that are as bad as hypnosis. I think there are things that are half as bad as hypnosis and there are things that are done which have nothing to do with hypnosis, and I think different lawyers have different standards and different ways of operating, and I think different concepts of what integrity means." D.A. Jordan asked, "What would you use as an example of things that are as bad as hypnosis yet don't involve hypnosis?" Dr. Diamond, "Well, I have knowledge of circumstances where lawyers have coached witnesses and gave them shamefully explicit really, hints, that they shouldn't talk about certain things or that they should about certain things." D.A. Jordan, "Tell them what to testify to?"

Dr. Diamond, "And tell them what to testify to without actually coming out and spelling it out in one syllable words, but the witnesses or the defendant gets the point quickly enough and testifies falsely. At other times, I think a lawyer can in good consciousness help a witness to recall facts and sort out what's relevant, what is not relevant and what may have happened and just maybe guess what happened." D.A. Jordan, "How might that be done, to sort out what is relevant and what is not relevant and truthful?" Dr. Diamond," Well, I think all witnesses have a tendency to talk about irrelevant things. I, in my testimony here more than once have brought in irrelevant details, and this can be confusing, it takes up time and makes it harder for the jury to pick out what is really important, so I think a good attorney can assist a witness in knowing what is important for the legal process, and very few witnesses understand what the law is after, and on the other hand, this can be done in a context which grossly distorts, so that between – I am unable to draw a firm line from my experience between simple coaching and subordination of perjury in such cases, and this concerns me greatly."

D.A. Jordan, "Let me ask you about this: What would your feelings be about a situation where a lawyer and perhaps a defendant goes on TV and makes statements, now, as far as contaminating the jury panel?" Dr. Diamond, "Well, I would be very condemning of that."

D.A. Jordan asked, "Now how many times — and you may have already answered this, but I don't recollect it - did you say you've testified, 12 times in 12 different cases? Dr. Diamond responded, "In hypnosis?" D.A. Jordan, "Yes." Dr. Diamond, "No, more than that now. I think there is, about 10 or 12 in California, and I have testified in Boston, New York, Colorado and Anchorage, Alaska." D.A. Jordan, "15 or so?" Dr. Diamond,"15 or more." D.A. Jordan, "But as many as 20?" Dr. Diamond, "No, somewhere between 15 or 20, I suspect." Dr. Diamond, "The 12 cases were cases where I personally hypnotized the defendant for purposes of my psychiatric examination, that's what I referred to." D.A. Jordan, "Sometime in the '60's was the last time you did that?" Dr. Diamond, "Sirhan Sirhan was the last one." D.A. Jordan, "But you have continued to testify?" Dr. Diamond, "Yes." D.A. Jordan, "But you have not done any more hypnosis for any purpose since then?" Dr. Diamond, "Not for forensic purposes, I-"

D.A. Jordan, "Have you for any purpose?"

Dr. Diamond, "Yes. I occasionally demonstrate hypnosis, the hypnotic technique to students." D.A. Jordan, "Now, what type of students are we talking about?" Dr. Diamond, "Post-Graduate, Psychiatrist, they are taking their psychiatric training, I think the last was four or five years ago." D.A. Jordan, "Have you conducted any research experiments in forensic hypnosis?" Dr. Diamond, "Yes, just prior to getting started in this, I don't want to divert - I had one spectacular case where an Army Officer was accused of planting a bomb and mailing it to his wife, and he had quite confessed and agreed that he must have done it, but he didn't have any memory, and I used hypnosis for the purpose of having him relive the experience, and what got me going on this project, I hypnotized him about five or six times and he gave a different version of the bomb every time, and in that case, I knew what the bomb was like and I knew that all five were very false, and a few years back I was sort of replicating this on two patients who agreed to be hypnotized as to whether I would get different versions on different occasions, and I found I did, and so that I would hypnotize somebody and they described a certain event and a week later I hypnotized them and they described it differently. What I'm interested in is what Reiser should be doing and isn't, and maybe I ought to persuade him he should do it, if I ever get the chance, he is judging the reality of his subjects according to what comes out in Court. What I would like him to do, if he ever got a chance, is to re-hypnotize each of these subjects and see whether they come up with the same story or whether the stories have been changed by hypnosis and how many alterations can be produced, so I did some of that."

D.A. Jordan, "It is your understanding that Reiser principally goes to taking the word of the witness and then presenting those to the jury rather than taking the words and making outside corroboration?" Dr. Diamond, "Well, Reiser believes that there is a very high level of corroboration between what comes up with hypnosis and what the true facts are, I forget the figure he proposes, but to me I don't believe it."

D.A. Jordan, "What percentage of cases does he say that useable information comes to of forensic hypnosis?" Dr. Diamond, "It was 85 percent that he feels useful information comes from and that it is valid. I think there is an article here." D.A. Jordan," I don't recollect it." Dr. Diamond, "Yes, I think it is, maybe not. Anyhow, you can ask him, but I know it is a substantial number that he feels fully justifies the use for investigative purposes." D.A. Jordan, "All right, is it your understanding that he does or does not make an effort to corroborate by outside evidence what he is told?" Dr. Diamond, "He does, he makes definite efforts and testifies about the corroboration. I challenge what he and I differ is what is corroborated." D.A. Jordan, "Now, would you give us an example of what you are talking about there?" Dr. Diamond, "Well, let's say the police are convinced that Kenneth Bailey committed this crime, so they question a witness about certain aspects of this which correlate with Bailey, then the witness under hypnosis comes up with information which corroborates what the police say. Well, Reiser, I think, would assume that the identity of this information which the police and Bailey proves accurate, supposing in the trial Bailey confesses." D.A. Jordan, "All right."

Dr. Diamond, "That certainly corroborates the – what the hypnotically enhanced witness says, but it doesn't in any way prove that the witness had any independent knowledge. The witnesses of her memory may have come from the previous interrogation, it may have come from reading the newspaper articles, this is strictly true in cases of identifications made under hypnosis where sometimes the line-up is with the hypnotized person. What the person may identify is a picture they saw in the newspaper and think it's the real person. Now, that may turn out to be true, but it - put it this way, if the corroboration is so substantial and proves what comes up, you needn't need that witness and there should be no objection to leaving out that witness because you have all the other evidence, so I don't - I just don't agree with Reiser that he has the corroboration of the witnesses, I find it's exceedingly difficult to find out what really happened. Reiser seems confident that in the majority of cases he knows what the real truth is, I don't understand how he does that."

D.A. Jordan, "Let me ask you this: As a hypothetical matter, if the evidence in this case would show that Dugger heard the gunshot and made the observation of an individual that she could not specifically identify as a person but could identify and describe as to general description, general characteristics as well as the automobile, and then at a subsequent time a gun is found that had definitely fired the death projectile, and also fired cartridges found in the possession of the defendant, would that not be corroboration?"

Dr. Diamond, "No. No, I don't see it has anything to do with it. All it indicates is that the witness heard or thought she heard a shot. What that has got to do with reality may or may not have any connection with reality, I just don't know."

D.A. Jordan, "Let me just ask you this for clarification. It appears your answer and your evaluation and reasoning go to the pure scientific approach and analyzing observations and memory, I suppose, rather than the practical application of a jury making a decision. Would that be a true statement?" Dr. Diamond, "No. Actually

I'm much more practical than that. I'm more concerned with the practice suspected of it. To me, the practice aspect of it, as far as I know, the criminal justice system relies very heavily on witnesses, that is the essential part. Circumstantial evidence is very desirable, but is not always available. Scientific evidence as such is very desirable, but seldom available in limited amounts, so we rely on witnesses. There is a possibility always of distortion anywhere from none to gross distortion of many witnesses, that's beyond dispute."

D.A. Jordan asked, "Hypnotized or not?" Dr. Diamond answered, "Hypnotized or not. Variously techniques have developed in the judicial system, namely, Direct, and Cross-Examination, and other interrogation methods for attempting to determine how much weight and validity should be attached to particular witnesses. These are not by any means infallible, they don't always work, and sometimes gross errors are made. Nevertheless, they're all we have. Now, in that context, the police have introduced a new or a different technique of interrogation and investigation which we have substantial objective scientific reason to believe greatly increases the chances that the undesirable kind of distortion may have occurred. It is also a technique in which the degree of the interference is not easily defined, and in most cases, I think it is impossible to define, so one can't tell from any kind of known procedure whether there has been a lot of contamination or gross contamination, and also that it interferes with the markers which traditionally for better or worse we use to judge contamination." D.A. Jordan asked, "Now, you are referring to –"

Dr. Diamond went on, "Demeanor, contamination, hesitancy, non-verbal language. What that means from a practical standpoint is should such technique be permitted, and it is my opinion that the harm or the dangers of it are so great as measured from the value of it for investigative purposes that I think it should not. Obviously, others would think differently and they would weigh these things differently. One of the elements which place a very important role in my feeling is a belief which I hope to research someday, but probably won't because I'm no longer in a situation where I have free access to the police like I did at one time, is whether there are other ways of getting the same information without hypnotizing people."

D.A. Jordan, "Now, what would you have in mind?" Dr. Diamond, "I think there are techniques of interrogation which modern psychologists are discovering and experimenting with which I think promise –

D.A. Jordan, "Would you describe that?"

Dr. Diamond, "I have yet to have a case or I have yet to see a anybody else's case where what came up in hypnosis, as far as I can guess or judge, could not have been achieved without hypnotizing the person and without introducing that, which is such a strong element of contamination. It puzzles me why a person like Mrs. Dugger was hypnotized in the first place. If I were asked to participate in that case, there are a great many things I would have done before I would have hypnotized her, and I see nothing which came up under hypnosis of a kind or nature which couldn't have come up without this danger of contamination had they been a little more patient and given her a chance. There are techniques like the techniques of free association and psychotherapy where it has been demonstrated over and over again, where not only can you find out what happened without hypnosis, you can get more information."

D.A. Jordan, "Would that technique be suggestive?" Dr. Diamond, "I think it can be, I think you can do it in ways that contaminate and ways that are unlikely to contaminate." D.A. Jordan, "So this gets down to the efficiency of the operator?"

Dr. Diamond, "Well, actually a valuable form of research which is developing now, they are doing this at Stanford, is find out what is more likely to contaminate and what is more likely not, and the conclusions are that the most accurate memories come when you just ask a person, 'Tell me what you remember, tell me the story,' and shut up. "You will get the most accurate memory, and also the most complete memories. Then if you ask questions like lawyers do, you get the most complete memories and the least accurate memories, and the trick is what kind of balance between these two techniques will give you the maximum memories with the minimum distortion, and they are actually doing research on this subject now, and I think they will come up with ideas that would maximize interrogation techniques and which would be of real value to the police in reducing distortion and increasing completeness. Obviously, they will never do what the police want, which is to read people's minds and to know the real truth, but I would like you to know that it is my opinion, and this is from talking to the researchers in this field and other famous people in hypnosis and the like that really if ever anything is elicited from hypnosis that could not be elicited without hypnosis."

D.A. Jordan asked, "Now, is there a body of data you can refer to that proves that scientifically?"

Dr. Diamond, "In terms of the alternatives?"

D.A. Jordan, "Yes."

Dr. Diamond, "Not yet, it's premature."

D.A. Jordan, "Okay, it's still in the investigative stage at this point?"

Dr. Diamond, "Yes."

D.A. Jordan, "Would you agree that the fields of psychology and psychiatry are really still in their infancy?"

Dr. Diamond, "No. No, the fields are – these are fairly advanced. This infancy business is a cliche."

D.A. Jordan, "All right, let me rephrase that."

Dr. Diamond went on, "There are a lot of things about human psychology we don't know anything about. There are a lot of things we have a very sound idea. It's as valid as anything in physics."

D.A. Jordan, "Do you feel we have learned as much as there is still to learn?"

Dr. Diamond, "In the areas that are relevant to criminal investigation, there is an astonishing deficiency of knowledge."

D.A. Jordan, asked, "So really in those areas as a society, we have very limited knowledge?"

Dr. Diamond, "Let me put it this way, I think an ignorant person is defined as not as much a person who doesn't know things as a person who knows many things that are not true, and I think the problem, their problem is not knowing things, but they know things that are not so, and there is a tendency to adopt simplistic views and also by theories that fit their needs, very, very much."

D.A. Jordan, "Do you believe that it is true in human experience we do from history determine from experience that certain things do work?"

Dr. Diamond, "Yes, it's a curious fact that the modern psychology in terms of what is the best way to interrogate may turn out to be a time-honored way that experienced police interrogators have always used. Certainly, I have known interrogators who have relied always, and who would say in response to what I have just said of the Stanford work, of course, this is the right way to interrogate people, and I have done this all my life."

D.A. Jordan, "That is the way you would tell the story?"

Dr. Diamond, "Yes, and when the story is told, they are very, very good at sorting out and comparing versions, so there is nothing new about this."

D.A. Jordan, "Would you feel that trained police investigators are professionals within their area?"

Dr. Diamond, "Well, having been occupied with training police at various times in my career, there are problems. The problem of police training is an open one. There are very strong differences of opinion about how police should be trained."

D.A. Jordan, "Are there problems in training all professionals?"

Dr. Diamond, "Well, there are special problems in training the police, and I am not a good person to ask. I, of course, for many years was associated with the School of Criminology at Berkeley, which was founded as part of a radical idea originally by Chief Aylmer (phonetic) on the Berkeley Police department. The theory was that policemen have been as highly trained as doctors and architects, and every policeman should be a minimum of a college graduate and trained in their work just like any other professional. The School of Criminology was founded in the '30's for that purpose," he continued, "and there was a time when that goal of having every policeman as a trained professional, college trained, scientifically trained, was almost realized in the Berkeley Police department." But, he continued, the practice died in World War II. "The shortage, the draft and everything else meant they weren't able to use college trained people," he said. "The changing role of the university created problems, we had many police who were enrolled in our school who were not really qualified to do high level academic work, and somehow the whole idea has sort of fallen apart.

"Now, the police rely very heavily on the so-called police academies. The biggest problem is the John Jay College of Criminal Justice in New York City, and their student body is some 3,000 policemen who are getting various college training.... Some people, even their own professors, admit that in the past John Jay has been a kind of Junior College for cops, and they are in the process of upgrading it."

D.A. Jordan, "Perhaps my question should be better phrased, not the typical street policeman, but the well qualified investigative officer?"

Dr. Diamond, "The well-qualified investigative officer is much more apt to be somebody who became well-qualified with on-the -job training and from his own experience."

D.A. Jordan, "All right, and learned that from trial and error primarily?"

Dr. Diamond answered, "Trial and error, Yes."

D.A. Jordan, "Because of your belief that hypnosis contaminates a witness, do you believe that a defendant should not be hypnotized?"

Dr. Diamond," Well, there is a conflict of legal principle here. There are reasons why what is done to a Defendant has to be less restrictive, what is done to a Defendant by his own attorney has to be less restricted than what is permitted to a witness."

D.A. Jordan, "Are you referring to any specific body of law?"

Dr. Diamond, "Yes."

D.A. Jordan, "What specific body of law?"

Dr. Diamond: "In California there are a series of cases, first of all permitting that if a defendant's attorney was to have his defendant hypnotized, the jailor must permit it. That's People versus Modesto, which says if a technique is normally used by a psychiatrist for clinical evaluation, it can be used to form the basis of the expert's opinion, so in California at least it is legally permissible to do that, and I have done that as I have indicated to you. My present posture is you shouldn't do it, and in my opinion, it does contaminate the evidence of a defendant in ways which are inimical to justice, and a psychiatrist should not permit it to happen. So my position, I tell a defense attorney that I will not hypnotize their defendant no matter what, and if you have him hypnotized, you can't use me in your case because I don't know what is true and what is not.

D.A. Jordan, "Is there a constitutional provision that the state, the People, are entitled to a fair trial as much as the defendant is entitled to a fair trial' Do you feel that the same rule should apply?"

Dr. Diamond, "Well, see, fairness to the defendant and fairness to the state doesn't mean identity to the state. There are imbalances of power and money and investigative things, so I think in certain cases the law has to permit things for the defense that are not permissible to the prosecution, and that's proper in order to result in fairness."

D.A. Jordan, "You are presuming that in this case the State has more resources available than the Defendant?"

Dr. Diamond, "Well, there are different purposes for the State, say, a common example which everybody accepts, although the defense attorney has a perfect right to withhold critical information from the trial, the prosecutor has no such right, and I think it is right and proper."

D.A. Jordan, "So different rules would apply and that would be fair?"

Dr. Diamond, "Also different rules apply to the expert. The defense attorney may wish that I shouldn't reveal certain things as an expert, but I as a physician may have an ethical position that puts me in a dishonest position, so I refuse to comply with it, I shouldn't comply with it."

D.A. Jordan, "I assume that gets back to the problem that you had with the equating of the hypnotic evidence with the perjury problem, I assume this would be your reasoning to get into this area?"

Dr. Diamond, "There are lots of ways of committing perjury rather than just the conscious willful thing."

D.A. Jordan, "All right."

Dr. Diamond, I'm more worried about inadvertent than I am about intentional falsification."

D.A. Jordan, "How long has hypnosis been in existence?"

Dr. Diamond, "Well, surprisingly we really don't know. The first documented case of hypnosis was reported by Marquis de Puysegur in France, who inadvertently hypnotized a peasant boy by the name of Victor. It was reported in 1780 something. It would be incredible that this was the first example of it, but this is the first documented example. There are a lot of earlier things that strongly suggest that hypnosis existed, one which is cited is so-called Temple Sleep in ancient Rome, in ancient Greece. What you would do, you would go to the temple to pray, you would then go to sleep and you would have a dream that would tell you what is going to happen and whether your prayers would come true, and there is no proof despite a great deal of research into this, that the priests hypnotized the patient, but the context strongly suggests that it may have been natural hypnosis."

D.A. Jordan, "At least they might have been very susceptible to it?"

Dr. Diamond, "Yes, what one would expect under those circumstances. The Oracle of Delphi in Greece – the traditional states that the Oracle was intoxicated by fumes which came up from the earth. Geologically it seems improbable, it is not like Sebastopol in California up here where fumes do come up, and it's possible that the Oracle or the one who receives the messages was hypnotized, but the first proven case was in the eighteenth century."

D.A. Jordan, "What qualifications are required for a person to become a hypnotist?"

Dr. Diamond, "Apparently none, I find there are no regulations."

D.A. Jordan, "How long has the American Medical Association, for instance, even recognized its existence?"

Dr. Diamond, "Oh, for quite a long time, I would say 20 years or more A.M.A. – let's put it this way recognized that there is such a thing as hypnosis and some psychiatrists feel it is a very valid therapeutic technique."

D.A. Jordan, "Do you belong to any associations or societies dealing with the limited specialty of investigative and clinical hypnosis?"

Dr. Diamond, "No."

D.A. Jordan, "Are there such societies?"

Dr. Diamond, "Yes."

D.A. Jordan, "And what might they be?" Dr. Diamond, "Oh, I hesitate to give their specific names, there are three or four of them I've heard about, I forgot what the names are, I don't belong to any of them."

D.A. Jordan, "Is it important for a doctor to belong to various societies within his specialty for the interchange of ideas?"

Dr. Diamond, "Yes."

D.A. Jordan, "Is the purpose of these associations to exchange views?"

Dr. Diamond, "Well, I hesitate to give an opinion about their purpose. I regard them as rather dubious, I'm not sure that is the purpose, but I have to - it is not fair of me to comment about them."

D.A. Jordan, "I take it you have not actually participated in the exchanges, so therefore you are speaking from lack of knowledge there?"

Dr. Diamond, "No, I have actually been invited to participate before them. A couple of months ago I presented my position about hypnosis and I did so by an association of police hypnotists in the Bay Area, so I have had some contact with them, but I really don't know what – I think they are different, some are better than others, some of these groups are solely kind of a pseudo-status to the hypnotists who don't have licensees. Others are interested in exchanging ideas."

D.A. Jordan, “Are there societies or associations of psychiatrists and psychologists only which are limited to examining hypnosis?”

Dr. Diamond, “No, to expand that, the psychiatrists, psychologists or physicians, I think there are such groups.”

D.A. Jordan, “For physicians?”

Dr. Diamond, “Yes.”

D.A. Jordan, “All right, and I assume this would get into the dentists who would use it for anesthesia?”

Dr. Diamond, “Or the dentists, because a number of the more prominent hypnotists are not psychiatrists, I think it seems to me more hypnotists are not psychiatrists and belong to other medical specialties, chiefly dentists and obstetricians and gynecology.”

D.A. Jordan, “These people are legitimately using it, but they are not getting into using it for the purpose of getting or determining information; is that correct?”

Dr. Diamond, “Yes.”

D.A. Jordan, “Have you ever been hypnotized?”

Dr. Diamond, “Yes.”

D.A. Jordan, “How many times?”

Dr. Diamond, “Oh, I think it was maybe three times.”

D.A. Jordan, “All right.”

Dr. Diamond, “I say maybe, because of the third one I wasn’t sure whether I was hypnotized.”

D.A. Jordan, “All right, when and by whom?”

Dr. Diamond, “This was by fellow residents years ago when I was in training.”

D.A. Jordan, “All right. Is it possible that an experienced hypnotist cannot always tell if a person is hypnotized?”

Dr. Diamond, “There may be difficulties, Dr. Arons is particularly famous for a piece of research he did years ago. What he proved is that it is possible to train a subject to simulate hypnosis, and that even a highly trained hypnotist, when asked to judge whether a particular person is a simulator - that is, a trained simulator or a true subject, failed to make such distinctions, so certainly you can fake hypnosis in a way which is undetectable. From a practical standpoint, most who are hypnotized, you can either tell that they are hypnotized or they are not hypnotized or all you can say is maybe, and that can be fairly within those three possibilities, you can be pretty reliable, leaving out the specifically trained fakers.”

D.A. Jordan, “If you have an individual who is not a trained faker, just a lay person, who in fact is hypnotized and then the hypnotist asks a question which might be suggestive, do you see the tag number, this type thing, and the individual responds, no, I can’t see it; what would that indicate to you?” Dr. Diamond, “That doesn't indicate anything. A very curious thing which I discovered in reviewing a number of these tapes in other people's cases – not infrequently in hypnosis the individual expresses their critical judgement and says, "No, I'm not sure of this," and then as soon as they emerge from the hypnosis, they have lost their critical judgment, so the fact that the person seems to retain considerable judgment during the hypnosis does not mean that the hypnotist hasn't destroyed it, the loss may appear later, so I really can't say that you can make any conclusion from the instance you have cited."

D.A. Jordan, "Is there a difference between instructions used in induction and other instructions?"

Dr. Diamond, "Well, there is. Dr. Reiser trains his people in a technique which is different than was used here, and is worse than is used here. Dr. Reiser uses a technique which I believe, and he does not, I think greatly increases the likelihood of there being distortions, so-called television distancing documentary things in which you zoom in and it's my technique that this Reiser technique which he developed –

D.A. Jordan, "You are saying that technique is worse than that technique used on Dugger?"

Dr. Diamond, "Yes, it's almost guaranteed that it can be confabulation. Now, interesting to me in this case, Miss Roberts did not use the Reiser technique, she didn't do this."

D.A. Jordan, "Have you had any police investigative training?"

Dr. Diamond, "Well, I don't know what you mean by training. I've trained police investigators, I'll put it that way, I'm concerned with the problem of police investigation, scientific evidence, and so forth. I never attended a police academy. This was all done in terms of my academic professional work, particularly in the School of Criminology, but whether you would count this as training or not, this remains to be seen. Let's say I have some expert knowledge about police investigation."

D.A. Jordan, "This gets into your experience as a trainer then?"

Dr. Diamond, "Yes, and as a researcher in this area."

D.A. Jordan, "Now, when you say as a researcher in this area, I take it you are talking from the point of view of a research scientist rather than the criminologist who is out to solve a crime?"

Dr. Diamond, "No."

D.A. Jordan, "Have you worked in the area of solving a crime?"

Dr. Diamond, "Well, I've worked with police in developing techniques for solving crime, let's put it that way, but this is an academic setting."

D.A. Jordan, "I mean getting away from the academic and getting into an applied area?"

Dr. Diamond, "Well, the School of Criminology is an applied technique, people like myself, the way we see ourselves is as the bridge between the practical and the theoretical .... I'm not a pure research scientist, and I'm not a pure professional, I'm in between, and all my professional life I've had that kind of role and I've functioned in areas that was in between things, so I do that, but if you mean have, I ever been employed by a police department as an investigator, the answer is no."

D.A. Jordan, "All right. Have you received any formal training in your own hypnosis work, or was this an informal training?"

Dr. Diamond, "No, I was formally trained in hypnosis. When I graduated from medical school, I received a four-year fellowship to the Neuro-psychiatric Institute at the University of Michigan, and one of the senior members of the staff was a very strong enthusiast for hypnotherapy, I had already done hypnosis in psychology, but I received specific training in hypno-therapy from him over a period of several years.

D.A. Jordan, "You referred to Sirhan Sirhan a while ago I believe .... Was he a normal individual, or did he have what a layman might refer to as mental problems?"

Dr. Diamond, "No, I feel he was mentally ill."

D.A. Jordan, " In the course of your hypnosis work for criminal defendants, have you ever found through the use of hypnosis or otherwise that one of your clients who was publicly claiming his innocence was in fact guilty?"

Dr. Diamond, "Through hypnosis?"

D.A. Jordan, "Or otherwise?"

Dr. Diamond, "Or otherwise? Well, yes, otherwise once."

D.A. Jordan, "And in those cases, have you ever made that disclosure to a jury?"

Dr. Diamond, "Yes, I have."

D.A. Jordan, "What were the circumstances and how many times has that happened?" Dr. Diamond, "I don't know how many times it's happened, but, see, I wouldn't be testifying in a case unless they are willing to have so-called, what I call full disclosure, it's a principle in many articles that I have written. The basic principle is very simple, that although a defense attorney has a legal right, a constitutional right to withhold certain kinds of information, that that legal right is not appropriate to a psychiatric defense; that once you use a psychiatric defense, then the ballgame changes. What you are saying to the jury is, well, I have a legal right to not tell you what is in my mind, the Defendant, but I'm going to use a psychiatrist to tell you everything and if you know all there is about me and my psychology, then it will result in a fair decision, and I'm strongly opposed to what I regard as a kind of trickery where you use a psychiatrist to bring out certain things but withhold certain kinds of information that is legally proper. … And my principle is that you have a legal right not to testify, but you don't have a legal right to win your case, and the strategy of a psychiatric defense requires total disclosure, so I won't participate in a legal case as a psychiatric witness for the defense unless the defense agrees to put the Defendant on the witness stand, confess the whole thing, to admit everything that he told me, and if there is an important discrepancy between what I know and what the defense attorney is willing to tell the jury, I won't participate. In some cases, the defense attorneys will say, you are right, I'll let the jury know about what really happened. In other cases, the lawyers say, Good-bye, that's it, and in California there's a special law that protects the defense attorney, so if he uses me as a consultant basis, then the other side can't call me; if he doesn't call me, the prosecutor cannot call me, and I feel very strongly about that. So, in those cases where I know something relevant, I insist that either I tell or you tell the jury, that there mustn't be any deception."

D.A. Jordan, "In a sense is that what you anticipate in this case?"

Dr. Diamond, "Well, I don't know about this case, how this is being handled, I'm called in only remotely on this hypnosis issue. I know what I would prefer in this case, and my preference would be for that same kind of open thing. I don't regard this, what I'm doing now, as a psychiatric defense, but it is close enough that I would prefer that to happen."

D.A. Jordan, "Have you performed hypnosis on behalf of law officials, law enforcement officials?"

Dr. Diamond, "No law enforcement official has asked me to hypnotize him as a witness. Of course I would refuse. Surprisingly, for the very first time, a prosecuting attorney up north has asked me whether I would be willing to work for the prosecutor on a hypnosis issue, and I said, "Sure," and it's pending. … That's the only case. … I might say prosecutors don't look upon me kindly."

D.A. Jordan, "I wonder why that is, Doctor."

Dr. Diamond, "I think many prosecutors are beginning to agree with me and can be concerned about the indiscriminate messing up of a case."

D.A. Jordan, "Did you ever talk to the State's hypnotist in this case?"

Dr. Diamond, "I know nothing about it whatsoever other than the records here."

D.A. Jordan, "Do you believe hypnotically enhanced memories are always false and distorted?"

Dr. Diamond, "No, I believe that they may be false or distorted."

FLIGHT FROM SAN FRANCISCO TO LOS ANGELES

As District Attorney, I had lived this case. I had carefully prepared for the deposition of Dr. Diamond. On the flight from San Francisco to Los Angeles to take the deposition of Dr. Martin Reiser with the Law Enforcement Hypnosis Institute I realized that I had not given any thought to what I would ask Dr. Reiser when we took his deposition that afternoon. As I thought about it, I felt sure that the defense counsel, Mr. Taylor, thought I would ask Dr. Reiser questions that would give him more ammunition to use at trial. Instead, I didn't ask any questions involving the hypnosis used in the Bailey case. Instead, I asked questions to educate the judge who would be hearing the case.

DEPOSITION OF MARTIN REISER, ED.D., ABPP

Dr Reiser started out, "I have a Bachelor of Arts Degree, 1950: a Master of Education Degree in Clinical Psychology, 1956: and a Doctor of Education Degree in Psychology, 1961. All from Temple University."

Dr. Reiser went on. "I am currently the Director of Behavioral Science Services for the Los Angeles Police Department. I am also the Director of the Law Enforcement Hypnosis Institute, and I have been employed by the police department for the past 13 years as a psychologist providing counseling and therapy for officers and family members. I teach at the Academy in various ways, do research of various kinds on police-related topics, consult with managers and other police people at the department, and also consult with detectives in major crimes for psychological profiling for hostage-negotiation situations, and also for investigative hypnosis purposes."

Asked about his training Dr. Reiser related, "Well, I've had numerous – probably more than a dozen seminars in clinical hypnosis sponsored by the American Society of Clinical Hypnosis, and numerous other seminars. ... I have taught investigative hypnosis since June of 1976, first at the Los Angeles Police department in our original program, and since then, through the Law Enforcement Hypnosis Institute to over 1,000 justice professionals nationally. I have read probably 100 or more books on hypnosis – clinical hypnosis and other applications of hypnosis – hundreds of articles on hypnosis. I subscribe to several journals of hypnosis and I have published several articles on investigative hypnosis and a textbook, in 1980, called the 'Handbook of Investigative Hypnosis', which is considered one of the leading texts in that area."

Then he was asked if he held any professional certificates or diplomas that he had not covered and he responded, "I'm a diplomat in clinical psychology of the American Board of Examiners in Professional Psychology and a board member of the Western Regional Board of that organization. This is the board group for the upper 10 percent of psychologists who pass that examination in the country. ...I'm a licensed psychologist in the State of California. ...I can also give you additional memberships... ... I was an assistant Professor of psychology at the Pennsylvania

State University from 1961 through 1964; a Clinical Psychologist at Camarillo State Hospital, 1964-1965. A Senior Clinical Psychologist at the San Fernando Valley Child Guidance Clinic, 1965 through '68, and I've been the Director of Behavioral Science Services for the Los Angeles Police department from December 1968 until the present time. … I'm a Fellow of the American Psychological Association. I'm a past President of the Los Angeles County Psychological Association. I'm a past President of the Los Angeles Society of Clinical Psychologists. I'm a faculty consultant with the California School of Professional Psychology and have been since 1973. I am a faculty member and training analyst with the Los Angeles Institute for psychoanalytic studies from 1970 until the present time. … I have memberships in the American Society of Clinical Hypnosis Division 30, which is the Hypnosis Division of the American Psychological Association; the Southern California Society of Clinical Hypnosis; and I am a founder and member of the Board of Directors of the International Society for Investigative and Forensic Hypnosis. … I have published over 60 papers and four books – seven papers of which and one book have been on the subject of investigative hypnosis. … We initiated the investigative hypnosis program in 1975 at the Los Angeles Police department, and during the one-year research demonstration project, 70 cases were handled by those people with positive results. … I personally have conducted over 70 investigative hypnosis cases with witnesses or victims of major crimes and have consulted with several hundred others who have done investigative hypnosis cases." Dr. Reiser also submitted 10 pages of qualifying material.

D.A. Jordan, "Have you participated in any research or experiments in those areas?"

Dr. Reiser, "Yes. I have participated in considerable research of a psychological nature, beginning with my doctoral dissertation, which was completed in 1961. While at the Los Angeles Police department, I and many of my psychology interns under my supervision have conducted doctoral-level dissertation research and other research during the past 13 years."

D.A. Jordan asked, "… Have you had people assist you as a consultant in any of your work? …"

Dr. Reiser, "Not really, no. I think that for the reason that I seem to have been in this specialty rather early and have gained apparent background of knowledge and expertise. It's usually people coming to me for assistance. … Well, I have consulted with several hundred agencies over the years, including agencies such as the F.B.I., the Treasury Department, the Secret Service, the Bureau of A.T.F., numerous state and local criminal justice agencies…"

Dr. Reiser noted that he had a list of 15 cases in which he had testified as an expert witness in a variety of civil and criminal court jurisdictions including: State of Arizona vs Richard Francis Young, CR106652, Maricopa County, 1978; People vs Robert Edward Crane, CR-39733, Orange County, California, 1979; People vs Eddie Tyler Burnett, Orange County, California, 1979; State of Indiana vs Eugene Peterson, Noble County, Indiana, 1979; State of Indiana vs David A Mossman, Noble County, Indiana, 1979; State vs Anthony Peterson, CCR79-003, Stockton, California; Commonwealth vs Scott Colihan, Superior Court, No. 030302, Suffolk County, Massachusetts, 1980; Commonwealth vs James Watson, No 028954, Suffolk County, Massachusetts, 1980; People vs Gallegos, Sacramento County, California, March 1981; State of New Mexico vs Ronald Lee Beachum, Chaves County, New Mexico, March 1981; People vs Eugene Richard Cruz , 67336, Municipal Court, San Diego County, April 1981; People vs Louise Victor Hayes, No C 9306, San Mateo County, June 1981; Commonwealth vs Clay, Superior Court, Suffolk County, Massachusetts, 8/7/81; State of Alaska vs David Ziegler, No 3-81-147CR, Anchorage, Alaska, 8/10/81; People vs Steven, Guadalupe Superior Court, A-143438, Van Nuys, California, September 21, 1981; People vs Buono, Superior Court, Los Angeles, California, and I believe that was October 1981 - just recently.

D.A. Jordan then asked, “What is meant by the term ‘forensic hypnosis’?”

Dr. Reiser responded, “Forensic hypnosis is the use of hypnosis in court-related situations, such as for determining the state of mind of a defendant at the time a crime was committed.”

D.A. Jordan then asked, “And what is meant by the term ‘investigative hypnosis’?”

Dr. Reiser, “Investigative hypnosis is that specialty in hypnosis where the specific purpose is of enhancing recall of a witness to a crime”

D.A. Jordan then asked, “Do people ever spontaneously go into a state of hypnosis or any similar state?”

Dr. Reiser, “Yes, all the time. People mostly, without being aware of it, go in and out of hypnosis when day-dreaming, when staring into a fire on a winter evening, when driving down the highway on a warm summer day with the mind being a thousand miles away, when listening to a stirring speech and forgetting where they are. The same thing with watching a moving, emotional movie or television program. These are just a few of everyday spontaneous hypnosis experiences that many people have.”

D.A. Jordan, “Do people ever spontaneously come out of hypnosis?”

Dr. Reiser, “yes, they come out all the time.”

D.A. Jordan, “Is it possible for a person to deliberately hypnotize himself?”

Dr. Reiser, “Yes. As a matter of fact, self-hypnosis is taught in many seminars.

There are many books on the subject. It has been described as being helpful for educational purposes, for relaxation purposes, for learning purposes, study and examination purposes and – incidentally, many lawyers have used hypnosis and self-hypnosis for passing Bar examinations."

D.A. Jordan asked, "And are you the head man as far as the L.A. police department is concerned in this area; is that correct?"

Dr. Reiser, "Well, I'm the originator of the investigative hypnosis project that was started in June of 1975, and I am still a consultant to the program at the police department and also conduct cases on referral from our project coordinator-director, who is Captain Nielson. He operates the program on a day-to-day basis."

D.A. Jordan, "I have a list that you gave me of statistics indicating, 'Los Angeles Police department Hypnosis Survey 1975 through June 1981. Total sessions conducted - 624.' Does this item set out essentially what the statistics have been?"

Dr. Reiser, "Yes, this is a compilation of information that we think is meaningful over the first six years of our investigative hypnosis program at Los Angeles Police department ."

D.A. Jordan, "Are you familiar with any cases where a professional psychiatrist or psychologist who is not trained as a police investigator has been involved in hypnosis - investigative hypnosis of a witness?"

Dr. Reiser, "Yes. ... Well, of course, it's difficult to generalize and I think you have to examine each case on its merits, but there have been some horror stories of psychiatrists who have had training in therapeutic or clinical hypnosis who have done work in investigative cases and run into serious problems. I think one kind of prime example of that was the Hurd case in New Jersey, wherein the hypnosis was done by a psychiatrist, a very prominent psychiatrist, and the court found that there were many errors including leading and coercive kinds of questions both by the hypnotist and a police investigator who was present during those times. ... I think that many of the examples of the bad things that can happen with investigative hypnosis that two of my main antagonists to investigative hypnosis – namely, Doctors Diamond and Orne, give, typically involve psychiatrists or psychologists without specific training in the investigative hypnosis area. ... Dr. Diamond would preclude anyone from doing hypnosis with a witness wherein that case might get into court, and he doesn't discriminate between mental health professionals and criminal justice professionals. ...It's Dr. Orne who has attempted to assert guidelines in a variety of court situations, and his first guideline indicates that hypnosis should be done only by a psychologist or psychiatrist with training in forensic or investigative hypnosis. ... Now, originally, Dr. Orne did not include the specific training in investigative hypnosis; however, recently he came to recognize that that's important no matter who does the hypnosis. ... I've attempted early on to correspond with Dr. Orne and kind of enlighten him about the facts and the realities of investigative hypnosis since he had been quoted in the media saying things that, based on my experience were kind of off-the-wall and not accurate; however, I was unsuccessful in this correspondence, apparently, to get into meaningful dialogue with him that seemed productive to me, and I have encountered Dr. Orne in court situations on, I think, it was two or three occasions. …I've met Dr. Diamond. I've read a couple of his articles, including the California Law Review article. I've also read his 1961 Stanford Law Review article as well."

D.A. Jordan, "When you talk about the California Law Review article, I assume you're talking about the one entitled, 'Inherent Problems in the use of Pretrial Hypnosis on prospective Witnesses'?"

Dr. Reiser, "Yes."

D.A. Jordan, "What is your definition of 'suggestion'?"

Dr. Reiser, "Well, I think there are many definitions of suggestion depending on the context. I think that in a general sense, suggestion would be any communication that tends to influence a person in one direction or another. …In the area of hypnotic suggestibility, there's a lot of confusion about it. I think people confuse instructions in hypnosis with suggestibility, and they can be quite different. There are even people like Dr. Diamond who try to equate all instructions in hypnosis with suggestibility, which I think is incorrect. … But, on the issue of suggestibility, I think we have to look at suggestibility in general and we're all highly suggestible in normal everyday life. An example is that the advertising industry spends billions of dollars a year to influence us to buy products, which we may or may not need, and no hypnosis is required for that and we are very suggestible in buying those products. … A confidence man may fleece victims out of thousands of dollars all of the time in "get-rich-quick" schemes, and no hypnosis is required, and those people are very suggestible, so that suggestibility is an everyday common kind of event or experience and potential that we all have, and we are all suggestible depending on who it is we're talking with and what kind of communications are given to us. …I think the early definition of hypnosis started by a psychologist named Clark Hull back in 1933, in his book called 'Hypnosis and Suggestion,' really tries to equate hypnosis as a state of heightened suggestibility and even to define hypnosis as a state of heightened suggestibility. That's not true. There may or may not be heightened suggestibility and in varying degrees, depending on the motivation of the subject, the relationship to the hypnotist and the expectations which are established in the transaction that is involved."

D.A. Jordan, "Could you give us an example of this relationship? In other words, are you getting at the fact that a doctor should not treat his own family member? Does that type of relationship have any bearing in your - in this context?"

Dr. Reiser, "Well, yes. I think it has a bearing in that because of personal emotional involvement, a doctor and likewise an attorney is not - cannot be as objective and maintain a professional relationship to someone with close personal attachment or investments. … Well, what I am talking about, as far as hypnosis is concerned, is the kind of rapport that is established between the hypnotist and the subject and whether or not there is a positive working relationship, and I think that that's really nothing unusual. That's required at any interview situation, in any kind of professional transaction, and it doesn't have to involve hypnosis."

D.A. Jordan asks, "Does suggestion, in your view, relate to memory in any way?" Dr. Reiser, "Well, it may. It depends on the context, I think. … If, for example, we structure a recall session in investigative hypnosis and part of the instructions are that the person will review the crime event on a television set, watching a documentary film of the crime event in question and the person is able to sit in the chair, remaining calm and relaxed and review that documentary film – this is the metaphor for memory – then that instruction or suggestion has a useful purpose. It sets up an expectation and lets the person know what the transaction is all about."

D.A. Jordan, "Now, today, earlier, we took the deposition of Dr. Diamond and we got into the theories of memory and, specifically, talked about the technique that you use that you've just alluded to - the TV screen. … And he said … He testified – and correct me, Counsel, if I'm in error – but in essence, that that theory is a faulty theory and a faulty premise from which to start. Do you have any comments to make on that?"

Dr. Reiser, "Yes, I would like to see Dr. Diamond's data for that. You know, it is really interesting to me that people who identify themselves as scientific persons speaking for themselves and sometimes for the so-called scientific community, make assertions and flat-out statements about what is feasible or not feasible in the absence of any data to support those statements. That is directly contrary to the scientific method of how we operate. I think that based on my personal experience, since 1970, with the Los Angeles Police Department and other police agencies around the country using the television technique, I can state – and we have some statistical data and you have some on the sheet that I think we passed along earlier – that indicates not only does the TV technique work in a certain number of cases, but that the information that is recalled by the witnesses gets corroborated in a highly significant number of cases, indicating that by and large much of that information seems to be accurate. So, I don't know where Dr. Diamond gets those statements from other than his own knee-jerk assertions.

D.A. Jordan, "Now, I asked him a hypothetical question earlier today along the line that I'm about to outline here. A witness makes an observation; that witness then relates that observation: that witness is then subsequently hypnotized; the witness again, relates the same observation without material changes. I asked him if it was likely that that person's memory had been affected by hypnosis - contaminated. … He kept referring to 'contamination' – or if that was corroboration, and the thrust of his testimony, as I understood it, was that absolutely, it would be contaminated and that would not be sufficient corroboration. …Do you have any comments on that?"

Dr. Reiser, "Oh, I think that's an absolutely ridiculous position from my point of view, and, I think, that this same argument was presented by Dr. Diamond in a California case, People vs Diggs, and the court also indicated that Dr. Diamond's testimony notwithstanding that hypnosis is proper when conducted properly; that has to be looked at; that it's not a matter of admissibility, but how much weight to give the testimony, and that's up to the jury to decide and not up to a psychiatrist to decide. I just don't see that happening based on my personal experience in many, many cases in major crimes wherein we used hypnosis for recall purposes.

D.A. Jordan, "Going back to something you testified about a little bit earlier on the suggestion business with that hypnosis, the fact that we all - every day run into suggestions and, specifically, in the advertising area, are there instances where we are subject every day to suggestions without even knowing that we've been suggested?"

Dr. Reiser, "Well, yes, as a matter of fact. I think many of the commercials that we watch on television are designed to be extremely subtle. Many of the printed media commercials, particularly for alcoholic beverages, are designed to be - to be subtle and have so-called subliminal messages included in them, and they're very, very effective. It reminds me of a well-known experiment that was done some years back wherein the researchers selected a movie theater and used a tachistoscope [an instrument to expose objects to the eye for a brief measured period of time] to flash split-second messages on the screen that consciously were not perceived by the audience, but were perceived subconsciously that to the effect they would be hungry; that they would buy popcorn, candy and peanuts; and using different groups of audiences, some of which they flashed these messages on the screen and some of which they did not, there was no question but that the sales of peanuts, popcorn and candy - the message that had been subliminally presented - zoomed tremendously, statistically significant. Whereas, those audiences where the message had not been flashed on, they were much lower and typical for that theater as far as sales were concerned.

D.A. Jordan, "Let me shift gears here a little bit. If a hypnotist offers a suggestion, and that subject, under hypnosis, rejects that suggestion in an affirmative manner, such as, 'I do not see the car tag,' this type response or, 'I can't see that,' is that an indication that what the subject is relating is not likely to be the product of hypnosis?"

Dr. Reiser, "Yes. I think it clearly indicates that the subject has possession of critical faculties and judgment and is able to discriminate between what the person knows from his or her own memory in answering the question."

D.A. Jordan, "Today, Dr. Diamond testified — and correct me, counsel, if I'm in error on this - that on numerous occasions he had discussed your program with you, the way you do your hypnosis, though in more recent encounters you each have realized that neither one is going to change the other. … Could you expand a bit on your side of this how much interplay and discussion have you all had?"

Dr. Reiser, "To the best of my knowledge, Dr. Diamond has never discussed my program or my work with me. We have merely encountered each other on about two occasions and, in passing, said, 'Hello' to each other, and on one occasion, that I recall vividly in a courtroom in Roswell, New Mexico, where we listened to each other's testimony in a particular case, Dr. Diamond approached me after the session and indicated that one day he would have to come down to Los Angeles and convince me to give up my nonsense."

D.A. Jordan, "Now, today he testified that he had been engaged in the training of police officers in the past as well as in the law schools and also medical students. Do you recognize him as an authority in investigative hypnosis?"

Dr. Reiser, "No, I don't think that I do. I think that Dr. Diamond denies that there is such an area as investigative hypnosis, which there is, and it has all of the criteria of a specialty; and he also indicated in prior testimony, for example, in Anchorage, in State of Alaska vs David Ziegler–

Mr. Taylor, "Are we getting ready to testify as to what Dr. Diamond has said? If we are, I'm going to object to it being hearsay, talking about what somebody else has said."

D.A. Jordan, "Well, I simply was relating what had been said to get his response to it."

Mr. Taylor, "Well, if we're getting ready to get into things that Dr. Diamond has said, I think I would object to it being hearsay."

Mr. Taylor, "I believe that Dr. Diamond testified this morning that he had had a couple of conversations with you, not about your program here at L.A. Police Department, but just conversations generally about hypnosis, and he testified that it never went into any depth and that you both knew that you couldn't influence the other to change his mind and for that reason there was never any in-depth conversation about it. He never said that he visited with you and conferred with you about your particular program here at L.A. Police Department, and the deposition will speak for itself."

D.A. Jordan, "Yes, it will speak for itself. I agree with counsel on the final conclusion, but I was thinking he did go ahead and testify otherwise earlier… You started to allude to a transcript of a case in Alaska?"

Dr. Reiser, "… it's my recollection that Dr. Diamond indicated that he didn't agree that there was a specialty of investigative hypnosis; that all hypnosis is essentially the same and, therefore, he didn't feel that any special qualifications were necessary in this area, of course, I disagree with that completely, and he also added that if indeed there was a specialty, then it's possible that he would not have those qualifications."

D.A. Jordan, "… If a person goes to a police department and meets a hypnotist and then subsequently goes to a courtroom where that person is hypnotized, do you have any comments on whether or not that would possibly lead to suggestion that might contaminate the memory?" …

Dr. Reiser, "Not at all. I think it's traditional and expected that interviews involving crimes are done by police or criminal justice people and, frequently, in police stations and other legal-criminal settings, and I think that is how it is done every day, so I don't see that as being atypical or suggestive. I think that the suggestive part would come in how the person doing the interviewing conducted the interview."

D.A. Jordan, "…it is my understanding that it is Dr. Diamond's position that once a person has been hypnotized, that he cannot accurately distinguish between his own true memories and the memories that were possibly implanted as the result of hypnosis. Do you have any comments on a thought like this?"

Dr. Reiser, "Yes, I disagree with that completely. Based on my own personal experience and the experience of many investigative hypnotists at the Los Angeles Police department as well as other people, we find typically that witnesses can discriminate among what they knew before hypnosis, during hypnosis, and after hypnosis; however, if a person is scatterbrained and typically has poor memory and can't find his car in the parking lot, hypnosis will not cure that. So, we have to take into account the individual and his normal cognitive functions in addition to whatever happens during the hypnosis session. But that's not a hypnosis issue. That's an issue of witnesses generally."

D.A. Jordan, "Does the fact of hypnosis, in your view, have any particular impact on testimony? Does it do anything to the way a person would testify - a witness?"

Dr. Reiser, "It may. What we have found is that – because we use hypnosis in so-called dead-end cases, where we're looking for additional leads – that in a significant number of our cases and I think our latest data indicate that, oh – in over three-quarter of the cases, we do get additional information with the use of hypnosis by witnesses and victims in major crime cases; however, we do not find that these witnesses are unable to discriminate about their memories and can testify from present memory refreshed in court."

D.A. Jordan, "It's my understanding that Dr. Diamond's position is that the hypnosis itself can result in the destruction of evidence to the effect of possibly affecting the memory as to which was hypothetically suggested and implanted and which was the true memory and then also in the area of the demeanor – the confidence of the witness. Those things which might be important to cross-examination. Do you have any comments on that?"

Dr. Reiser, "On the first issue, if anything is implanted by the interviewer, that's an improperly conducted interview. In the old days, they used – I hear– a rubber hose and a spot light to implant memories, or whatever they wanted to from witnesses, so that's not really a hypnosis question."

D.A. Jordan, "The demeanor of the witness after hypnosis as compared with the demeanor of the witness before hypnosis. In other words, Dr. Diamond, took the position – if I am correct counsel – that the witness is much more likely to be much more confident and have much more – better eye contact, much more firmness, make a stronger witness by the fact of hypnosis. Do you have any comment on that?"

Dr. Reiser, "I have not found that to be the case generally and, once again, my observation is that it's more a function of the personality style of the individual with or without hypnosis as to what kind of a witness they make, and I have been in court on numerous occasions and listened to hypnotized witnesses, those who have been previously hypnotized and many of them were very unsure and unclear. Many of them denied that they were in hypnosis at all."

D.A. Jordan, "Is that any indication that they may, in fact, not have been in hypnosis?"

Dr. Reiser, "It may or may not, depending on the situation. It is not uncommon for people who are untrained in hypnosis, particularly early on, to feel that they have not been in hypnosis."

D.A. Jordan, "Is it possible for a trained hypnotist to always discern which individual is, in fact, truly in hypnosis and which individual is only pretending hypnosis?"

Dr. Reiser, "Well, first to answer the question on its face, no. I think that the studies on simulation of hypnosis are clear that a highly-trained simulator of hypnosis is almost impossible to detect even by an expert; however, in working with witnesses and victims in crime cases, we are not dealing with simulators or people trained to deceive the hypnotist but quite the contrary. They are cooperative, motivated and are there only because they choose to be there. We don't work with people who don't want to assist in the investigation."

D.A. Jordan, "Where would the simulator come in? How does this come about? Where do you run into that?"

Dr. Reiser, "Well, I think that's more an issue with defendants when they are hypnotized by a hypnotist to assist in determining the state-of-mind issues around the time of the commission of the crime and, I think, then that's because alibis are important to defendants and other kinds of things that faking or simulating hypnosis becomes a real issue in those cases."

D.A. Jordan, "Now, is it true, Doctor, that there can be post-hypnotic suggestions in hypnosis?"

Dr. Reiser, "Oh, yes."

D.A. Jordan, "Now, what is that and how does that differ from what you've been testifying about here?"

Dr. Reiser, "Post-hypnotic suggestions are suggestions given by the hypnotist while the subject is in hypnosis to be carried out by the subject after hypnosis has been terminated in the non-hypnotic state. An example of that might be that with a highly traumatized rape victim, I might give post-hypnotic suggestion, during the hypnosis session, that this woman might well find herself sleeping better, feeling less anxious, feeling less anger and hostility toward men subsequently, as a way of assisting with the traumatic aspects of the rape situation."

D.A. Jordan, "Dr. Diamond today testified about law enforcement people making extravagant claims; that he has read most of the literature published by the C.C. Thomas Publishing Company aimed primarily towards police and not towards psychiatrists and other professionals – sociologists or psychologists – and that virtually all of it is totally unscientific, unethical, and illegal even. Do you have any reaction to that kind of comment?"

Dr. Reiser, "Well, I think Dr. Diamond is totally incorrect, first of all, in his characterization of the Thomas Publishing Company. If he were more familiar with the literature that they publish, he would know that they are one of the largest publishers of medical and psychiatric literature in the country, and I wouldn't be at all surprised if the number of volumes they publish for physicians and psychologists and clinical social workers outnumbered the number of volumes that they publish for criminal justice professionals."

Mr. Taylor, "I'm going to have to interrupt here. His comments were not directed at the publishing company, but rather at the two authors who we were discussing – Teitelbaum and Arons. His comments were directed toward those authors and not the publishing company. I don't want to get Dr. Diamond into a libel case."

D.A. Jordan, "I am glad you interjected that."

Dr. Reiser, "I'd like to continue with that, because Dr. Diamond has made similar statements in other cases on thc record and I think the record should be clear on these issues from my point of view. … I think– Now, my intent is not to get Dr. Diamond into trouble with the publishing company, but to point out that he's making statements that are really inaccurate. – On the issue of scientific, I think that Dr. Diamond needs to talk, specifically, about my book, for example, the 'Handbook of Investigative Hypnosis' and point out wherein I make unscientific statements, because my book is based on standard hypnosis and psychological and psychiatric literature as well as on my own experience and findings in the area of investigative hypnosis, essentially, at the Los Angeles Police Department. Other reviewers, for example, in England, Switzerland, seem to feel quite differently from Dr. Diamond about my book, and they have given it very good reviews."

Mr. Taylor, "Dr. Diamond has not made any comment about Dr. Reiser's book. I would like to point that out for the record. He's never mentioned Dr. Reiser's book. – This deposition is becoming a critique of Dr. Diamond rather than the subject of this case. I'm going to object here as to the relevancy of critiquing Dr. Diamond's every statement rather than the issue of this particular case, State vs Bailey."

D.A. Jordan, "But, of course, I feel it's relevant or I wouldn't be going into it, but I am sure the court will rule on it. Doctor, you are familiar with the Identi-Kit?"

Dr. Reiser, "Briefly."

D.A. Jordan, "Do you know what it is?"

Dr. Reiser, "Yes."

D.A. Jordan, "Do you have any thoughts or comments as to whether or not it is of itself subject or not subject to implanting suggestions in a subject's mind?"

Dr. Reiser, "I think it depends on the operator and how the different facial possibilities are presented to the subject as to whether suggestions are given or not and, I think, that it really is quite similar to how any interview would be conducted in terms of cueing or leading the subject during the interview."

D.A. Jordan, "How many different theories are there of memory?"

Dr. Reiser, "Well, there are literally at least a couple dozen theories of memory extant."

D.A. Jordan, "Forgetting hypnosis for a moment, what about accuracy of memory? Are there problems inherent in memory?"

Dr. Reiser, "Yes, there are all kinds of problems, and the research and literature on eyewitness issues – eyewitness testimony and the memory of eyewitnesses – clearly indicates that there are all kinds of problems with that, yes."

D.A. Jordan, "Does the fact of hypnosis change that in any way?"

Dr. Reiser, "About the only way that hypnosis changes that is that in a certain number of cases we may be able to enhance memory or to get what we call 'hypermnesia' which is increased memory with hypnosis, although not in every case. …May I add something here?"

D.A. Jordan, "Sure."

Dr. Reiser, "I have been taken to task for using what is called the 'Cybernetic' model of memory, likening the mind or brain to a tape-recording system, which is akin to work that was done by a neurosurgeon in Canada named Penfield over about a 15-year period and, also, grows out of the Cybernetic work of people like Norbert Weiner, and I think it's important to note that even after a 100-year period in the area of research of memory, no one really knows how the memory really works to date. There are merely series and models that people have proposed in attempting to account for the data on memory. A couple of the current theories on information-processing models, such as the one proposed by Craik and Lockhart, involves the depth of processing concept – that is, how deeply information is processed, depends on its meaningfulness to the person, the context in which it is perceived, and whether or not this information goes into what is called 'short-term memory,' which is a relatively brief memory store, supposedly; or to 'long-term memory,' which is described as being rather permanent and processed at a very deep level within the individual. There are many, many variations on the information processing models that we could get into we wished to." …

D.A. Jordan, "How would you go about going through a hypnotic session? What kind of a plan or format would you use of a witness to a crime? I'm specifically talking about in terms of investigative hypnosis?"

Dr. Reiser, "yes. Well, first of all, there would probably be contact between the case investigator and our project director, Captain Nielson, in regard to the feasibility of hypnosis in that particular case, and Caption Nielson would review the case, including the investigative work that has been done and make a determination that hypnosis is indeed appropriate in the case. He might then refer the case to me if it were, perhaps, a highly traumatized child rape victim, for example. I get quite a few of those cases because of the psychological implications. …I would then talk with the case detective and get a brief summary of the crime event, including the location, the time, the kind of activities, whether it's a rape case or homicide, and, also the kind of information that the case detectives are hoping to elicit from the person. We would then set up a time, assuming that the witness was agreeable and motivated for the hypnosis session. We would then have a pre-induction session with the witness before hypnosis is induced and during that time a lot of issues would be covered with that person including myths and misinformation about hypnosis, prior to the hypnosis, prior hypnosis experiences, whether they are in therapy for a particular problem and if so, there would be contact with the therapist about any particular difficulties that the hypnosis might present to that person. There would be discussion about the hypnosis session and a preview of coming attractions about the hypnosis session given to the person about what would be done and why. ...Those are some of the main elements of the pre-induction portion. ... We would then go into the hypnosis induction wherein hypnosis would be induced and, incidentally, I think it's important to mention because all hypnosis is really self-hypnosis and that we all have the innate capability and potential for experiencing it. It is not something which is imposed upon the subject by a Svengali-like hypnotist, but rather the hypnotist is a teacher or guide who teaches the naive subject to experience this state. So that the induction phase would teach the person how to go into this altered state of consciousness, which we call hypnosis, and I might or might not check to see where the person is in hypnosis. It's more of an academic issue than anything, because the level of hypnosis really doesn't matter except that we don't want the person to go too deeply in the hypnosis because the person becomes lethargic and may not want to talk or respond if too deep. A light or medium state is usually very adequate for our purposes. We would then get into the information-eliciting phase wherein we would set up the TV technique for the subject to review the crime on this special documentary film on the TV stand it would be explained that the film could be speeded up, slowed down, stopped completely. We can have a zoom-in close-up of anything and, incidentally, these are all things that most witnesses are familiar with from watching their own television sets and they're familiar with the technology that does exist for these kinds of experiences, so we haven't manufactured yet. ...In essence, we're merely utilizing this metaphor to assist the person in recalling, if indeed the person has this memory in the first place and we don't know that until we go through the process and see what, if anything, emerges; and then, of course, hopefully get corroborating evidence of whatever emerges because it's raw data at that point and we don't know whether it's un-factual or misperceived or factual or whatever. But it's information that needs to be processed further, hopefully."

D.A. Jordan, "Now, how do you determine whether you're getting faulty information, or truly accurate information?"

Dr. Reiser, "We don't know that, and this is why the witness in hypnosis is just like any other witness; that is, the typical non-hypnotized witness may not be giving true information. He may be giving information as perceived, but distorted originally on perception, or it may be accurate. You don't really know that and that's why it has to be evaluated hopefully, corroborated by other witnesses or physical evidence and, certainly, weighed by the trier of fact in a case if it gets into court to see just what that evidence is worth."

D.A. Jordan, "Based on your experience, do you believe that a jury can weigh the evidence from a previously hypnotized witness and consider it along with whatever experts may happen to be there for guidance and reach a proper decision as in any other case?"

Dr. Reiser, "Absolutely. There's no question in my mind, and I think there are numerous cases on the record already to show that that can be done and is being done. As a fact, the hypnosis process and the fact that the sessions are recorded allow more microscopic evaluation and examination of that kind of testimony than any other that I'm aware of, even though non-hypnotic witnesses' testimony is very questionable based on what we know about it and what the research has indicated. So, I think we are doing more in the area of investigatively elicited testimony using hypnosis than any other in the legal system."

D.A. Jordan, "Now, the procedure you outlined would be the ideal procedure that you would follow, I take it?"

Dr. Reiser, "Well, this is the procedure that I use and close to the procedure I think that we teach our students to use; however, you know, we have to recognize that we live in the real world, which is not ideal, and there are numerous agencies and organizations that have limited budgets and equipment and personnel and they can't all afford expensive video tape equipment and personnel to operate it and all the other things that would be nice to have if ideal. …For example, at Los Angeles Police Department, which is a very large agency with a large budget, we cannot afford to video every one of our sessions. We just don't have the equipment, the video tapes, or the personnel operate it, and so we have to settle for audio tapes of our cases."

D.A. Jordan, "Now, I suppose that some other hypnotist might vary the procedure somewhat and might still get valid information. Would that be a valid statement?"

Dr. Reiser, "Yes, there is an optimal legal procedure and approach, which is what we teach; however, it's also recognized that that may not happen in every case for a variety of reasons. If the errors or shortcomings, or whatever you want to call it, made are not fatal ones, and if there is adequate testimony given by people present, people involved, just as with any other witness, then, I think, those errors can be corrected to the satisfaction of the court and that information can then be weighed like any other testimony is weighed."

D.A. Jordan, "Now, let's assume this hypothetical. That a crime has been committed; investigating officers go to the scene and engage in the actual investigation; those officers call a hypnotist; relate verbally a brief, very brief sketch of what the crime was, leaving out most details and then turning the witness over to the hypnotist to elicit information. …Do you have any observations or comments on that type procedure?"

Dr. Reiser, "Well, it sounds like one that's not uncommon. It depends — Again, it depends on whether or not a department has its own program and its own structure for conducting these sessions or uses some different approach, and I could see where that could happen in certain agencies, which might differ from what we do at the Los Angeles Police Department, for example."

D.A. Jordan, "Do you see any contaminating effect of the hypnotist having less information than, apparently, you have?"

Dr. Reiser, "No, I think as long as the hypnotist has adequate information to conduct the hypnotic session to structure the crime scene with the subject … so that it can be reviewed adequately, I don't see any problem at all with that."

CROSS EXAMINATION OF DR. REISER

Mr. Taylor, "Dr. Reiser, do you in your teaching, you were talking about video tape and audio tape, do you feel that video tape is the preferable, the preferred method – to video tape the session?"

Dr. Reiser, "Oh, yes."

Mr. Taylor, "And should be done if possible?"

Dr. Reiser, "Well, I think it's the ideal way of doing it, if indeed one has the facilities for doing it, yes, I would prefer that."

Mr. Taylor, "Now, if a state agency – we're talking here about the Oklahoma State Bureau of Investigation, which is the statewide bureau of investigation – if they have a special projects unit, and they have hypnotists who have been trained and it's a statewide agency, would it be your professional opinion – advice to them that they videotape their hypnotic sessions?"

Dr. Reiser, "Well, you know, if their budgets were in better shape than ours here in Los Angeles, I think it would be a good idea. But, as I said earlier, we can't afford to do that, and we have a rather large agency, and that's one of the facts of the real world."

Mr. Taylor, "But at a minimum, at a bare minimum, you would require an audio tape?"

Dr. Reiser, "Yes, we do."

Mr. Taylor, "And that would be of the pre-induction, the session, and the post-induction?"

Dr. Reiser, "Yes. We teach and recommend that all contact with the witness should be on the tape. That's desirable, however, as I said earlier, recognizing that that may not happen for a variety of reasons, sometimes mechanical failures and other kinds of things, that if adequate remedies can be found through testimony of individuals who have been directly involved, then I don't think that it needs to be a fatal flaw in the process."

Mr. Taylor, "But now, as an instructor and as the Director of this Law Enforcement Hypnosis Institute, you personally feel that an audio tape of all contact with the hypnotist and the subject from the point they shake hands until they say, 'Good-bye', that should be taped."

Dr. Reiser, "That's what we teach, yes."

Mr. Taylor, "And that's what you, as an expert in this field, you feel that's a minimum standard?"

Dr. Reiser, "Well, I'm not saying that's a minimum standard. I'm saying that that's desirable and that's what we teach, but I recognize that it sometimes can't be done. But it doesn't necessarily, in my opinion, preclude information that may have been gained during the hypnotic session even though the complete session may not have been recorded. I think that needs to be examined before that judgment can be made."

Mr. Taylor, "You mentioned a mechanical problem. If there's a mechanical problem with the tape recorder, that would be, in your estimation, an excuse for not doing what you recommended?"

Dr. Reiser, "That's one of the things we have run into."

Mr. Taylor, "What about the hypnotist testifying that he or she just doesn't do that as a matter of course? Do you feel that is a wise step? That a hypnotist takes as a matter of course not to do that?"

Dr. Reiser, "I think it's preferable to tape the whole session." …

Mr. Taylor, "If a hypnotist, as a personal decision, says, 'I do not tape anything but the session itself; not the pre-induction or the post-induction,' there's no mechanical or budget considerations, just he or she does not do it, do you think that's wise professionally as the Director of the Law Enforcement Hypnosis Institute teaching police officers?"

Dr. Reiser, "As I said before, I think it's preferable and desirable to record the complete session; however, it's not necessarily a fatal error. It would depend upon an examination of the process by testimony and by whatever tape is available for the decision to be made, so that I would not automatically assume that because a pre-induction phase was not on the tape that something horrendous happened during that time or something after the person was dehypnotized was not on the tape that something insidious happened there, and, therefore, the information that was elicited, that was on the tape, could not be heard. I would not feel that."

Mr. Taylor, "Would you agree that not taping the pre- and post-hypnotic session, would you agree that that does not meet the generally accepted standards in your profession?"

Dr. Reiser, "Well, I don't know that there are generally accepted standards as such. I think there are preferred standards that we teach."

Mr. Taylor, "Let me ask you this: Would the failure to tape the pre- and post-induction sessions violate these preferred standards that you teach?"

Dr. Reiser, "Well, it would not provide as complete a verbatim record of the contact of the interview between the hypnotist and the subject as one that was taped from beginning to end, obviously."

Mr. Taylor, "Does the Los Angeles Police Department tape from initial contact with the hypnotist to closing?"

Dr. Reiser, "That's what we ask our people to do."

Mr. Taylor, "…and you have some control over the L.A. Police Department's hypnosis?"

Dr. Reiser, "No, Captain Nielson is the director of the hypnosis project, actually."

Mr. Taylor, "And they tape from the beginning to the end? Is that the regular procedure?"

Dr. Reiser, "Yes."

Mr. Taylor, "Are you aware of any time that the L.A. Police Department has not taped their sessions from beginning to end?"

Dr. Reiser, "Yes, I think this happened fairly often early in our program when it didn't seem to be as important when most of our cases were not getting into court; however, since cases have been going to court, and there has been a lot of argument and contention about this issue, we have become more sensitive to it, and so we have focused our attention on this point, and I would say that probably for the last-- oh, year or so, maybe a year and a half – that this has become a firmer issue than it was initially."

Mr. Taylor, "Are you aware of the F.B.I. standards on taping hypnotic sessions?"

Dr. Reiser, "Yes."

Mr. Taylor, "And, first of all, the F.B.I. recommends video tape, if possible, don't they?"

Dr. Reiser, "If possible."

Mr. Taylor, "And they recommend, at a minimum, that the entire session be audio taped; is that correct?"

Dr. Reiser, "Well, that's pretty close to what I recommend, too." …

Mr. Taylor, "Any procedure not employing an audio tape of the entire session, would then leave some question as to what happened before or after – and I'm not insinuating some horrendous something happened – I'm just saying it would leave a question about what went on before the session or after the session; wouldn't it?"

Dr. Reiser, "Well, it would not be as complete a record of the session, because you would have to rely on the testimony of those directly involved in the interview session rather than the tape recording of it."

Mr. Taylor, "And that would not be an ideal situation?"

Dr. Reiser, "Well, I think, given the climate, the kind of fighting that is going on in court on the issue of hypnosis sessions and so on, I don't think it would be wise, no."

Mr. Taylor, "Have you reviewed any materials in this case, the State vs Bailey?"

Dr. Reiser, "No, I haven't."

Mr. Taylor, "Have you visited or talked with Jackie Roberts, who is the hypnotist in this case?"

Dr. Reiser, "No, I haven't."

Mr. Taylor, "Have you heard the tape recording of the hypnotic session for this case?"

Dr. Reiser, "No, I haven't."

Mr. Taylor, "And you haven't read any transcript of Billie Jean Dugger, is that correct? … You've read no transcript of her testimony?"

Dr. Reiser, "No."

Mr. Taylor, "Have you read any transcript of Jackie Roberts, the hypnotist?"

Dr. Reiser, "No, I haven't."

Mr. Taylor, "And have you read any transcript of Harvey Pratt, the composite artist?"

Dr. Reiser, "No."

Mr. Taylor, "So your testimony here today is not based in any way on your knowledge of the State vs Bailey in whatever happened in the hypnotic session surrounding that case?"

Dr. Reiser, "Well, the information that I have about this case is brief information from the Prosecutor giving me a verbal sketch of the situation and who did the hypnosis and that's about it."

Mr. Taylor, "But you haven't read any transcript or heard any tapes in this case?"

Dr. Reiser, "No, not at all."

Mr. Taylor, "So you have no idea as to whether or not this session was done correctly or incorrectly?"

Dr. Reiser, "None at all."

Mr. Taylor, "You have no idea as to whatever suggestions may or may not have been made by the hypnotist?"

Dr. Reiser, "No, I don't."

Mr. Taylor, "Let me point out to you here in this particular case, the pre- and - post hypnosis was not done - was not recorded."

Dr. Reiser, "Yes."

Mr. Taylor, "So you have no idea about any of the situations in this particular case other than what Mr. Jordan has told you?"

Dr. Reiser, "Right."

Mr. Taylor, "What kind of mechanism do you use to record hypnotic sessions?

What kind does the L.A. police department – and you – recommend be used? Do you just put a tape recorder down on the table? Are there microphones? What do you do to ensure a good-quality recording?"

Dr. Reiser, "Well, I use my own recorder, because the Department's recorders are not very good and you get more air-conditioner noise than you do voices. I use a Sony TC-120 — I think it is — and two battery assisted lavalier type microphones that clip on, one for the subject and one for the hypnotist. Then, of course, if our police artist is involved in the case, then when he is communicating with the subject, I will, generally, clip my microphone on him so that he can be heard."

Mr. Taylor, "Now, when you use a police artist in conjunction with a hypnotic session, do you tape record whatever goes on between the subject and the police artist?"

Dr. Reiser, "Yes."

Mr. Taylor, "Is it part of the session?"

Dr. Reiser, "Yes."

Mr. Taylor, "And is that, generally, an accepted standard in your profession?"

Dr. Reiser, "Yes, it is."

Mr. Taylor, "That the police artist, if he is there, that whatever he and the subject say is tape recorded?"

Dr. Reiser, "Right."

Mr. Taylor, "Would you consider that to be a minimum standard? That it be tape recorded - audio tape recorded?"

Dr. Reiser, "Well, I don't know that I'd call it a 'minimum standard'. I think it is desirable that that be done."

Mr. Taylor, "The reason you use the clip-on-type microphones is so that everything that's said can be heard by whoever is interested later – the court or the jury or whoever might be interested?" Dr. Reiser, "Yes, I find you get much better voice quality on the tape when you use that kind of a system."

Mr. Taylor, "Sometimes, then, in a hypnosis session, the subject, because of the altered state of consciousness that they may be in, their voice may not be as loud as normal? They may become lethargic? They may start whispering and then they may speak unnormal?"

Dr. Reiser, "Yes: that's right."

Mr. Taylor, "When they start whispering, you want to make sure, if they do whisper, you want to make sure they hear it?"

Dr. Reiser, "Yes."

Mr. Taylor, "That it's on the tape?"

Dr. Reiser, "Yes."

Mr. Taylor, "It would disrupt thc process if, during the session, you told the hypnotized subject to speak up or to talk loud? That would not be conductive to a good session, would it?"

Dr. Reiser, "Probably not. We used to do that when we used the old Norelco things, which really were pretty bad. We had to do that on occasions. I think it's not desirable."

Mr. Taylor, "If the final product, the final tape recorder product - the audio tape, if it's of poor quality so that those who want to review it - if it is of poor quality and it is hard to hear, particularly questions asked by the hypnotist, would that give you some difficulty in evaluating the proficiency of the hypnotist and the quality of the session itself? If you couldn't hear part of what was going on?"

Dr. Reiser, "I think it would depend on how much would be missing and how much would be audible. I think that, say, in a two-hour session, which is, I guess, pretty close to our average time for the average investigative hypnosis session, if we had – oh, maybe 10 or 15 minutes unintelligible throughout the tape where words were either unintelligible or inaudible, I don't think that that would make too much difference, because the rest of that communication format would give you a pretty good idea of the style – the way the hypnotist frames questions, the response of the subject, and the interaction between the two of them so that I probably would not worry too much about that kind of situation."

Mr. Taylor, "But if there were a situation where not every 10 or 15 minutes, but regularly, you couldn't hear what is going on - I'm talking about where we have a tape recorder without microphones ... Where you can't regularly hear questions and what is going on, would that cause some concern?"

Dr. Reiser, "Well, it's certainly less desirable, because you have less of a record - a verbatim record - to review in this microscopic process."

Mr. Taylor, "Have you ever heard of the 'Yardstick Method,' where the hypnotist will tell the subject to look at a yardstick and give him the number that–"

Dr. Reiser, "That's one of the techniques we teach in our training program."

Mr. Taylor, "Whatever number they give from 1 to 36, tells the hypnotist what's the level of hypnosis they're in?"

Dr. Reiser, "At that particular instance, but, of course, you must recognize that hypnosis is not a steady state; that it's more like a sine wave and it fluctuates from lighter to deeper during the session, so that any kind of estimate by the subject or hypnotist is only an instantaneous one for that moment."

Mr. Taylor, "You've testified in several cases and you've told us about most of them. In those cases that you have testified in, have you had occasion to review the transcripts of the hypnotist or the subject who may have testified before you at a preliminary hearing or anything?"

Dr. Reiser, "On some occasions, yes."

Mr. Taylor, "And have you had occasion to, prior to testifying in court, of hearing the tape-recorded hypnotic session?"

Dr. Reiser, "In just about every instance, yes."

Mr. Taylor, "Can you think of any case where you have testified in a courtroom concerning this hypnosis process that you had not first heard the tape-recorded session that you're going to be testifying about?"

Dr. Reiser, "No, I think as far as courtroom testimony goes, in just about every instance, I have reviewed the tape and transcript and other materials that were available."

Mr. Taylor, "And you understand this case, even though we're not in a courtroom, you should view it the same way as being in a courtroom? That this is being taken down and will be used in court?"

Dr. Reiser, "Yes."

Mr. Taylor, "And is the same as testifying in court, as a matter of fact?"

Dr. Reiser, "Yes."

Mr. Taylor, "… And so you have no professional judgment or opinion as to whether or not the process used in this case, State vs Bailey, is correct or incorrect?"

Dr. Reiser, "No, I have no opinion about it."

Mr. Taylor, "Let me ask you this: If I told you that the hypnotist and the subject first met at the police station, after the subject had sat in the hallway for some time awaiting the hypnotist, and they went to the courthouse and had a pre-induction session and none of that was tape recorded, would that cause you some concern as a professional?"

Dr. Reiser, "Well, only in that it's much better to have things on tape; but unless I had some independent information of something improper or something that would be a deviant from standard procedure, I don't think I would be concerned about it."

Mr. Taylor, "Isn't the purpose of tape recording it, Doctor, to make sure that whatever went on – whether it's bad or good – that others can judge it later?"

Dr. Reiser, "That's right."

Mr. Taylor, "I keep using the term 'a minimum standard." Those words are used in all professions. We have certain standards that we follow and rules and procedures, and isn't it correct that audio taping a hypnotic session from start to end – you don't like the word minimum standard – but isn't it correct that that is a very widely accepted, generally accepted procedure?"

Dr. Reiser, "Well, as I said before, this is what we teach and this is what is desirable from my point of view."

Mr. Taylor, "As a professional and a teacher of those who are going to go out and practice this art and this science, that's what you tell them to do?"

Dr. Reiser, "Right."

Mr. Taylor, "And you have some very sound scientific and professional reasons for telling them to tape the entire session; don't you?"

Dr. Reiser, "Well, I don't think they're so much scientific as legalistic in that in the adversary-court process, this enables both sides to review in minute detail what went on during the interaction between the subject and the hypnotist and to them argue over or hash out any different points of view or opinions or disagreements with a verbatim record, which I think is more useful in that kind of situation."

Mr. Taylor, "And if there is no tape, then the adversaries and, particularly, those who are on the other side have no opportunity to view an objective record or an objective transcript of what happened? They have to rely on what other people who were there tell them what happened?"

Dr. Reiser, "They would have to rely on the witness personally, the one who was hypnotized, the hypnotist, and on any other persons who were present and then, of course, add it to any corroborating evidence that comes in from any other source that would tend to validate the information that was, if any, elicited during the hypnosis session."

Mr. Taylor, "And this tape recording in particular, is the reason you like it – and the reason it's suggested – is that it is an objective record, that you don't have to rely on what other people remember of this conversation that took place back in February?"

Dr. Reiser, "That's right. It's probably the most detailed account that one could have of what was verbally communicated."

Mr. Taylor, "And the fact of the matter is that this is the part of the very business that you're in because of the fact that people experiencing a conversation with another person and then they have to tell somebody about it, if it's not tape recorded, then you have to tell somebody about it later, and it never is as accurate as if it were tape recorded? Eyewitness testimony we're talking about."

Dr. Reiser, "It may not be, right."

Mr. Taylor, "People who were there and then – you know, this session took place back in February and the trial of this matter is going to be in November – so without a tape recording, we're relying on somebody saying in November what happened in February?"

Dr. Reiser, "It kind of throws it into the same area as most other eyewitness accounts where there have not been recordings of interviews, conversations, and so on, which means that one must then rely on written reports that were made by police, by the subject, the witness, and by the others who have percipient knowledge of the situation."

Mr. Taylor, "In an adversary process – and in this case, there was certainly an adversary process. This is a murder case. The man's life is at stake. His liberty is at stake – I want to get back to minimum standards. At a very minimum, wouldn't, in your opinion. the defendant be – at a very minimum, it be fair that the defendant has an opportunity to listen to the tape recording of a potential witness?"

D.A. Jordan, "Certainly, Doctor, I want you to go ahead and answer that, but, for the record, I do want to interpose an objection because I believe that requires actually a legal decision rather than a professional decision. But, yes, go ahead and answer the question."

Mr. Taylor, "I'm asking you as a professional and an investigative hypnosis expert and as a teacher of police hypnosis, don't you think that a minimum we ought to be able to hear a tape recording of what went on in the hypnotic session?"

Dr. Reiser, "I think that would be an important issue if the hypnosis elicited information critical in the particular case; that is, if a lot of information came out in hypnosis that was not available either prior to hypnosis or from other sources: however, in those cases where – and this happens not infrequently – where nothing essentially new or different comes out during the hypnosis session and the witness's memory is essentially unchanged, then I really don't see it as a big issue."

Mr. Taylor, "But don't you let the L.A. police department do that? You don't – Captain Nielson doesn't let his people conduct hypnosis sessions without audio tapes; does he?"

Dr. Reiser, "No, as I've said earlier, we tape each of our sessions."

Mr. Taylor, "And the people who come from all over the country to your school, you don't want them to leave your school, as a graduate of your school, and go out in the field and conduct hypnotic sessions without audio taping them as a minimum, do you?"

D.A. Jordan, "For the purpose of the record, I believe it's been asked and answered; but certainly, go ahead and answer it again."

Mr. Taylor, "You don't want them to leave your school and say, 'I'm a graduate of the Law Enforcement Hypnosis Institute, but I don't record any hypnosis sessions.' You don't want them to say that; do you?"

Dr. Reiser, "No, as I have indicated before, we emphasize, particularly in the last year and a half, that recording is very desirable and that it should be done in each case."

Mr. Taylor, "Have you ever heard of London Associates?"

Dr. Reiser, "Yes."

Mr. Taylor, "Do you know any of the people associated with the London Associates? Or do you have any opinion as to their standing in the field?"

Dr. Reiser, “Well, I know one of the principals in that organization, a person named Merrill Mellott – is a former director of Police Training in Ohio, was a trainee of mine who attended both basic and advanced seminars in investigative hypnosis, and, I believe, that the other instructor for that organization, Maynard Brazil, is a director of Police Training for the state of Kansas, and also attended both the basic and advanced seminars at my institute.”

Mr. Taylor, “So as students of yours, they would have been taught that the hypnosis sessions should be recorded from start to end?”

Dr. Reiser, “Yes.”

Mr. Taylor, “And you would expect them to teach their students to record the hypnotic session from beginning to end?”

Dr. Reiser, “Well, that would be desirable.”

Mr. Taylor, “Do you feel like a person who has been hypnotized can then – their demeanor, their confidence, their appearance of honesty and integrity, do you feel it’s bolstered after they have been hypnotized?”

Dr. Reiser, “I don’t understand your question – ‘honesty and integrity’?”

Mr. Taylor, “The appearance of honesty and integrity and their confidence in what they’re saying?”

Dr. Reiser, “Well, as I said on direct examination, I think that’s more a function of the individual’s personality, initially, than of the hypnosis session. I have observed numerous witnesses who have been through an investigative hypnosis process who were extremely uncertain after the hypnosis, so I don’t equate certainty with hypnosis, no.”

Mr. Taylor, “Are you aware and do you recognize that there are other experts in the field, not only Bernard Diamond, but other experts, Martin Orne, who do believe that, and it is their professional opinion that once a person has been hypnotized, their self-confidence and their demeanor may be stronger and firmer than it would have been otherwise?”

Dr. Reiser, “Well, I don’t consider Dr. Orne as an expert in the area of investigative hypnosis. He certainly has done considerable research in laboratories with college students on issues around hypnosis, but I don’t believe that he’s particularly qualified in this specialty and real crime cases. I know that Dr. Orne and some others have been making that assertion; however, they don’t have the data from real crime-case situations to back that up, in my view, and my experience is contrary to that in about a ten-year period.”

Mr. Taylor, “Let me just ask you this: Have any appellate courts adopted your viewpoint here in the last year and a half, to your knowledge?”

Dr. Reiser, “Which viewpoint do you mean?”

Mr. Taylor, “Your viewpoint about investigative hypnosis, based on either your testimony or some literature that you've authored?"

Dr. Reiser, "Well, I'm having trouble with the term 'adopted' my viewpoint."

Mr. Taylor, "Let me rephrase the question. Are you aware of the Arizona Supreme Court case, the State vs. Mena?"

Dr. Reiser, "yes."

Mr. Taylor, "And in that case, the Arizona Supreme Court adopted and cited throughout the decision Bernard Diamond's California Law Review article. Is that your understanding?"

Dr. Reiser, "Well, it's my understanding in the Mena case that there was really an extremely poor record; that there was no expert testimony on the record; and that the Supreme Court did liberally quote Dr. Diamond's Law Review article as authority. However, it's also my understanding that as of – I believe it was September 23rd, they have agreed to hear a new case with a good record where expert testimony was sufficient, and so the Mena case may or may not be the last word of the Arizona Supreme court."

Mr. Taylor, "But as it stands right now, they have, basically, adopted the Diamond – Bernard Diamond's thesis?"

Dr. Reiser, "That's correct."

Mr. Taylor, "Now, you said they have a case pending that has a good record where experts have testified. When experts testifying in a case like that, they have, first of all, reviewed the tape recording of the session and other transcripts that may be relevant to the session, haven't they, prior to testifying?"

Dr. Reiser, "Yes."

Mr. Taylor, "And that's what we're talking about - a good record.?"

Dr. Reiser, "Yes, and that was not done in the Mena case."

Mr. Taylor, "But when you're talking about experts testifying and having a good record, before they testify, they've reviewed the tapes and the transcripts?"

Dr. Reiser, "Yes, both sides have looked at all of the information detail and have had an opportunity to review the sessions completely and testify on the record from their point of view about it and so the court then is in a position to look at both points of view." Mr. Taylor, "It's presumed that the session in question would have been tape recorded in its entirety to have a good record so that the experts have reviewed it?"

Dr. Reiser, "Yes, but I don't think that was done in the Mena case."

Mr. Taylor, "But in the case where – in any case where there's a good record, that presumes that there is a tape recording of the hypnotic session, isn't that correct, the entire hypnotic session?"

Dr. Reiser, "Well, I think that's desirable; but I think when I use the term 'good record,' I'm talking more about the opportunity for expert testimony on both sides to enlighten the court on the myths and misinformation, as well as the facts about investigative hypnosis." Mr. Taylor, "And that's after those experts have reviewed the tapes and transcripts available in that particular case; isn't that correct?"

Dr. Reiser, "Usually, yes."

Mr. Taylor, "And you have not, in this case, reviewed any of the tapes or transcript?"

Dr. Reiser, "As of yet, I have not, no."

Mr. Taylor, "You're testifying here today in court and you have not?"

Dr. Reiser, "Well, it's my understanding that I may have an opportunity to do that at some future time should the prosecutor feel it's desirable to do that."

Mr. Taylor, "Prior to this testimony to this court"—

Dr. Reiser, "No, I have not."

Mr. Taylor, "– you have not?"

Dr. Reiser, "No"

Mr. Taylor, "You understand there will be an Evidentiary Hearing based on this deposition?"

Dr. Reiser, "Yes"

Mr. Taylor, "And that's the purpose of this deposition to enlighten the judge?"

Dr. Reiser, "Well, I think we are getting into legal strategies and issues that I'm not really qualified to answer on."

Mr. Taylor, "Would it be a fair statement, Dr. Reiser, that you are, in your profession, police oriented?"

Dr. Reiser, "Yes."

Mr. Taylor, "And in these cases, you've named several, cases that you have testified in. Have they all been testimony for the state, for the prosecution?"

Dr. Reiser, "Right."

Mr. Taylor, "Have you ever testified for the defendant?

Dr. Reiser, "No." Mr. Taylor, "- in a hypnosis case?"

Dr. Reiser, "No, I haven't. One of the problems in that area is that we don't use hypnosis with suspects or defendants, and so we rarely get an opportunity to get into that area."

Mr. Taylor, "But your expertise has not been called upon by a defendant to testify for him?"

Dr. Reiser, "That's correct."

Mr. Taylor, "And you're aware that the highest Appellate Courts of Michigan and Minnesota have adopted, basically, the Orne philosophy safeguards, and they had excluded hypnotically enhanced testimony? Are you aware of those decisions? The Mack and I forgot the name of the other one."

Dr. Reiser, "I'm aware of the Mack case. I'm not as familiar with the other one."

Mr. Taylor, “I believe it’s a Michigan case. Are you aware of the fact that Michigan has excluded hypnotically enhanced testimony?”

Dr. Reiser, “No, I’m not aware of that.”

Mr. Taylor, “If they have – Michigan has excluded hypnotically enhanced testimony, then, I take it, that you will disagree with the Court in Michigan?”

Dr. Reiser, “Yes, I would disagree if that’s a decision that they’ve made.”

Mr. Taylor, “And you’re familiar with the Mack case, the Supreme Court of the State of Minnesota? I assume that you would disagree with the Supreme Court of Minnesota in their decision in the Mack case?”

Dr. Reiser, “Well, unfortunately, the Mack case was a very bad case and bad cases, as you know, make bad law, and I think that unfortunately the Minnesota Supreme Court was basing its judgement on a very poor case in that situation.”

Mr. Taylor, “Was this, again, a case of a poor record?”

Dr. Reiser, “It wasn’t so much a case of a bad record as a case of a lady who was intoxicated at the time that some injury, apparently, occurred to her, and the whole issue of whether her assailant was a friend of hers or was in some way attempting to retaliate against her was unclear. The hypnosis in that case, as I recall, was done by a self-taught hypnotist. There were many, many problems with the circumstances in the Mack case, which raised legitimate questions about the facts in that case; I think that the Court’s inferences and generalizations about hypnosis, based on the facts in that case, from my point of view – How shall I put it? Unfortunate, because it was a bad case.”

Mr. Taylor, “They relied on Dr. Orne’s expertise in his field; didn't they?”

Dr. Reiser, “I believe so, yes.”

Mr. Taylor, “And I also take it that you disagree with the Supreme Court of Arizona in their Mena decision?”

Dr. Reiser, “Well, I think I’ve already mentioned that I think, unfortunately, the Mena case didn’t have any record to speak of.”

Mr. Taylor, “Well, I’m just asking: Did you disagree with the holding in that case?”

Dr. Reiser, “Yes.”

Mr. Taylor, “You’ve published a book, the ‘Handbook of Investigative Hypnosis’; is that correct?”

Dr. Reiser, “Yes.”

Mr. Taylor, “Do you know Dr. Charles Mutter of Miami, Fla?”

Dr. Reiser, “I know of him.”

Mr. Taylor, “Would you consider him to be an expert on this subject matter?”

Dr. Reiser, “I really don’t know what Dr. Mutter’s qualifications in this area are. I know that in some of the things he has written; he claims to be a forensic psychiatrist."

Mr. Taylor, "Are you aware that he has reviewed your book, 'Handbook of Investigative Hypnosis'?"

Dr. Reiser, "Yes, I'm aware of Dr. Mutter's review. I think it's a rather unfair review partially based on his bias against police officers using hypnosis."

Mr. Taylor, "His review was published in the 'American Journal of Clinical Hypnosis,' October 1980. Is that correct?"

Dr. Reiser, "Right."

Mr. Taylor, "And in that review he said that, approximately, two-thirds of the contents of your book are gained from basic textbooks of hypnosis and described hypnotic phenomena in an oversimplified manner. Isn't that a statement he made?"

Dr. Reiser, "I think Dr. Mutter incorrectly makes those statements."

Mr. Taylor, "Well, I'm just asking if that was a part of this review in the journal here?"

Dr. Reiser, "Yes, he said that."

Mr. Taylor, "He also said, 'That the language in the textbook is generally simplistic and combined with lay terms': is that correct?"

Dr. Reiser, "Well, he says on, as I recall, in that review at other places the language in the text is overly – Maybe you can just read what he says out of that."

Mr. Taylor, "Okay. 'The language is generally simplistic and combined with lay terms, but at times it becomes more technical and out of the layman's reach, although the author attempted to design this book for the lay person. There are certain incongruities in the chapter on ethics.' He points out 'The hypnotic investigator' - excuse me, 'hypno-investigator should refuse to perform a procedure if the hypnosis is deemed inappropriate or contrary to the subject's best interest, yet the contents of the book do not offer the foundations for proper training to enable the investigator to make that evaluation. There are some useful chapters, but this reviewer feels that there is a dearth of information for those who wish to use these procedures strictly for investigative purposes.'"

D.A. Jordan, "Counsel, would you please cite what you're reading from?"

Mr. Taylor, "I'm reading from the 'American Journal of Clinical Hypnosis,' October 1980, published by the American Society of Clinical Hypnosis at page 138-139."

D.A. Jordan, "Thank you."

Mr. Taylor, "Are you a member of the American Society of Clinical Hypnosis?"

Dr. Reiser, "Yes, I am. I'd like to mention, if I may?"

Mr. Taylor, "Yes."

Dr. Reiser, "That Dr. Mutter has been an outspoken antagonist to the police use of investigative hypnosis and that I have a couple of other reviews in my book. One of them, I believe, from the British Society of Clinical and Experimental Hypnosis, which is very favorable and has quite a different point of view from Dr. Mutter's, so that I guess it depends on whose objection is getting gored and as to what one's point of view is."

Mr. Taylor, "But this particular review is not very favorable; correct?"

Dr. Reiser, "I don't think he was too friendly."

Mr. Taylor, "And this is published in a journal of a society to which you belong?"

Dr. Reiser, "I've been published in the same journal several times."

Mr. Taylor, "The fact of the matter is that you had some articles published in this very volume, this very issue?"

Dr. Reiser, "An article, yes."

Mr. Taylor, "A seminar article, I believe it was?"

Dr. Reiser, "Right."

Mr. Taylor, "Are you aware – Again, we're getting away from Dr. Diamond and Dr. Orne – are you aware that not just them, but other professional organizations have passed resolutions saying that police use of hypnosis, police hypnotism - they've condemned it? Other professional organizations."

Dr. Reiser, "Well I'm very familiar with that, and I also know that Dr. Orne is the author of that identical resolution that was passed by both societies; namely the Society for Clinical and Experimental Hypnosis and the International Society of Hypnosis, and that these two therapeutic societies, whose charters involve therapy and research, were attempting to legislate against investigative hypnosis, an area in which I don't think they are qualified to do that. I'm also a member of the International Society of Investigative and Forensic Hypnosis, which passed its own resolution deploring the resolution of these two societies, and I'll point out that they're out of their ball park."

Mr. Taylor, "Now, we've talked about the F.B.I. guidelines earlier, and I want to get back to the F.B.I. guidelines. Are you aware of the F.B.I. guidelines – And I'm here at page 449 of the international Journal of Clinical and Experimental Hypnosis? This is an article on F.B.I. Guidelines by Richard Ault, who is with the Behavioral Science Unit of the Federal Bureau of Investigation Academy. …One sentence out of the guidelines of the F.B.I. guidelines is: 'You should consider utilizing only a psychiatrist, psychologist, physician, or dentist who is qualified as a hypnotist.' Are you aware of this F.B.I. guideline?"

Dr. Reiser, "Well, first of all, Mr. Ault is one of my trainees, as are several other F.B.I. people from the Behavioral Science Unit at the Academy and numerous field agents around the country. I'm also aware that one of the reasons for the way that the F.B.I. guidelines were established, were political issues – post–Watergate and"

Mr. Taylor, "Let me interrupt you."

Dr. Reiser, "I want to add one thing before you ask me another question."

Mr. Taylor, "But you have – "

Dr. Reiser, "Let me finish, please. That is, when you include a dentist as one of the health professionals who may be qualified to do an investigative hypnosis session, I think it's obvious on its face that the notion of extra qualifications by way of psychological or psychiatric expertise is not an issue, because dentists don't have that kind of training and are no more qualified to do investigative hypnosis than anyone else."

Mr. Taylor, "Well, my question was: Is it correct that the F.B.I. has established a guideline recommending the utilization of the kind – of all of the above in the profession?"

Dr. Reiser, "For the induction phase and the dehypnotization phase, yes; however, they use a trained field agent to do the actual interviewing for information-eliciting purposes, which is really the core of the hypnosis session, and even Dr. Orne has acknowledged that the hypnosis induction is the simplest part of the whole process because you can train the average person to do a hypnosis induction in about an hour or less. So, I think it becomes more apparent that there are other issues involved, such as political issues involved in the guidelines that they're using."

Mr. Taylor, "You would disagree with those F.B.I. guidelines, I take it?"

Dr. Reiser, "Well, I think a trained criminal justice professional who has specific knowledge and experience with investigative hypnosis is much more qualified to use hypnosis with witnesses than are doctors, dentists, and psychologists without that specific training."

Mr. Taylor, "My question is: you would disagree with the F.B.I. guidelines on this matter?"

Dr. Reiser, "On that point, yes.

Mr. Taylor, "When you bring a subject out of the hypnotic state and immediately go into a session with the police composite artist, do you feel that should be tape recorded?"

Dr. Reiser, "Yes, that's not exactly how we do it, but the answer to your question is that whatever interaction the police artist has, we normally include that on the tape."

Mr. Taylor, "And you feel that's a professionally wise standard of practice to follow?"

Dr. Reiser, "Well, I think, then, that it reduces the likelihood that certain parties in the legal process will infer that something improper was done because it can be looked at."

Mr. Taylor, "That protects everybody's interest and assures a fair process?"

Dr. Reiser, "yes, it's a more available record."

Mr. Taylor, "And it makes it a fairer process for everybody involved?"

Dr. Reiser, "I think it's more satisfying to all parties."

Mr. Taylor, "Would you agree that it's a fairer process?"

Dr. Reiser, "Well, I think fairness is another issue."

Mr. Taylor, "Would it be fairer to tape record all of this rather than not do it?"

Dr. Reiser, "I think it's desirable to do it, but it depends on the particular case and the circumstances of a case. I think in certain cases it is less important than it is in other cases. As I said before, in those cases where no new information was elicited under hypnosis and nothing substantial changes from the initial crime report, I don't see that it's really that big an issue because if nothing came out of it, so what's the big deal about revealing the hypnosis session?"

Mr. Taylor, "Again, I'll ask the question. Would it be a better and more fair process for everybody involved to tape record a composite artist's interview immediately after the hypnotic session?"

D.A. Jordan, "For the record, we certainly –

Mr. Taylor, "That question has been asked and it has not been answered. I've gone around it, but I'm asking you would it be?"

D.A. Jordan, "Simply for the record, I feel it has been answered. Thank you. Go ahead."

Mr. Taylor, "Okay. Would it be more fair and more proper professionally to tape record it?"

Dr. Reiser, "I think it's very desirable to do it."

Mr. Taylor, "When you talked about subliminal suggestions in your direct examination, that's just another form of planting suggestions in the human mind; isn't it?"

Dr. Reiser, "It can be, yes."

Mr. Taylor, "And it's one of the methods of planting suggestions in the human mind?"

Dr. Reiser, "Yes, I think the subliminal thing is important, because many people don't seem – aren't aware that we perceive things not only consciously, but subconsciously at the same time, and we don't necessarily have to pay attention directly to something for it to get perceived at a subconscious level, and I think that the example of that theater research that I gave you was on that issue."

Mr. Taylor, "I want to go back to Dr. Orne for just a minute. You're familiar with Dr. Orne's four safeguards as he's set out in his affidavit to the United States Supreme Court? Are you familiar with those? I think he filed an Affidavit in the State of – in the case of Quaglino vs. California in 1978. He filed his affidavit in the United States Supreme Court, and he set out in that Affidavit four safeguards. Are you familiar with those four safeguards?"

Dr. Reiser, "Well, I'm familiar with the fact that the Supreme Court did not accept that case, so that they did not review his guidelines, which were submitted as part of an amicus, I believe. But, yes, I know of his guidelines."

Mr. Taylor, "Certiorari was not granted in the Quaglino case?"

Dr. Reiser, "Yes; that's right."

Mr. Taylor, "Are you aware of the New Jersey Appellate Court decision adopting Dr. Orne's safeguards?"

Dr. Reiser, "Well, my understanding of the decision in the Hurd case in New Jersey was that they took note of his guidelines, but didn't specifically adopt them."

Mr. Taylor, "You're familiar with those four guidelines, I suppose?"

Dr. Reiser, "Yes."

Mr. Taylor, "Do you agree with them or disagree with them?"

Dr. Reiser, "No, I disagree with, I think, three of them."

Mr. Taylor, "No.1 is that hypnosis should be carried out by a psychiatrist or psychologist with special training in its use. I assume you disagree with that standard?"

Dr. Reiser, "Yes, I definitely disagree with that based on my own experience."

Mr. Taylor, "All contact with the hypnotist with the subject should be videotaped from the moment they meet until the entire interaction is completed?"

Dr. Reiser, "Well, I can't agree with that, because in our own experience at the Los Angeles Police Department, we can't afford to videotape all sessions."

Mr. Taylor, "So you would modify this standard to read, 'All contact with the hypnotist and the subject should be, at a minimum, audio-taped?"

Dr. Reiser, "It should be taped using audio or video."

Mr. Taylor, "So this particular safeguard, rather than saying you just flat-out disagree with it, you would amend it to say that it should be videotaped or audio taped?"

Dr. Reiser, "Right."

Mr. Taylor, "From the moment they meet until the entire interaction is complete?"

Dr. Reiser, "That's desirable, yes."

Mr. Taylor, "So you would alter that safeguard? You would agree that video tape is preferable if the budget will allow it?"

Dr. Reiser, "Yes, it's nice to have."

Mr. Taylor, "But you would further amend this safeguard to say that if it can't be videotaped, it should be audio taped?"

Dr. Reiser, "Right."

Mr. Taylor, "No 3 is that, 'No one other than the psychiatrist or psychologist and the subject to be hypnotized should be present in the room during and before the session."

Dr. Reiser, "Well, I don't think that is feasible, because we want to get a composite drawing of a suspect. In other instances, in cases where small children have been raped, we may need to have a parent sitting in the back of the room for security purposes in order to do the session, and in other instances, it's important to have the case detective present, particularly, if the hypnotist has only a thumbnail sketch of the situation and information emerges during the session that the case detective would find meaningful, but the hypnotist wouldn't. The case detective should be able to pass a note to the hypnotist so that it can be pursued if desired."

Mr. Taylor, "No 4: 'Tape recording of the prior interrogations of the subject are important to document that a witness has not been cued.' Would you agree or disagree with that?"

Dr. Reiser, "I think that's kind of naive in terms of expecting police arriving at the scene of a crime and taking an initial report to tape record every word, every statement from the person because Dr. Orne is afraid that in some way they're going to shape or cue this person into saying something when there's no suspect in mind. There's no suspect in custody. There's nothing to implant or to cue at this stage of the game. I think that's based on Dr. Orne's lack of familiarity with the investigative process."

Mr. Taylor, "So you disagree with that?"

Dr. Reiser, "Yes."

Mr. Taylor, "You testified in your direct examination that the L.A. Police Department used hypnosis, and I quote "in dead-end cases." What do you mean by that?"

Dr. Reiser, "Well, it's not a substitute for good investigation, and when the investigators run out of leads and are at a dead-end and they have the impression that a witness likely perceived or has more information than they're able to recall at the moment, then that may be a suitable case for a hypnosis session if, in Captain Nielson's opinion, adequate investigation has been done previously."

Mr. Taylor, "And when you get to this dead-end point in the case, then that triggers what, apparently, is a very thoughtful process on your part and Captain Neilson's part as to whether or not hypnosis should be employed in that particular case?"

Dr. Reiser, "I'm not involved in that decision. Captain Neilson is the Project Director and makes that kind of an assessment."

Mr. Taylor, "Then Captain Neilson enters into this thoughtful process of whether or not the hypnosis should be used in that particular case?"

Dr. Reiser, "Yes, he reviews, with the case detective, the whole situation and what has been done and why the detective thinks that hypnosis might be useful and then arrives at a judgement about doing it or not."

Mr. Taylor, "And sometimes you are consulted on these decisions; aren't you?"

Dr. Reiser, "Occasionally."

Mr. Taylor, "What I'm getting at is before the L.A. Police Department uses hypnosis, first they run out of all their leads and get to the dead-end point, and then they sit down and decide whether or not they should use hypnosis?"

Dr. Reiser, "That's the usual situation. There are exceptions to that; however, there are certain cases where time is of the essence, and it may be one somebody's life is in jeopardy or such as a kidnapping situation where hypnosis may have to be done rather quickly. That's another possibility."

Mr. Taylor, "But when we're not in the emergency or life-and-death situation, then hypnosis is used – and I don't mean to sound like this is a last-ditch effort. I don't mean that in a derogatory manner – but it's something that's used after all the standard police procedures have been employed?"

Dr. Reiser, "Yes, yes."

Mr. Taylor, "Is that what you teach your students at the Institute? That hypnosis should be used after they've employed all the other police techniques?"

Dr. Reiser, "That's correct, yes."

Mr. Taylor, "And if you would not recommend that hypnosis be used immediately when there's not a life-or-death situation, that other standard procedures be exhausted first?"

Dr. Reiser, "It depends on the case, you know."

Mr. Taylor, "As a general rule?"

Dr. Reiser, "Generally, there's no rush to do hypnosis if no one's in danger."

Mr. Taylor, "And I'm having to speak in general terms here, because you haven't reviewed this particular case, and so you don't know what happened in the Bailey case, so I'm just asking you for general rules."

Dr. Reiser, "Yes."

Mr. Taylor, "Do you feel like a judge ought to instruct a jury on hypnosis? Do you think that's wise if a witness testifies in court and that witness has previously been hypnotized? Do you feel it's wise for the judge to instruct the jury about that - that it has taken place and, perhaps, give some cautionary instructions on hypnosis?"

Dr. Reiser, "Well, assuming that the hypnosis session has been conducted properly and that there is adequate cross-examination, I think that the judge should instruct the jury that a hypnosis interview is like any other interview that is properly conducted, and the jury needs to weigh this evidence like any other evidence and decide how much weight to give it."

Mr. Taylor, "But if the judge can't be sure, because of a lack of tape recording of the session, as to whether or not the session was proper or improper, then, would you agree that then an instruction might be necessary when there is no tape of the session?"

Dr. Reiser, "No, my bias is that in our system of justice, I think the jury should be the body to decide on evidentiary issues, and, I think, that they need to hear any kind of evidence in the case with the instruction that they be able to weigh that evidence based on certain factors that they obtain in a particular situation. But they should have the opportunity to hear that evidence and weigh it and weigh it like any other evidence, and I think that if certain so-called experts try to preempt that and get into the jury's roll of deciding who will testify and who won't testify, I think that's a perversion of the criminal justice process."

Mr. Taylor, "Do you feel it's the jury's role to decide who will testify and who won't testify?"

Dr. Reiser, "No, I think the judge makes that decision; however, I think that if anything, the weight should be on the part of letting the jury hear whatever there is to hear and then giving them instructions about what that - how they might weigh that kind of evidence."

Mr. Taylor, "Now, is your opinion somewhat changed in a case where there is no tape recording – a complete tape recording of the hypnotic session? Does that influence your opinion?"

Dr. Reiser, "No, I think that although it doesn't allow as minute an examination of the process, as I said before, in practically all other eyewitness situations, we don't have that kind of tape-recording situation existing, and the jury has to make up its mind based on the testimony of individuals. So, we're not really talking about anything different than the average eyewitness situation."

Mr. Taylor, "But you teach your people to tape record everything?"

Dr. Reiser, "Yes, of course."

D.A. Jordan, "For the record, asked and answered."

Mr. Taylor, "Dr. Reiser, you are the Director of the Behavioral Science Unit of the Los Angeles Police Department?"

Dr. Reiser, "Yes."

Mr. Taylor, "And then you're the Director of the Law Enforcement Institute?"

Dr. Reiser, "Yes."

Mr. Taylor, "Are those in any way related?"

Dr. Reiser, "No, the Law Enforcement Hypnosis Institute is a profit-making California corporation, which is not connected with the police department."

Mr. Taylor, "And this Law Enforcement Hypnosis Institute, you say it's a profit-making corporation? Who are the stockholders?"

Dr. Reiser, "My wife and I are the two stockholders in the corporation."

Mr. Taylor, "Any other stockholders?"

Dr. Reiser, "No."

Mr. Taylor, "And it's purely a private venture on your part; is that correct?"

Dr. Reiser, "Well, it's not a public corporation, so I guess it would be private."

Mr. Taylor, "And I assume you are paid a salary and also profits on whatever?"

Dr. Reiser, "Hopefully."

Mr. Taylor, "A salary plus dividends or profits from the overall business; is that correct?"

Dr. Reiser, "No, I am supposed to get a salary, and I also have a profit plan, rather, as part of my compensation. There are no profits other than those things."

Mr. Taylor, "So your salary and the pension plan, are these profits you derive?"

Dr. Reiser, "That's right."

Mr. Taylor, "How long has this been in existence?"

Dr. Reiser, "July, 1977."

Mr. Taylor, "And how long have you been involved directly with investigative hypnosis?"

Dr. Reiser, "Since early 1970."

Mr. Taylor, "Since you haven't reviewed the records in this case, I'm going to make you aware of the fact that the defense has filed a motion to exclude the testimony of the subject that was hypnotized, and our goal in filing that motion is to exclude her testimony and prevent her from testifying. ...If hypnosis were outlawed, if it became the trend in the United States that hypnotically enhanced testimony could not be introduced in court, adopting the Diamond and Orne viewpoint, then your Institute and you personally would suffer financially; isn't that correct?"

Dr. Reiser, "Well, I don't know about that. Neither Dr. Diamond nor Dr. Orne claims that hypnosis is not a good investigative tool. I think there's a unanimous opinion that it is. I think that most police agencies are using it as an investigative tool, which they would continue to use in any case. I think they would just have to be more careful about the possibilities of witnesses going to court and that kind of thing. So just how much that might affect the number of people who come for training and so on, I don't know."

Mr. Taylor, "If the Mena and Mack decisions become the trend and persons who are hypnotized by the police could not testify in court, wouldn't you expect the police use of hypnosis would substantially drop?"

Dr. Reiser, "That could happen."

Mr. Taylor, "Because under those decisions if they have hypnotized a witness, they have preempted the use of that witness in the courtroom in prosecuting a case, so if that did become the law, then the police use of hypnosis would substantially drop; wouldn't it?"

Dr. Reiser, "Yes, but if the implication is that, you know, I'm involved in investigative hypnosis for the sheer fact of making money out of it, I think that is a false implication because in terms of what it boils down to – just since this kind of thing has been asked of me before by other defense attorneys in terms of tremendous amounts of money that I'm supposedly making out of this business, I sat down and figured out what it is. I make approximately $25.65 an hour for the amount of time and work I put in at the Institute, including all of the compensation I get, which would compare to $60.00 to $100.00 an hour if I were in private practice, or more, doing similar kind of work. I don't think that would constitute a very good money-making scheme on my part."

Mr. Taylor, "What was your annual income from this Institute last year?"

Dr. Reiser, "Well, my salary is $20,000.00 a year."

Mr. Taylor, "And then your pension plan. But if the police couldn't use in court a witness that they have hypnotized, then they'd quit hypnotizing a lot of people?"

Dr. Reiser, "That's possible."

Mr. Taylor, "Are you being paid for your testimony here?"

Dr. Reiser, "Yes."

Mr. Taylor, "I don't have any further questions."

D.A. Jordan, "To clarify a few points, Doctor, does tape recording affect credibility of information? Or does it only allow additional opportunity to weigh and evaluate that testimony or that hypnotic session?"

Dr. Reiser, "Well, I don't think that tape recording changes any testimony in any way. I think it just allows a more minute examination in detail of what was communicated verbally during the session."

D.A. Jordan, "Well, can the facts surrounding the hypnosis be taken together with the tape recording and evaluated in their entirety to evaluate the session?"

Dr. Reiser, "Yes, and, as I have said on numerous occasions now, I think that's the typical situation in most eye-witness cases that don't involve hypnosis. That's the process we go through."

D.A. Jordan, "Now, counsel asked you about tape recording the session with the artist, and, I believe, that you responded your practice is to have the artist present while the witness is actually hypnotized; is that correct?"

Dr. Reiser, 'Yes."

D.A. Jordan, "Now have you established any guidelines or had any experiences or do you have any comments with reference to the situation where the hypnotic session ends and then the person works with the artist?"

Dr. Reiser, "Yes."

D.A. Jordan, "All right."

Dr. Reiser, "Yes, that's not an uncommon situation. There are some who prefer not to do the composite artist work during the session itself, but do it after the person is out of hypnosis based on whatever might have been elicited and recalled during the hypnosis session so that, in essence, the composite art work is done in a non-hypnotic state. … I think the reason we do it the way we do is that I think it may increase the likelihood of a composite being more like the suspect, but, you know, that's just our opinion."

D.A. Jordan, "Does the quality of the tape used or made during a hypnotic session, does that problem differ from the evaluation of the quality of the tape in a non-hypnotic interview?"

Dr. Reiser, "I think it is the same problem."

D.A. Jordan, "And in the absence of anything else which would raise concern, would concern arise if a witness related an observation, then was hypnotized and still related the same observation without material changes?"

Dr. Reiser, "Well, I think it would suggest that the hypnotic session had very little effect on the witness and, therefore, wasn't as material in that case."

D.A. Jordan, "In a case of that type, would it be necessary to completely evaluate what the people heard, what was related before the hypnotic session from all the various sources?"

Dr. Reiser, "Well, I think it would be important to review all of that information from whatever witnesses and reports were available."

D.A. Jordan, "If a police officer, for instance, took the report, the incident report, and made a record of it, would that be useful in evaluating the total hypnotic session? … Now, this evaluation we're talking about, this initial report being made before the hypnotic session?"

Dr. Reiser, "I think it would be useful in determining whether or not additional important information was elicited during hypnosis or what was reported initially on the original report."

D.A. Jordan, "And, again, if in fact there is very little difference between what was reported before and what was reported after hypnosis, would that be significant or would there be any problem indicated there?"

Dr. Reiser, "Well, it would suggest to me that the hypnosis session probably made very little, if any, difference in that case."

D.A. Jordan, "Now, you've used the term 'record' in responding to counsel's questions. Would other things beside the tape be included in the term 'record' as you've used that word?"

Dr. Reiser, "My use of the term 'record' would indicate all information whether written, tape recorded, or by verbal testimony from witnesses would be part of the record."

D.A. Jordan, ''Now counsel asked you about the Michigan ruling, and I took it from your response that you are not completely familiar with that case, and I don't recall hearing a citation on it. Would you need to consider the full record, the full facts in that case in order to fully respond to defense counsel's question?"

Dr. Reiser, "Yes, I think I would."

D.A. Jordan, "Now, I believe you indicated that you disagree with the holding of the Arizona Supreme Court, and let me ask you this: Are you talking about disagreement as to the blanket rule? Or is your disagreement with the details of the court's reasoning?"

Dr. Reiser, "My disagreement is with the blanket rule in generalizing from what I consider a very poor record in the very bad case."

Mr. Taylor, "Just one question and that is, Mr. Jordan asked you about a composite artist meeting with the subject immediately after the hypnotism?"

Dr. Reiser, "Yes."

Mr. Taylor, "You feel, even though that procedure may very well be proper, that it should be tape recorded?"

Dr. Reiser, "Well, that's the procedure that we use at the Los Angeles Police Department, but I don't – I'm not claiming that that's the only procedure. I think that others have – from other agencies, have reported to me good success with doing composite artist work after the hypnosis session, I don't have any quarrel with that."

Mr. Taylor, "I'm not talking about whether it should be done during. I'm asking you: If it's done immediately after the session, would you agree that that should be taped recorded?"

Dr. Reiser, "Well, if this is a non-hypnotic process and the person is not in hypnosis at that point, I don't see that there's any special need more than in any other interview to tape record it."

Mr. Taylor, "Wouldn't that be part of the post-induction session? That you recommend be taped - the post-induction session be taped?"

Dr. Reiser, "Well, I think the post induction session is with the hypnotist, and I think that the whole issue, as I understand it from the defense side, has been on the issue of cueing or leading or suggesting things by the hypnotist to the witness. I haven't really encountered the situation where defense attorneys are claiming that the police artist has been suggesting things to people."

Mr. Taylor, "Well, in a case where the police artist sat in the room throughout the session and then immediately after the subject was brought out of hypnosis, immediately the police artist then got with the subject and started going through the

Identi-Kit, do you feel like that - Would you recommend, in your professional opinion, that that be tape recorded as part of the session?"

Dr. Reiser, "Well, I suppose that if that followed immediately after the hypnotic session and the equipment were already present, probably it would be just as well to leave it running."

Mr. Taylor, "I'm only asking you for your opinion as to a general rule, because you haven't reviewed this case. So, I can only ask you now as a general rule, would you feel that it would be the best practice to tape record that - what happened immediately after the person was brought back out of hypnosis - counted down to the here-and-now, and then the police artist goes into the composite?"

Dr. Reiser, "I think it might be useful to do that, although I don't know that that's exactly the same issue as the one, we were talking about where the hypnotist supposedly can influence or suggest things to the subject."

Mr. Taylor, "You advocate or teach that the post-induction session should be tape recorded?"

Dr. Reiser, "With the hypnotist."

Mr. Taylor, "With the hypnotist?"

Dr. Reiser, "Right."

Mr. Taylor, "And if the composite-sketch session becomes a part of the post-induction session, then that also should be tape recorded?"

Dr. Reiser, "I think it would be useful to do that, but I don't think if it is not done–"

Mr. Taylor, "I'm not asking you if it's not. I'm asking you, as an expert, Dr. Martin Reiser, would it be your expert opinion that it would be the best practice to tape record it?"

Dr. Reiser, "Well, again, I think it would be useful to do that."

Mr. Taylor, "Would it be, in your professional opinion, the best practice to tape record it? yes or no?"

Dr. Reiser, "Well, if I thought I was going to be attacked by the defense on the issue, I certainly would want to do that."

Mr. Taylor, "So you feel it would be the best practice?"

Dr. Reiser, "Well, I think it would help the defense to allay any anxieties or fears they might have about improper communication."

Mr. Taylor, "And that's what you would teach any students that you had under your – in your school?"

Dr. Reiser, "Well, we really focus on the interaction between the hypnotist and the subject and what we teach in terms of recording. We really don't get into ancillary issues as to when the composite drawing will be done or whether an Identi-Kit is used as opposed to the artist doing a free-hand sketch, and that kind of thing. It varies with different situations."

Mr. Taylor, "But, again, back to the hypothetical. You feel that it would be 'desirable' to tape record it, using your words?"

Dr. Reiser, "Well, I think we're really talking about hindsight here, and I think, I guess I'm reacting that, yes, you know, from the point of hindsight it probably would have been desirable to do that, but the persons involved may not really anticipate that this would become an issue."

Mr. Taylor, "Well, if it's part of the post-induction session, then it should be tape recorded, shouldn't it?"

Dr. Reiser, "Well, that's what we recommend. We teach that."

Mr. Taylor, "I have no other questions."

D.A. Jordan, "If the hypnotist were not even present at the time the artist did his work with the hypnotized subject, would that make any difference in your answer?"

Dr. Reiser, "Well, yes, I think from a technical point of view, that would no longer be a hypnosis session. That would be a different part of the process."

D.A. Jordan, "Would it make any difference if the artist and his equipment sat silently behind the witness during the hypnotic session and said absolutely nothing? Would that make any difference?"

Dr. Reiser, "In what connection do you mean?"

D.A. Jordan, "As far as suggestibility, creating problems with the hypnotic session?"

Dr. Reiser, "I don't see how it would be."

D.A. Jordan, "It would be irrelevant then?"

Dr. Reiser, "Yes."

Mr. Taylor, "Is it good practice for a hypnotist to bring a person down out of hypnosis and then get up and leave the room without having any post-induction session with the subject? Do you teach that? Or do you teach that they should have a post-induction session?"

Dr. Reiser, "It depends on the situation. Sometimes all we say is, 'Thank you very much,' and 'Good-bye.' At other times, depending on what went on during the session, there may be some further discussion about – we may even make a referral for therapy with a particular witness, if that seems desirable. It depends on each case."

Mr. Taylor, "The 'Thank you very much,' and 'Good-bye,' is on your tape, isn't it?"

Dr. Reiser, "Hopefully, yes."

Mr. Taylor, "If the hypnotic session was conducted solely for the purpose of producing and coming up with a composite sketch, if that was its purpose, the stated purpose of the hypnotic session, then do you believe that it would be the best practice to tape record the session with the composite artist that took place immediately after the person was counted down? Would that be the best practice?"

Dr. Reiser, "I don't really think it's as important an issue, because it's not really part of the hypnotic session."

Mr. Taylor, "Well, I'm not asking whether you think it's an important issue or not. I'm asking you - I'm giving you a hypothetical and that hypothetical is that the hypnotic session was set up for the purpose of getting a composite sketch, and the composite artist was present during the session, then the composite artist and the subject got together immediately after the subject was counted down. Do you feel that it would be best practice, useful, desirable, whatever word you want to use, to tape record that part of the session?"

Dr. Reiser, "Well, I think I answered that before by saying that I think it would be useful to tape record that; however, as I stated a moment ago, I think it's a different situation when you have a non-hypnotic police artist interview with a witness to get a composite drawing than if we have a police artist participate during the hypnotic session with the witness, as he is in hypnosis, with the hypnotist participating in it also. Then I think that that should be on the tape, because it's part of the hypnotic process. But you're talking about a post-hypnosis process, and now you're saying that, you know, that – Well, at least as I'm getting it, that it would be important to consider that part of the hypnosis process and, therefore, tape it. I don't see it that way. I think that's post-hypnosis if the hypnosis has been terminated. The hypnotist has dehypnotized the subject and has left the room, which is an indication that we're talking about police artist interviews with the witness who happens to be the same witness who was previously in a hypnosis interview."

Mr. Taylor, "What if the stated purpose of the hypnosis was to compile a composite sketch? Does that, in any way, alter your opinion or would your answer be the same?"

Dr. Reiser, "I think that the stated purpose of the hypnosis would be to refresh the memory of the witness."

Mr. Taylor, "I'm asking if the stated purpose of the hypnosis session was to compile a composite sketch?"

Dr. Reiser, "The only way that could be done would be to refresh the person's memory."

Mr. Taylor, "And, in that case, then, you've testified earlier that it would be desirable and useful to tape record that session? Is that your testimony?"

Dr. Reiser, "Well, I think it would be more satisfying to both sides, I guess, if that were on tape."

Mr. Taylor, "No other questions."

D.A. Jordan, "Very briefly, Doctor, you have referred to important issues. Are those important issues, as you have viewed them, based on practice experience?"

Dr. Reiser, "Well, I think the issues that I have referred to are based on about 10 years of my own personal involvement with investigative hypnosis in real crime cases and about six years of involvement in investigative hypnosis teaching, consulting, and working in the field very intensively probably hundreds of cases."

D.A. Jordan, "Thank you."

Mr. Taylor, "No other questions."

IMPORTANT WIN

Mr. Taylor advised Dr. Reiser that "…defense has filed a motion to exclude the testimony of the subject that was hypnotized, and our goal in filing that motion is to exclude her testimony and prevent her from testifying …" We presented enough evidence to the court that we were properly allowed to have her testimony considered.

"It does need to be pointed out that Dr. Reiser responded to the question by D.A. Jordan," And in the absence of anything else which would raise concern, would concern arise if a witness related an observation, then was hypnotized and still related the same observation without material change?"

Dr. Reiser, "Well, I think it would suggest that the hypnotic session had very little effect on the witness and, therefore, wasn't material in that case."

FURTHER EVENTS BEFORE TRIAL

It was again suggested that I withdraw from the trial of this case and let a District Attorney from a larger district try the case. Obviously, he would have more resources to call upon such as other lawyers to help him. I gave serious consideration to this suggestion. I decided against the suggestion because no District Attorney from out of my district could know the people as well as I did and I certainly recognized that there were many things I did not know but after evaluating this question it seemed clear that I knew more than anyone available could know.

There was also the fact to be considered that I was the only District Attorney that I knew of trained in Investigative Hypnosis and if we were not very careful, we would find ourselves without our only eyeball witness to the escape of the killer. This was such an important issue that I really had no other choice. My duty was to protect the citizens in Okmulgee and McIntosh Counties and to provide the very best prosecution possible.

A fact known only to me was that during this time K.D. Bailey, the attorney father of the defendant in this case, came to me and asked that I not put off the trial of his son because he had already spent all of his money and would not be able to pay for a defense for his son if trial was delayed as some wanted. It seemed to me and continues to seem to me that the purpose of our judicial system is to protect our citizens and not to attempt to force any of them into financial insolvency.

I knew the case inside and out. I made the decision to try the case myself even though I would not be provided with any assistance from the staff of a District Attorney from a larger district.

I had the help of the Oklahoma State Bureau of Investigation, the best available. And they had demonstrated a willingness to devote resources to this case. When I first became District Attorney, I was cautioned that the O.S.B.I. was very political and to be careful when dealing with them. Before I made the decision to retain control of the prosecution of this case, I asked the agents if there was going to be anything learned if we delayed or if we knew everything we were ever going to know and I was assured that we knew everything we would ever know. I felt that I had good honest cooperation from the O.S.B.I..

In addition, I had to consider the fact that witnesses die or become unavailable to testify over time, an important reason not to delay trial.

Ultimately the decision was one I had to make and after a lot of soul searching I made the decision to retain control of the prosecution of this case and proceed with prosecution.

I did all of my trial preparation at my house where nothing could slip out. I devoted my full time to this case and let my assistants take care of all other District Attorney matters during this preparatory time.

Pretrial

Summons had been issued to prospective jurors.

Of all things my wife, the wife of the District Attorney, and the wife of the victim of this crime, a witness to appear in the trial, were sent summons to come and be part of the jury panel. Judge John Maley called both ladies to the courthouse well before time for the jury to report and ordered them to not even come to the courthouse at that time. There was no way either wife could serve on the jury, and if they appeared there would be a chance that would be enough to poison the panel and cause delay of the case for another term.

I had previously served as Special Judge and at times had tried two full D.U.I. jury cases a day so I was familiar with pulling names from the jury wheel. At times the same names would be repeatedly pulled to hear a case. I watched very closely and never found anything improper about the same names being repeatedly pulled and I finally decided that it was just the luck of the draw.

After the jurors were selected, I tried to learn as much as I could about each of them. I wanted to know if there was any reason to believe that any one of them would be prejudiced and not have an open mind to hearing the evidence and rendering a fair trial to the state as well as to the defendant.

A LESSON LEARNED

When I first arrived in Okmulgee as an Assistant District Attorney I used a yellow tablet in trials and preliminary hearings with notes to be sure I didn't miss anything. Some of the established lawyers didn't think that looked professional, to not just speak without notes.

When I became Special Judge hearing all misdemeanor trials and felony preliminary hearings, I discovered that some of these same lawyers who though it did not look professional to work from notes would at times leave out some important fact. I specifically remember one lawyer who proved that a crime had been committed and there was probable cause to believe that the defendant in the case had committed the crime. However, he failed to prove where the crime had happened. Either I asked him or he remembered and asked the witness who was still on the stand where the crime had occurred and proved by his testimony that the crime had occurred outside our jurisdiction. Therefore, I could not give him the relief asked for, but had to dismiss the case.

DETAIL TRIAL PREPARATION

Before the trial I put together my personal trial notebook. The following appeared in this trial notebook.

I wrote out the chain of custody for each piece of evidence to be presented in the case. This included the death projectile, three expended .38 casings, the death gun, a second gun, three sandblasted projectiles, a zipper, and fiber.

I wrote down a few key statute sections that I thought could become important as we started the trial. These included: 22 OSA 719, which had to do with persons held as material witnesses; 22 OSA 723 having to do with witnesses from another state summoned to testify in this state, and 22 OSA 718, which had to do with fees to be paid to a witness from another state to testify in this state.

I wrote down the definition for the word Keen – to wail in lamentation over the dead. All kinds of things come up in trials, and I wanted to be fully prepared.

I had a list of everyone who might appear as a witness together with full addresses so we could contact them if necessary.

I wrote out several statutes. The District Attorney's office did not have a photocopy machine, but we could go to the Court Clerk's office to make copies which was not convenient. While I was D.A., I did set up a Child Support Office to collect past due Child Support. That provided a small amount of earnings that could be used in my office. The very first income was used to buy a stapler and a couple of small items.

Some statutes that would be important in the trial included the following:

21 OSA 701.7A, Murder in the First Degree. It provided, "A person commits murder in the first degree when he unlawfully and with malice aforethought causes the death of another human being. Malice is that deliberate intention unlawfully to take away the life of a human being, which is manifest by external circumstances capable of proof."

21 OSA 701.9A, "A person who is convicted of or pleads guilty or nolo contendere to murder in the first degree shall be punished by death or by imprisonment for life."

21 OSA 701.10 had to do with sentencing proceedings.

21 OSA 701.11 had to do with instructions to the jury and jury findings of aggravating circumstances.

21 OSA 702. A design to effect death is inferred from the fact of the killing, unless the circumstances raise a reasonable doubt whether such design existed.

21 OSA 703. A design to effect death sufficient to constitute murder may be formed instantly before committing the act by which it is carried into execution.

21 OSA 704. Homicide committed with a design to effect death is not the less murder because the perpetrator was in a state of anger or voluntary intoxication at the time.

21 OSA 705. Homicide perpetrated by an act imminently dangerous to others and evincing a depraved mind, regardless of human life, is not the less murder because there was no actual intent to injure others.

21 OSA 731 had to do with excusable homicide.

21 OSA 732 had to do with justifiable homicide by an officer.

21 OSA 733 had to do with justifiable homicide by any person.

22 OSA 585 had to do with postponement for investigation of claimed alibi.

22 OSA 601a had to do with alternate jurors.

22 OSA 655 had to do with peremptory challenges; that is excusing a prospective juror without stating a cause. In a first-degree murder case, there were nine such challenges.

22 OSA 745. Upon a trial for murder, the commission of the homicide by the defendant being proven, the burden of proving circumstances of mitigation, or that justify or excuse it, devolves upon him, unless the proof on the part of the prosecution tends to show that the crime committed amounts only to manslaughter, or that the defendant was justifiable or excused.

22 OSA 831 (1) Clerk or District Attorney reads the information (The information is the written-out charge against the defendant.)

(2) No limit on time unless the lawyers agree.

22 OSA 62 had to do with the issue of sanity at trial.

22 OSA 1163 had to do with sanity hearings.

22 OSA 1164 set out the order of trial.

22 OSA 1161 note 4 cited cases re the test of responsibility for crime.

The Maggot case, 599 P2d 1110, contained the comment that the prosecutor's remarks during void dire as to definition of "reasonable doubt" was not error where the prosecutor was trying to make certain that prospective jurors understood the burden placed upon the state.

The Lee case, 600 P2d 344, provided that if a witness were unavailable a preliminary hearing transcript could be used.

The Mayberry case, 603 P2d 1150 held that in proceedings in which the defendant was convicted of indecent proposal to a child, argument in which the prosecutor read a passage from the Bible was within the bounds of proper closing argument.

It is not necessary to establish the chain of custody for photos but only necessary to establish that they are faithful reproductions, as pointed out in the case at 602 P2d 237.

12 OSA 2102. This code shall be construed to secure fairness in administration, elimination of unjustifiable expense and delay and promotion of growth and development of the law of evidence to the end that the truth may be ascertained and proceedings justly determined.

12 OSA 2105 A Preliminary question concerning the qualifications of a person to be a witness, the existence of a privilege or the admissibility of evidence shall be determined by the court, subject to the provisions of subsection B of this section.

B. When the relevance of evidence depends upon the fulfillment of a condition of fact, the judge shall admit it upon, or subject to, the introduction of evidence sufficient to support a finding of the fulfillment of the condition.

C. ...admissibility of a confession ...out of the hearing of the jury. Hearings on other preliminary matters shall also be conducted upon out of the hearing of the jury when the interest of justice require or when requested by an accused who is a witness.

D. The accused does not subject himself to cross-examination on other issues in the case by testifying upon a preliminary matter.

E. This section does not limit the right of a party to introduce before the jury evidence relevant to weight or credibility.

12 OSA 2106 When evidence which is admissible as to one party or for one purpose but not admissible as to another party or for another purpose is admitted, the court shall upon request restrict the evidence to its proper scope and instruct the jury accordingly.

12 OSA 2107 When a writing or recorded statement or part thereof is introduced by a party, an adverse party may require him at that time to introduce any other part or any other writing or recorded statement which should in fairness be considered contemporaneously with it.

12 OSA 2202 A. This section governs only judicial notice of adjudicative facts.

B. A judicial noticed adjudicative fact shall not be subject to reasonable dispute. It shall be either:

1. Generally known within the territorial jurisdiction of the trial court, or

2. Capable of accurate and ready determination by resort to sources whose accuracy cannot reasonably be questioned.

C. A court may take judicial notice, whether requested or not.

D. A court shall take judicial notice if requested by a party and supplied with the necessary information.

E. …In a criminal case, the court shall instruct the jury that it may, but is not required to, accept as conclusive any fact judicially noticed.

12 OSA 2304 had to do with presumptions in criminal cases.

12 OSA 2401 "Relevant evidence" means evidence having any tendency to make the existence of any fact that is of consequence to the determination of the action more probable or less probable than it would be without the evidence.

12 OSA 2402 All relevant evidence is admissible, except as otherwise provided by the Constitution of the United States, the Constitution of the State of Oklahoma, by statutes or code.

12 OSA 2403 Relevant evidence may be excluded if its probative value is substantially outweighed by the danger of unfair prejudice, confusion of the issues, misleading the jury, undue delay, needless presentation of cumulative evidence, or unfair or harmful surprise.

12 OSA 2404 A. Evidence of a person's character or a trait of his character is not admissible for the purpose of proving that he acted in conformity therewith or on a particular occasion, except:

1. Evidence of a pertinent trait of his character offered by an accused or by the prosecution to rebut the same; …

12 OSA 2405 A Where evidence of a person's character or trait of character is admissible, proof may be by testimony as to reputation or by testimony in the form of opinion. Inquire is allowable on cross-examination into relevant specific instances of conduct.

B. …

12 OSA 2406 Evidence of a person's habit or of an organization's routine practice, whether corroborated or not and regardless of the presence of eyewitnesses, is relevant to prove that the conduct of the person or organization on a particular occasion was in conformity with the habit or routine practice.

12 OSA 2504 A. A communication is confidential for purposes of this section if it is made privately by any person to his spouse and is not intended for disclosure to any other person.

B. An accused in a criminal proceeding has a privilege to prevent his spouse from testifying as to any confidential communication between the accused and the spouse. …

12 OSA 2510 has to do with Identity of informants.

12 OSA 2513 A. A claim of privilege, whether in the present proceeding or upon a prior occasion, is not a proper subject of comment by a judge or counsel. No inference may be drawn therefrom.

B. In jury cases, proceedings shall be conducted, to the extent practicable, so as to facilitate the making of claims of privilege without the knowledge of the jury.

C. Upon request, any party against whom the jury might draw an adverse inference from a claim of privilege is entitled to an instruction that no inference may be drawn therefrom.

12 OSA 2601 Every person is competent to be a witness except as otherwise provided by this code.

12 OSA 2602 A witness may not testify to a matter unless evidence is introduced sufficient to support a finding that he has personal knowledge of the matter. Evidence to prove personal knowledge may consist of the testimony of the witness himself. This rule is subject to the provisions of Sec. 2703 of this code.

12 OSA 2606 B. ...A juror may testify on the question whether extraneous prejudicial information was improperly brought to the juror's attention or whether any outside influence was improperly brought to bear upon any juror. ...

12 OSA 2607 The availability of a witness may be attacked by any party, including the party calling him.

12 OSA 2608 A. The credibility of a witness may be attacked or supported by evidence in the form of opinion or reputation, subject to these limitations:

1. The evidence may refer only to character for truthfulness or untruthfulness; and

2. Evidence of truthful character is admissible only after the character of the witness for truthfulness has been attacked.

B. Specific instances of the conduct of a witness, for the purpose of attacking or supporting his credibility, other than conviction of crime as provided in Section 2609 of this code, may not be proved by extrinsic evidence. They may, however, in the discretion of the court, if probative of truthfulness or untruthfulness, be enquired into on cross-examination of the witness if they:

1. Concern his character for truthfulness or untruthfulness;

2. Concern the character for truthfulness or untruthfulness of another witness as to which character the witness being cross-examined has testified.

C. The giving of testimony, whether by an accused or by any other witness, does not operate as a waiver of his privilege against self-incrimination when examined with respect to matters which relate only to credibility.

12 OSA 2609 A. For the purpose of attacking the credibility of a witness, evidence that he has been convicted of a crime shall be admitted if elicited from him or established by public record during cross-examination but only if the crime:

1. Involved dishonesty or false statement, regardless of the punishment; or

2. Was punishable by death or imprisonment in excess of one year, and the court determines that the probative value of admitting this evidence outweighs its prejudicial effect to the detriment of the defendant.

B. Evidence of a conviction under this section is not admissible if a period of more than 10 years has elapsed since the date of the conviction or of the release of the witness from the confinement imposed for that conviction, whichever is later, unless the court determines, in the interest of justice, that the probative value of the conviction supported by specific facts and circumstances substantially outweighs its prejudicial effect. Evidence of a conviction more than 10 years old, as calculated here, is not admissible unless the proponent gives to the adverse party sufficient advance written notice of intent to use such evidence to provide the adverse party with a fair opportunity to contest such evidence.

C. Evidence of a conviction is not admissible under this code if:

1. …pardon…

2. …pardon…

D. Evidence of juvenal adjudications is not admissible under this code. The court in a juvenal case may, however, allow evidence of a juvenal adjudication of a witness other than the accused if conviction of the offense would be admissible to attack the credibility of an adult, and the court is satisfied that admission into evidence is necessary for a fair determination of the issue of guilt or innocence.

E. The pendency of an appeal from the conviction does not render evidence of that conviction inadmissible. Evidence of the pendency of an appeal is admissible.

12 OSA 2610 had to do with religious beliefs and opinions.

12 OSA 2611 A. Subject to subsection B of section 611 of this code, the court shall exercise control over the manner and order of interrogating witnesses and presenting evidence as to:

1. Make the interrogation and presentation effective for the ascertainment of the truth;

2. Avoid needless consumption of time; and

3. Protect witnesses from harassment or undue embarrassment.

B. …civil action…

C. Cross-examination shall be limited to the subject matter of the direct examination and matters affecting the credibility of the witness. The court may permit inquiry into additional matters as if on direct examination.

D. Leading questions shall not be used on the direct examination of a witness except as may be necessary to develop his testimony. When a party calls a hostile witness, an adverse party, or a witness identified with an adverse party, leading questions may be used on direct examination.

12 OSA 2612 If a witness uses a writing to refresh his memory either while testifying or before testifying, the court shall allow an adverse party to have the writing produced at the hearing, to inspect it, to cross-examine the witness thereon and to introduce into evidence those portions which relate to the testimony of the witness. If it is claimed by an opposing party that the writing contains matters not related to the subject matter of the testimony, the court shall examine the writing in camera (out of the presence of the jury), excise any portions not so related, and order delivery of the remainder to the party entitled thereto. Any portion withheld over objection shall be preserved, made part of the record, and shall be available to the appellate court in the event of an appeal. ...civil.... In criminal cases where the prosecution elects not to comply, the order shall be striking the testimony or declaring a mistrial.

12 OSA 2613 A. In examining a witness concerning a prior statement made by him whether written or not, the statement need not be shown nor its contents disclosed to him at that time, but on request the same shall be shown or disclosed to opposing counsel just prior to cross-examination of the witness.

B. Extrinsic evidence of a prior inconsistent statement by a witness is not admissible unless the witness is afforded an opportunity to explain or deny the same and the opposite party is afforded an opportunity to interrogate him thereon. This provision does not apply to admissions of a party opponent as defined in subparagraph B of paragraph 4 of Section 2801 of this code.

12 OSA 2615 has to do with exclusion of witnesses.

12 OSA 2701 If the witness is not testifying as an expert, his testimony in the form of opinion or inferences is limited to those opinions which are:

1. Rationally based on the perception of the witness; and

2. Helpful to a clear understanding of his testimony or the determination of a fact in issue.

12 OSA 2702 If scientific, technical or other specialized knowledge will assist the trier of fact to understand the evidence or to determine a fact in issue, a witness qualified as an expert by knowledge, skill, training or education may testify in the form of an opinion or otherwise.

12 OSA 2703 The facts or data in the particular case upon which an expert bases an opinion or inference may be those perceived by or made known to him at or before the hearing. If a type reasonably relied upon by experts in the particular field in forming opinions or inferences upon the subject, the facts or data need not be admissible in evidence.

12 OSA 273 … expert may be required to disclose the underlying facts or data on cross-examination.

12 OSA 2801 … 3. Hearsay is a statement, other than one made by the declarant while testifying at the trial or hearing, offered in evidence to prove the truth of the matter asserted; and

4. A statement is not hearsay if:

a. the declarant testifies at the trial or hearing and is subject to cross-examination concerning the statement, and the statement is (1) inconsistent with his testimony, and was given under oath subject to the penalty of perjury at a deposition, trial, hearing or other proceeding, or (2) consistent with his testimony and is offered to rebut an express or implied charge against him of recent fabrication or improper influence or motive: or

b. the statement is offered against a party and is (1) his own statement …

12 OSA 2803 Hearsay is not admissible except as provided by law.

12 OSA 2804 Hearsay Exceptions; Declarant Unavailable.

…2. …Persists in refusing to testify …

…3. …lack of memory…

12 OSA 3001 … An 'original' of a photograph includes the negative or any print therefrom …

22 OSA 601a provides for up to two alternate jurors. The prosecution and the defense each get one peremptory challenge.

22 OSA 634 A challenge to the panel must be taken before the jury is sworn, must be in writing, specifying plainly and distinctly the facts constituting the ground of challenge.

22 OSA 655 provides up to nine peremptory challenges.

38 OSA 28 General causes of challenges are:

1. Conviction for felony.

2. A want of any of the qualifications prescribed by law, to render a person a competent juror, including a want of knowledge of the English language as used in the courts.

3. Unsoundness of mind, or such defect in the faculties of the mind or organs of the body as render him incapable of performing the duties of a juror.

38 OSA 28 Qualifications as electors

…B. Persons who are not qualified to serve as jurors are:

1. Justices of the Supreme Court or the Court of Appeals;

2. Judges of the Court of Criminal Appeals or the district court;

3. Sheriffs or Deputy Sheriffs;

4. Jailers or law enforcement officers, state or federal, having custody of prisoners;
5. Licensed attorneys engaged in the practice of law;
6. (Has to do with habitual drunkards)
7. Persons who have been convicted of any felony or served a term of imprisonment in any penitentiary …for the commission of a felony… (some provision to be able to serve if civil rights have been restored).

22 OSA 659 Particular causes of challenges are of two kinds:

1. …implied bias.
2. For the existence of a state of mind on the part of the juror, in reference to the case, or the other party, which satisfies the court, in the exercise of a sound discretion, that he cannot try the issue impartially, without prejudice to the substantial rights of the party challenging, and which is known in this chapter as actual bias.

22 OSA 660 Implied bias …

1. consanguinity or affinity within 4th degree
2. … member of family of the defendant…

22 OSA 691 All challenges of individual jurors must be taken, first by the defendant and then by the state alternatively.

22 OSA 745 Upon a trial for murder, the commission of the homicide by the defendant being proven, the burden of proving circumstances of mitigation, or that justify or excuse it, devolves upon him, unless the proof on the part of the prosecution tends to show that the crime committed only amounts to manslaughter, or that the defendant was justifiable or excusable.

22 OSA 831 Order of Trial

1. D.A. read Information (the charge against the defendant) and state the plea of the defendant.
2. State
3. Defense
4. Rebuttal testimony only, unless for good reason, in furtherance of justice, or to correct an evident oversight.
5. D.A. may submit written instructions.
6. No limit on argument.

22 OSA 835 …court may … restrict the argument to one counsel on each side.

22 OSA 855 If, before the conclusion of the trial, a juror becomes sick, as to be unable to perform his duty, the court may order him to be discharged. In that case or in the event of the death of a juror a new juror may be sworn, and the trial begin anew, or the jury may be discharged, and a new jury then or afterwards impaneled.

22 OSA 894 After the jury has retired for deliberation, if there be any disagreement between them as to any part of the testimony, or if they desire to be informed on a point of law arising in the cause, they must require the officer to conduct them into court. Upon them being brought into court, the information required must be given in the presence of, or after notice to the County Attorney (the office of County Attorney had been done away with and replaced with the office of District Attorney) and the defendant or his counsel, or after they have been called.

22 OSA 911 When the jury have agreed … their names must be called, and if all do not appear, the rest must be discharged without giving a verdict. … again tried ….

22 OSA 912 … felony, the defendant must, before the verdict is received, appear in person. …

22 OSA 914 has to do with the form of verdict, guilty or not guilty or not guilty by reason of insanity etc.

22 OSA 926 jury may fix punishment.

22 OSA 927 Court to set punishment when jury fails to agree or do not declare.

22 OSA 585 Whenever testimony to establish an alibi of the defendant shall be offered in evidence in any criminal case in any court of record of the State of Oklahoma, and notice of the intention of the defendant to claim such alibi, which notice shall include specific information as to the place at which the defendant claims to have been at the time of the alleged offense, shall not have been served upon the county attorney at or before five days prior to the trial of the case, upon motion of the county attorney, the court may grant a postponement for such time as it may deem necessary to make an investigation of the facts in relation to such evidence. Footnote 4 sat out that the filing of such notice was not mandatory and cited the case of Tubbs v State, 512 OkCr, P2 1385 (1973).

The Oklahoma Bar Journal reported at 54 OBJ 2227 that the court can discharge a jury for manifest necessity.

First Lesson by the Dean of the Law School

AT OKLAHOMA CITY UNIVERSITY

Dean Foster told us that if we had come to law school to learn what the law is that we were in the wrong place. In law school we would learn how to find the law, think like a lawyer and solve the problems of our clients.

That proved to be good advice as we started our studies.

VOIR DIRE

When we Americans think about selecting our rulers we usually think about elections. Voir Dire (the selection of a jury) is another process by which we select our rulers. The jury selected will rule on their findings and what should be done - as surely as any ruler ever ruled over any subject. Are you in the frame of mind to seriously consider what should be done in this case?

Then I would ask questions to get acquainted with each juror: where do you live, who do you live with, how long have you lived in Okmulgee County, do you own your home, number of children and grandchildren and their ages, do they attend Senior Citizens, what is their education and work experience, how long have they been on their present job, what are their duties and what hours do they work, hobbies, how do you spend your time when not working, have you had prior jury experience, civil or criminal, what kind of case, what was the outcome, do you believe that an experienced juror is more likely to see through a false claim, will you promise to not pay attention to anything other than sworn testimony and instructions from the judge and not pay attention to anything from the audience or anything else, has anyone told you anything about this case, lawyers are allowed to talk with witnesses - will you not hold it against us if we appear unfriendly, have you had experience with any of the lawyers on either side of this case, was it business, for pay or volunteer, buy sell etc., politics, involved on the same side of a political campaign or on the other side, social, anything in your experience that would make you feel for or against either side. Have you had contact with the D.A. James D. Jordan or any lawyer on his staff: Roy Powell, Peter Brangaccio, Everett Cotter, Don Pope, Fred Demire or attorneys for the defendant: K.D. Bailey, Mary Bailey Romaine, Dennis Seacat, Mrs. Seacat, Warren Gotcher, Jim Gotcher, Steve Taylor?

What has been your experience with crime, you, family, friend, or anyone close to you: victim or accused of crime, witnesses for or against the state, studied law in any way, have you ever been arrested or charged with a crime, anything that would make you feel for or against either side in this case? Do you have a religious or moral view that would keep you from convicting or punishing, experience in the military, experience with guns, do you own a gun, do you have experience loading, aiming and firing a gun, a hand gun or a long gun, a shotgun or a rifle, a revolver or an automatic pistol, have you been trained to use firearms, have you been taught the purpose of a firearm. Do you believe it is good that society has laws against one person killing another person, do you understand that it is not necessary for the state to prove why a person committed a crime - that you can convict if the state only shows that he was guilty in accordance with the instructions of the court; do you understand that in this case or in any other case the State may have one or more eyewitnesses who can tell you what they saw, or the state may have no eyeball witnesses to present and you may convict on circumstantial evidence alone, if the prosecution proves its case in accordance with the court's instructions. I anticipate in this case that the jury will hear the facts as to what happened, be instructed as to what law to apply to the facts. Will you listen closely to what the facts are, after the facts are laid out to you? Will you follow whatever the court instructs you with reference to the facts of what happened in this case? Will you not allow outside matters to influence you in this case? Do you understand that a trial is not a contest between lawyers, do you understand that the reason we are here is to determine the guilt of the defendant (or if there is objection to my question change it to determine the guilt or innocence of the defendant)?

Do you happen to be a hypnotist? Have you observed, had experience with or read about hypnotism, are you familiar with bio-feedback, yoga, transcendental meditation or other types of situations involving altered states of consciousness? Do you believe that hypnosis even exists, (if no) if during the course of this trial there is evidence submitted to the jury that one or more of the state's witnesses was hypnotized, by a law enforcement official, will you consider that evidence? (If yes) what do you know about the nature of hypnotism, if evidence is submitted that the nature of hypnotism is something different than you believe it to be, will you consider that evidence, and if you hear differences in the evidence as to the nature of hypnotism, will you listen to all of the evidence and apply your common sense to deciding what you believe the nature of hypnotism to be? Because hypnotism is a subject that people frequently know little or nothing about, there may be a problem of jurors or others listening closely to learn more about hypnotism than about the facts of what happened in this case. If you are selected to serve on this jury, will you listen closely enough to any evidence about hypnotism to understand its importance in this case? Will you continue to focus your attention on learning the facts of what happened in this case? Does it offend or prejudice you to be informed that one of the witnesses for the state was hypnotized?

Defendant Kenneth Dexter Bailey, Jr., is charged with the murder of Ray Courtemanche by shooting him Feb. 3, 1981, at his home at 1509 South Mission in Okmulgee, Okla. Do you know Kenneth Dexter Bailey, Jr. or during his life time did you know Ray Courtemanche? How were you acquainted? Do you know their families? Have you ever had any contact at all with either one of them? Did you see Defendant Kenneth Dexter Bailey, Jr. or Ray Courtemanche any time on Feb. 3, 1981? When and where? Were you in the area of 1509 South Mission in Okmulgee,

Okla., on Feb. 3, 1981 – or any time about that time? Did you see any cars or people or activity in the area then? Have you observed anything that had anything to do with this murder or this defendant? Has anyone talked to you about this case? Who? What have they told you? Have you learned anything from the news media about this case? TV, newspaper, radio or any other media? Do you understand that the news media do not decide guilt or innocence – that is the jury's job to do in a courtroom with proper evidence? Do you know what purport to be the facts in this case? These are some of the witnesses who may testify in this case; (read the list). Do you know any of these witnesses? Will the fact that you know part of the witnesses cause you to give more or less weight to their testimony?

Do you understand that you are not to give more or less weight to the testimony of a witness just because of occupation – that a preacher, policeman or any other witness starts off with an advantage or disadvantage? Will you hold it against the state if we call only those witnesses necessary to prove our case and not those who only know minor details or only know about something that someone else has testified about or is no longer necessary to prove?

As to the responsibility of the jury, I anticipate that you will learn from your observations of defendant Bailey that he appears calm, cool, collected, and not dangerous and perhaps even friendly. I anticipate that the judge will instruct you that you should not let sympathy, sentiment or prejudice enter into your deliberations. Can you follow such an instruction? I anticipate that the judge will instruct the jury that the jury is the judge of the evidence and the credibility of the witnesses. Will you give your best effort to deciding what the facts are and which witnesses you should believe? I anticipate that the judge will instruct you that the jury should consider the interest of any witness as to the outcome of the trial and their relationships to any party. Will you follow this type of instruction? Will you carefully listen to the witnesses who saw defendant Bailey and are familiar with him and his actions and give that testimony such weight as you feel it deserves?

If you hear witnesses whose testimony is diametrically opposed to each other, will you stay with the case and sort out the truth? If evidence comes to you that Ray Courtemanche may not have been perfect, will you keep your mind open and listen to all the evidence? If anyone talks to you about this case will you report that fact to the judge? Do you understand that the State must prove every material allegation beyond a reasonable doubt, but that does not require the state to prove anything which is not material?

The jury responsibility as to Reasonable Doubt: I anticipate that the judge will instruct the jury that defendant Bailey is presumed innocent until proven guilty beyond a reasonable doubt. Do you understand that you do not have to turn defendant Bailey loose if you have some doubt, but that you must convict him if the State proves to your satisfaction beyond a reasonable doubt that he committed murder in the first degree in accordance with the court's instructions? Or do you understand that the burden is on the state to prove its case beyond a reasonable doubt, but that does not mean beyond any doubt (or not beyond a shadow of doubt)? Do you understand that defendant Bailey is presumed innocent just like every other defendant tried in the courts of this state? Do you agree that the jury is the last wall between an orderly society and chaos?

Conclusion: At the conclusion of all you hear in this case, the evidence and the court's instructions, if you are satisfied beyond a reasonable doubt that defendant Bailey is guilty, will you return a verdict of guilty? If the facts and evidence support the verdict are you willing to send defendant Bailey to prison for the rest of his life? Do you have the courage to do that? If you find defendant Bailey guilty will you punish him? If anyone speaks to you about this case before the trial is over will you report that to the judge? Do you agree that this case is a search for justice?

After the lawyers have questioned the prospective jurors the lawyers may make challenges for cause to remove a particular juror, and each side has nine peremptory challenges which allow for the removal of prospective jurors without stating a cause.

NOTE: It is essential to be sure that all of our witnesses are present and available before the jury is sworn to try the case.

Moving on with My Trial Notebook

My trial notebook had every important thing written out before trial so that nothing would be overlooked.

Of course, I had a copy of the jury list, and I made inquiries about everyone on the list to learn as much about each prospective juror as possible. I talked with the Sheriff, police officers and anyone else I felt might provide understanding of how these prospective jurors might consider the question of the guilt of defendant Bailey. I was specifically looking for preconceived positions which might make a prospective juror have a closed mind and not be able to fairly consider all of the evidence. Were they related to the defendant either by family or friendship? Had they made statements that might show bias? We're there any business or social connections that might sway a vote on the question of guilt?

OPENING STATEMENT TO THE JURY

The Opening Statement by the state consisted of the reading of the Information (the charge against the defendant) to the jury and the statement that the defendant had entered a plea of not guilty to this charge and the issues were joined. The question for the jury to consider: was Kenneth Dexter Bailey, Jr. guilty of the crime of murder in the first degree? It was further stated that each and every material allegation set out in the information would be proved by competent evidence.

It was further stated that the State would prove:

Ray Courtemanche was murdered in cold blood.

The afternoon before the murder at about the same time as the murder that Kenneth Dexter Bailey, Jr was inside the home of Ray Courtemanche and that he left in a hurry when someone walked in on him.

It was further announced that it was anticipated that the jury would have the opportunity to go to the house where Ray Courtemanche lived and was murdered. It was pointed out that the jury should pay attention to: the driveway where the killer pulled in on the north side of the Dugger house, parked headed south and then drove out the south side headed south.

East door on the back of the house, which Ray was opening at the time he was murdered and the area just inside the door where he fell.

The Dugger house just south of the Courtemanche house, steps on the front of that house, driveway and yard and the distance from the steps to Ray's drive.

Width and roughness of Mission south of the Courtemanche house.

Width and roughness of the road going west from Mission to Wood Drive just south of the Courtemanche house.

At the ranch –

*Where the office area is

*Location of the house and shed out back.

*Location behind the house, fence has been moved.

*Color of houses changed.

The state will further prove that Kenneth Dexter Bailey Jr shot a pistol in his own backyard into a barrel during midmorning of the day on which Ray Courtemanche was murdered during the afternoon.

That the defendant, Kenneth Dexter Bailey Jr., borrowed a small red car shortly after 3:00 in the afternoon of the day of the killing and gave as his reason for borrowing the car the story that some person owed him money and had been avoiding him and he needed a strange car so that he could get close to the guy.

That a person meeting the general description of the defendant, Kenneth Dexter Bailey, Jr., was seen running from the scene of the murder just after a shot was fired and immediately drove south in a small red car matching the description of the car that had just shortly before been borrowed by Kenneth Dexter Bailey, Jr.

That within a very few minutes that defendant, Kenneth Dexter Bailey, Jr., returned the borrowed red car.

That within a very few more minutes after the murder the defendant, Kenneth Dexter Bailey Jr., had shaved off his mustache.

That the defendant, Kenneth Dexter Bailey, Jr., told the officers that he didn't remember when he shot a pistol in his back yard.

That a pistol that had previously been sold to the brother of the defendant, Kenneth Dexter Bailey, Jr., was found on a bridge, and ballistic examinations showed that this was the gun that killed Ray Courtemanche.

That expended casings were found in the area where the defendant, Kenneth Dexter Bailey, Jr., was observed shooting in his back yard on the morning of the day of the killing, and ballistics examinations showed that these expended casings were fired in the same gun that fired the projectile that killed Ray Courtemanche.

That Kenneth Dexter Bailey, Jr. murdered Ray Courtemanche.

At the conclusion of the trial the state will ask for conviction in the interest of justice.

TRIAL QUESTION

In my trial notebook I listed each witness who might be called to testify at trial. I wrote out every question I expected to ask along with what I expected the answer to be. If there was any chance that a witness might not remember the facts he had previously testified about I noted the prior testimony and where it was located, in the event, I needed to pull it out and ask the witness to explain any material differences.

The following is a brief summary of my questions.

Helen Courtemanche, the wife of the deceased court reporter. She testified where she and Ray lived in Okmulgee County, how Ray earned his living (Court Reporter, Bank Director, County Excise Board and rental buildings). She also testified that Ray was at home the day before the murder when she arrived about 5 or 5:15, and the defendant, Kenneth Dexter Bailey, Jr., was there. He jumped when she arrived as if she had startled him. He was nervous and in a rush to leave. Dexter was bareheaded, had a mustache and his hair was loose, not plastered down. Ray told her that Dexter was there asking Ray to help him find a job. I noted Steadman v. State, Okla Cr 568 P2 350 (1977) if there was a hearsay objection.

She would also identify pictures of the house and testify that the pictures showed the house as it looked the day of the murder.

Ron Froman could testify that he had conversations from time to time with Ray exchanging job recommendations with the Creek Nation and the state Senator's office. He knew Dexter, and after a conversation with Ray he told Chief Cox that he believed it would be a mistake to hire Dexter.

Kenneth Butler was a lawyer who shared an office with Ray. Kenneth knew that Ray was Chairman of the County Excise Board and he was engaged in various businesses with Ray including a convenience store business and rental property. He went to lunch with Ray the day he was murdered and last saw him at the office about 2:30. He could identify a picture of Ray.

Mack Kelly was a bail bondsman who was a social friend of Ray and his wife.

Cheryl Womble last saw Ray about 3:30 on the day he was murdered.

Betty Reynolds worked at the convenience store partly owned by Ray. On the day he was murdered she last saw him about 4 or 4:35 when he came into the store.

Amos Dixon drove a truck for the state highway department on the day Ray was murdered. The truck was kept at the highway Department barn near the New Morris Road and Wood Drive. He knew Ray and saw him at the convenience store at 4:10 and then saw Ray turn left off of Wood Drive onto the New Morris Highway at 4:20. He knew the time because he looked at his watch and was not to return to the barn before 4:30. He saw a red car behind Ray's car on the New Morris Road.

Patty Harris was serving as dispatcher for the Okmulgee Police Department on Feb. 3, 1981, when she received a call from EMSA ambulance service at 4:32 p.m., which she entered in the log. She dispatched a unit to the residence of Ray Courtemanche. She noted that Officers Grable and Boyd arrived on the scene at 4:37 p.m. and Captain Don Rade at 4:42 p.m.

Billie Jean Dugger lived next door south of the Courtemanche residence. She saw Ray pull up to his mail box, and she wanted to explain to him about why her trash cart was on his property. She checked the baby two times. She went out the front door, down the stairs and heard a noise. She saw a person run from the back of Ray's house. The person looked at her, had something by his leg. The person was startled, turned back around, continued to run and pulled on a red ski mask. The person jumped off the level to the driveway and pointed a gun at her. She turned and heard the car speed out to the south. She turned back and ran toward the street and tried to get a tag number but could only see white. She went to Ray's back door, saw Ray and called the ambulance and then called her husband. She saw Ray and he still hadn't moved. She went to the street and stopped Jim Newport and they both looked at Ray. She described the killer as being in his 30's, about 6 feet tall, dark hair, no deformities noted, he was in motion and his hair caught in the wind, he had an athletic build, was about 170 to 175 pounds, medium length hair, dark eyes and eye brows, gun in right hand behind his leg. She described the body style of the car as being like a Mercury Capri, a red car with black trim around the windows and on the bumper. The tag had a light background and dark lettering. She gave this information to Captain Don Raid and O.S.B.I. agents Estes and Mr. Ottwell and Okmulgee detective Ledbetter. Captain Raid typed up her observations, which she signed.

After she had given the statement written out by Capt. Raid and signed by her Billie Jean Dugger was hypnotized by an O.S.B.I. agent in an effort to get the most accurate composite drawing of the killer who pointed the gun at her, and she felt that the hair and face weren't right; the hypnosis session was tape recorded. Her observations before hypnosis and after remained without material change. The hair and the face were not right in the drawing. After the killing she saw a car which looked like the red car that left the scene, but the left front tire was not right.

Richard Powell drove south on Mission about 4:10 to 4:15 to visit a friend at Mission Lane Mobil Home. He was there only about three to five minutes because his friend was asleep. Then he drove north on Mission where he observed a small red car come out of a drive headed south and swerve toward him. That swerve toward him got his attention. Mr. Powell had to pull over a bit. The driver of the red car was holding something red, which he seemed to be throwing into the back seat. The driver of the red car was a white male with medium length brown hair. The car was either a Capri or a Mustang, with black molding around the bottom. He did see a lady down by the road turning around toward the house. He saw the car again during lunch one day of the preliminary hearing. (During the trial he saw the driver in the hall and identified him for the jury.)

Hadley Cook had been driving a bit after 4:00 p.m. on Feb. 3, 1981, on U.S. Highway 75, then turned East onto 36th Street. A car traveling at a high rate of speed met him coming over a hill, and he had to pull over. Highway 75 is also known as Wood Drive or the Beeline. The car he met was a small red car, not a foreign car and a late model. The driver was white with brown hair and he believes it was a man. The driver's hair was not like in the drawing; it was a fluffy length reaching to his ears.

Jim Newport was part owner of Star Drug and Gibson Pharmacy. He would usually take lunch from 4:30 to 6:00 p.m.. He knew Billie Jean Dugger; her husband worked for his store. Newport's home was about a half mile south of the Dugger residence. On Feb. 3, 1981, he saw Billie Jean Dugger in her driveway as he was driving home for lunch. She was waving her arms, running down the driveway and yelling something. He pulled into her drive and they went to Ray's back door. He saw that Ray had been shot, checked for a pulse, and there was none. He went outside and told Billie Jean that he was dead and she burst into tears; she said, "I didn't get the tag, don't know if I could recognize, he had short hair but not a crew cut." She added that she heard a noise, saw a guy with a ski-mask and gun, and that the car was a small red Ford – she thought a Mustang.

Dennis Grabel was an officer with the Okmulgee, Police department in 1981. On the afternoon of Feb. 3, 1981, he was dispatched to the residence of Ray Courtemanche on South Mission where he saw the lady next door, the ambulance and the body lying on the floor. He called for a detective. He had been right behind the ambulance on the way to the residence. He had only been about two or three blocks from the Courtemanche residence when he received the call. He preserved the scene until Detective Fields arrived.

Don Rade was shift Captain with the Okmulgee Police department on Feb. 3, 1981. He arrived at the Courtemanche residence and broadcast a brief description of the suspect. He took a statement from Billie Jean Dugger, which he typed and she signed.

Roy Fields was a Lieutenant Detective with the Okmulgee Police department on Feb. 3, 1981. About 4:25 that afternoon he arrived at the Courtemanche residence. He saw Ray Courtemanche on the floor. Officer Grabel was there. Detective Fields ran off the ambulance people and then took charge, protected and secured the scene. He entered the residence with Chief Hodge after stationing Vic Fry at the east door of the residence, which went into the kitchen, to prevent anyone from coming into or leaving the residence. They searched the house for other victims. There were none. He took photographs of the scene, which he identified at trial, and had Leon Hudson, an Oklahoma Highway Patrol Trooper, make a drawing. Dr. Anderson, the Medical Examiner, arrived. Detective Fields left the residence for 10 to 15 minutes leaving Chief Hodge in charge while he was away. O.S.B.I. Agent Roger Chrisco arrived and helped with the collection of evidence and investigation at the scene.

Perry Harkrider of the Okmulgee Police department knew the defendant, Dexter Bailey Jr, and knew where he lived. He was searching the area near the trash cans on the property where Kenneth Dexter Bailey, Jr. lived. He found a sandblasted projectile. O.S.B.I. Agent Chrisco was present. Mr. Harkrider knew that a 55-gallon trash barrel and galvanized trash barrel were removed from the premises. He was handed the projectile and identified it. The condition of these items did not change while in his possession.

Don Conners went to the Bailey ranch home where defendant Kenneth Dexter Bailey lived on Feb. 20, 1981, with a bunch of officers where they searched and he found a sandblasted projectile which he gave to O.S.B.I. Agent Ottwell. He identified the projectile and testified that its condition had not changed while in his possession.

Bob Powell of the O.S.B.I. went to the Bailey ranch on Feb. 5, 1981, visited with Mike Stacy and went to a location between the houses near a shed area. A bullet hole in a trash can caught his eye. Agent Powell saw a spent .38 casing in the trash can, which he removed. As he was doing so ice and goo clung to the casing and exposed another .38 casing, which he also removed and marked for identification.

He was handed the death gun, which he identified; he explained the chain of custody, having received the gun from Agent Ottwell and delivered to Tom Jordan and received it from Tom Jordan and agent Looney, who was with him at that time. Nothing changed about the condition of the death gun while in his possession.

Oklahoma Highway Patrol Trooper Leon Hudson made drawings of the crime scene.

Joel Anderson, testified as Medical Examiner as to what he observed, and he confirmed that the pictures were accurate representations of what he saw. Ray was dead, and he ordered an autopsy.

Chester Hodge, Chief of Police for Okmulgee, Okla., testified about what he saw at the crime scene. He also testified that the evidence room at the police department had a lock on the door and he told who had keys to the lock. He described items of evidence and related who had custody of these items and their condition.

Rodger Chrisco of the Oklahoma State Bureau of Investigation testified that when he arrived at the crime scene, he talked with Okmulgee detectives Fields and Ledbetter and made sure the scene was secure. He was at the scene until about 9:00 P.M. and took possession of the death projectile, which he kept in his custody until he delivered it to O.S.B.I. agent Robin Estes. About 7:00 A.M. on Feb. 8, 1981, he talked with Kenneth Dexter Bailey at his home. Dexter had been at Ray's home the day before the murder talking about getting into court reporting school because he could not rodeo forever. On the day of the murder, he left the ranch about 3:00 p.m. after borrowing his ranch hand's car. He was going to his father's office to talk about race horse bills. Before he went to his father's office, he went to the County News and purchased a newspaper and then went to People's Bakery, where he bought a cream puff, and ended his outing about 4 or 4:15 P.M. and returned to the ranch, where he took a shower and shaved off his mustache. He didn't remember when he last fired a pistol behind his house. Later that day he talked with Dexter at the Okmulgee Police department; this time he gave a different reason for taking a shower, he had diarrhea, ran to the house, but the door was locked and he had an accident. He testified that photos were accurate and showed what was seen.

M.F. Merchant testified that during the month of February 1981 he was State Medical Examiner. He set out his education, training and experience and testified that he was licensed to practice medicine in Oklahoma. He testified about having performed an autopsy on Ray Courtemanche and stated that the cause of death was a gunshot to the head. He testified that one name of an associate was in error in that Roy was actually Ray. He further confirmed that the photo presented to him was the man on whom he performed the autopsy, Ray Courtemanche.

Jackie Roberts testified that she was an agent of the Oklahoma State Bureau of Investigation and was a hypnotist. She described her basic and advanced schooling. She testified that she came to Okmulgee on Feb. 4, 1981, to hypnotize Jeannie Dugger in order to secure the best possible composite picture of the killer. Before the hypnosis session she received brief information so that she could ask appropriate questions. She made a tape recording of the hypnosis session. Harvey Pratt, the O.S.B.I. artist, was also present in the room during the hypnosis session. Agent Pratt was behind Mrs. Dugger. When Agent Roberts completed her work, she left. On cross-examination Agent Roberts testified that the purpose of the session was to get Mrs. Dugger relaxed to tell what she saw. Mrs. Dugger was in a light and medium hypnosis state. The effort was to get a composite picture of the killer.

Harvey Pratt testified that he was an agent with the Oklahoma State Bureau of Investigation and that he was an artist and that his experience included having done 1,300 composite drawings. He came to Okmulgee on Feb. 4, 1981, to make a composite drawing. He received information from Jeanie Dugger on which to base his drawing. He used an Identikit Mark II and showed the jury the equipment he used. He was handed the composite drawing he had made and testified that it was in the same condition as when he made it. He further testified that a composite drawing is not intended to be an exact drawing of a person but is intended to rule out people who do not look like the subject.

Mike Stacy testified that in February 1981 he worked on the Bailey ranch. He knew Kenneth Bailey and lived next door to him. He testified that he had testified at the preliminary hearing. He further testified that at times while working on the ranch his work took him off the ranch, and one time he went with Kenneth Dexter Bailey to Oklahoma City, and there was a conversation about guns and silencers. He further testified that on the morning of Feb. 3, 1981, about 9:30 or 10:00 A.M. he heard sounds that he did not hear every day on the ranch. He heard shots, and he went where he could see. He saw Kenneth Dexter Bailey with something in his hand which he presumed was a gun. Dexter said that he had had the gun for a long time and he wanted to see if it still shoots. On Feb. 3, 1981, he left the ranch about 12:00-12:30 and returned about 3:30 p.m. Sue Bailey and Richard Coleman were at the ranch.

Later he saw Kenneth Dexter Bailey wearing jeans and a shirt walking to his house. He talked with Kenneth Dexter Bailey after he came to the barn about 15 minutes later. The conversation had to do with the fact that Kenneth Dexter Bailey had shaved off his mustache; there was kidding about having a new hand on the ranch. At some point Kenneth Dexter Bailey said that if his father ever said anything about gambling that he was to say that he knew nothing about it. Richard Coleman's red car was at the ranch on Feb. 3, 1981; it had milky film on it like road film thrown from the wheels but he saw no mud on it. Dexter got home about 4 or 4:30 p.m.; he did not wear a watch. He further testified that he talked with law enforcement officers and told them the only places he could not let them go was Dexter's house and personal area. Mr. Stacy gave the officers permission to look around. They specifically looked in the area where Dexter had shot the gun. He was asked if he had ever used the name Remington, and he said he had asked to be identified as Mr. Remington if he called the Police department because he had some problem with one of the officers and didn't want him to know he was calling.

He pointed out and identified Kenneth Dexter Bailey, Jr and testified that he had his own trash can and never burned anything in the trash can behind Dexter's house.

Sue Bailey testified that she is married to Dexter. She discussed family matters and identified family members and spouses including Laura Neal and Randy White. She was asked if she had told someone about something Dexter had done on Feb. 3, 1981, between about 4:30 and 5:00. She testified that she had told Mrs. Stacy that Dexter had burned newspapers that she was planning to use to train a new puppy. Sue was also asked if on Feb, 8, 1981, while officers were at the ranch if she mentioned something to someone and she confirmed that she had said to not mention that Dexter had been shooting in the back yard.

At this point in my trial notebook, I had notes regarding a wife testifying against her husband.

The objection might be made that a wife can NOT testify against her husband where a crime was not against her or the children.

22 OSA 702 specifically provided: "Except as otherwise provided in this and the following chapters, the rules of evidence in civil cases are applicable also in criminal cases; Provided, however, that neither husband nor wife shall in any case be a witness against the other except in a criminal prosecution for a crime committed one against the other, or except in a criminal prosecution against either the husband or wife, or both, against the minor children of either the husband or the wife, but they may in all criminal cases be witnesses for each other, and shall be subject to cross-examination as other witnesses, and shall in no event on a criminal trial be permitted to disclose communications made by one to the other except on trial of an offense committed by one against the other or except on a trial of a felony committed by one, or both, against the minor children of either the husband or the wife."

This statute has been repealed by implication by the enactment of the Oklahoma Evidence Code effective Oct. 1, 1978. Lavick v. State, 632 P2 1234 (1981).

12 OSA 2102 "This code shall be construed to secure fairness in administration, elimination of unjustifiable expense and delay or promotion of growth and development of the law of evidence to the end that the truth may be ascertained and proceedings justly determined."

12 OSA 2103 "… this code shall apply in both criminal and civil proceedings…"

12 OSA 2501 "Except as otherwise provided by constitution, statute or rules promulgated by the Supreme Court no person has a privilege to:

1. Refuse to be a witness;
2. Refuse to disclose any matter;
3. Refuse to produce any object or writing: or

4. Prevent another from being a witness or disclosing any matter or producing any object or writing."

12 OSA 2504 Husband and wife privileges

"A. A communication is confidential for purposes of this section if it is made privately by any person to his spouse and is not intended for disclosure to any other person.

B. An accused in a criminal proceeding has a privilege to prevent his spouse from testifying as to any confidential communication between the accused and the spouse.

C. The privilege may be claimed by the accused or by the spouse on behalf of the accused.

D. There is no privilege under this section in a proceeding in which one spouse is charged with a crime against the person or property of:

1. The other;
2. A child of either;
3. A person residing in the household of either; or
4. A third person when the crime is committed in the course of committing a crime against any other person named in this section."

Evidence Subcommittee's note following 12 OSA 2504 provides "…Most significantly it limits the marital communication privilege to preventing a spouse in a criminal proceeding from testifying as to any confidential communication between the accused and the spouses." …

"This has led a majority of the jurisdictions to abandon the spousal privilege though a majority of the states do recognize a privilege of an accused to prevent his spouse from testifying as to any confidential communication between them and was the one aspect of marital privilege that the Advisory Committee to the Proposed Federal Rule 505 felt was warranted in continuing. This policy was carried forward in the Uniform Rules of 1974 and was recommended by the subcommittee for the retention of the marital privilege only to the extent provided in this statute."

DeWolf v State, 95 Okl Cr 287, 245 P2 107 (1952) "Where nature of information sought is peculiarly within the knowledge of one spouse and is not acquired through confidence of the marital relation, or when communication is in presence or hearing of a third person, such communication or knowledge is not within the rule of confidential or privileged communication."

What I planned to examine Sue Bailey on went to statements she had made to other persons.

Judy Stacy is the wife of Mike Stacy, who testified earlier in this trial. She testified that on Feb. 3, 1981, she lived on the Bailey ranch, and on that morning about 10:00 or 10:30 she heard a sound that caught her attention, and she observed that Dexter Bailey caused the sound. She saw that he had a gun in his hand, and he opened the cylinder.

If Sue Bailey did not admit that she talked about Dexter burning newspapers and that she asked Judy Stacy not to talk about the shooting, I would have asked Judy Stacy the following questions: Did you know a person by the name of Sue Bailey? Did you have a conversation with her about 4:30 or 5:00 P.M. on Feb. 3, 1981? What did Sue Bailey say? (Dexter burned newspapers) What was she doing while you were talking to her? (Watching the fire) On Feb. 8, 1981, while O.S.B.I. agents were on the ranch, did Sue say anything to you? What did she say? (Don't mention Dexter shooting)

If Judy Stacy had any problems remembering I would ask the following questions: Do you know a person by the name of Steve Cox? Did you talk to him on Oct. 30, 1981? Did you tell him about Sue Bailey telling you about Dexter burning papers? Did you tell him about Sue telling you not to mention that Dexter had been shooting in the back yard?

Then I would have Judy Stacy point out Dexter Bailey and Sue Bailey. I would also ask her about any burning she had done in the trash can.

If Judy Stacy did not remember accurately, I would call Steve Cox and ask him the following questions: State your occupation on Oct. 30, 1981? (Investigator for the District Attorney of Okmulgee and McIntosh Counties) Do you know a person by the name of Judy Stacy? Did you talk with her on Oct. 30, 1981? What was the thrust of the conversation? (She talked about talking to Sue Bailey on Feb. 3, 1981, talking about Dexter burning and on Feb. 8, 1981, Sue asked her not to talk about Dexter shooting) Did you make any type of record of that conversation? (Tape recording) Then have Steve listen to the tape and confirm that it is the same one without any changes. Then offer the tape recording into evidence. If there should be any objection, I had made a note of 12 OSA 2607 which provided that the reliability of a witness may be attacked by any party, including the party calling him.

Richard Coleman. I would have asked his occupation in February of 1981. (student at Oklahoma State tech and ranch hand on the Bailey ranch) Did he have a car and describe it. (1980 Mustang, red with black trim, four speed transmission) Hand him a photo of his car and have him identify it and confirm when and where the photo was made and that he was present when it was made and explain why the left tire looked different than the others. Have him confirm that he worked for the Bailey ranch on Feb. 3, 1981, and ask him about what time he arrived. (3:00 to 3:10) Have him describe what other vehicles were parked and where when he arrived. Then ask him if anyone other than himself drove his car sometime after 3:00 P.M. on Feb. 3, 1981. (Dexter asked to borrow his car because some fellow owed him money and was avoiding him; if he used a vehicle the guy didn't recognize, he might be able to catch him.) Then have him confirm that there were other vehicles at the ranch that Dexter could have used. Ask what Dexter's appearance was when he borrowed his car. (He was wearing a navy blue goose down jacket and jeans, but he didn't remember about the mustache.) When was the first time after 3:00 P.M. on Feb. 3, 1981, when he noticed Dexter without a mustache? (That evening.) What time did Dexter ask to borrow your car? (3:15 - 3:20, very shortly after Coleman arrived at the ranch, 5 or 10 minutes.) Ask if there were any damage to any tires before Dexter borrowed his car. (no) What time did Dexter leave with your car? (3:15 to 3:20) When and where did you next see Dexter? (at the ranch at 4:30) How did you know the time? (Looked at his watch) At the time you looked at your watch where were you and who were you with? (in the tack feed room with Mike Stacy) When Dexter returned, where did he go? (to the feed room. Dexter was still wearing the dark blue goose-down jacket and blue jeans.) During the course of the evening of Feb. 3, 1981, did you notice anything different about Dexter? (Dexter had shaved off his mustache. Dexter said he was tired of it.)

Did you do anything besides your usual work before you left the ranch? (Turned out calves for Dexter and ate supper with them. Left the ranch in his red car about 7-7:30. His first stop was about 100 yards outside the gate because he had a flat tire; there was a tear in the tire. He put a little cheap tire on instead of the flat one.) When did you last make a trip in your car? (Previous Sunday returned from South Dakota, and the car was covered with chloride, which was being used in South Dakota to clear out ice, snow and slush) What was the last thing you remember Dexter did before you left? (He talked to his father.) Point out Dexter Bailey.

If Coleman turned out not to be a good witness, ask the following questions: Describe Dexter's appearance the day of the killing. Did Dexter go anywhere a short time after the killing? (Went to Kentucky to a rodeo) Describe his appearance on his return. How did his hair compare before the killing and as soon as he returned from the rodeo? Did you ever tell anyone that his hair looked different? Did you ever tell anyone that he got a haircut? Did you ever tell anyone that after the killing he got a red neck hair cut? (Paul Witt).

If my memory is correct Coleman turned out to be a good witness and I did not need to call Paul Witt, but I was prepared to call him if I needed to establish that Dexter had changed his appearance shortly after the killing.

Robin Estes testified that she was an O.S.B.I. agent. She testified about having various items of evidence in her possession, chain of custody and to David Dixon to check for trace evidence, then to Larry Mullins to check for fingerprints, then to Tom Jordan to do a ballistics check and finally returning the death gun to Harry

Ledbetter at the Okmulgee Police Department; the death gun was never out of her presence. She was also shown the death projectile which she identified. Nothing happened to either item of evidence while in her possession to change the condition of the item.

Jim Pratt testified that he was an O.S.B.I. agent in February 1981, described his education and talked about his involvement in the case against Dexter Bailey on trial. Agent Pratt went to the Bailey ranch about mid-day with Agent Powell on Feb. 5, 1981, in response to a call from Mike Stacy. At that time Pratt, Powell and Stacy went to an area between the house and the shed area. A shinny indented hole in a trash can caught Agent Pratt's eye. He got close enough to examine the hole and while doing so he spotted a casing in the can. Mr. Powell removed one casing, Mr. Pratt removed one, and Mr. Powell removed the third one. The casings were given to O.S.B.I. Agent Kevin Ottwell. Mike Stacy used a fake name when calling the police department, which he called about 10 to 15 times. While looking in the trash can did anything else in the immediate area catch your attention? (the rusted trash can, galvanized trash can burnt inside, remnants of newspapers, zipper)

The rusted trash can with the hole in it, the galvanized trash can with ashes in it, the expended casing, and photos from the preliminary hearing were presented to agent Pratt to identify and confirm that nothing had happened to change the condition of the items since February 1981. He was also presented with the melted zipper from the trash can, which he confirmed had not changed condition since February 1981, and it was submitted to the O.S.B.I. lab in a sealed container. While not under arrest Dexter Bailey saw agent Pratt in possession of the burnt zipper and said that Stacy was always burning in the trash can.

There was a second gun similar to the death gun, which Dexter claimed to have won in a poker game.

Claude Berry was an O.S.B.I. criminologist. After he described his education, training and experience he identified the burnt zipper, which he had received in a sealed container. Its condition had not changed.

Kevin Ottwell testified that in February 1981, he was an O.S.B.I. agent and was involved in the investigation of the murder of Ray Courtemanche. He identified a photo of Mr. Coleman's car and stated that it was a true representation of what the car looked like. He also testified about items of evidence and the chain of custody.

Ken Pierce was the court reporter at the preliminary hearing and had custody of some evidence. I had questions about the chain of custody.

James Looney, an O.S.B.I. agent, testified about chain of custody of evidence.

Raymond Caudill testified that in February 1981, he lived west of Okmulgee, west of the Deep Fork River. He also testified that at that time he was employed by G&W Body Shop in Okmulgee and that about 7:30 on the morning of Feb. 4, 1981, he was driving his pickup to work, and as he drove over the Deep Fork River bridge, he saw a pistol lying on the bridge. He stopped and picked up the gun with a pencil and put it in his pickup seat. He went to the West Side Cafe for breakfast and left the pistol locked in his pickup. After breakfast he drove to work on West Sixth, told his boss about the pistol he found, and his boss called the police. He turned the pistol over to Detective Harry Ledbetter of the Okmulgee Police department. The gun was handed to him, and he recognized it from scratches on the grip and cylinder. Nothing happened to the gun while in his possession to change its condition.

Mr. Ledbetter set out his occupation in February 1981, and testified that he saw Raymond Caudill at G&W Body shop in Okmulgee on Feb. 4, 1981, where he received a pistol removed from Mr. Caudill's locked pickup, which was parked in back of the shop. Detective Ledbetter testified that the pistol could not be seen inside the pickup because there was a cloth over it. Detective Ledbetter picked up the pistol with a pen and placed it in a sack. He made sure the pistol was unloaded, filled out a form and sealed the envelope. He gave the gun in the sealed envelope to O.S.B.I. Agent Robin Estes, who returned it to him that evening and locked it in the property room. He next saw the pistol on Feb. 24, 1981, when he gave it to O.S.B.I. Agent Kevin Ottwell. He was handed the pistol and identified it. He further testified that the only keys to the evidence room were in the possession of the Chief of Police, Chester Hodge, and himself.

I made some notes about Billy Wilson from DeQueen, Ark., who had another gun stolen from him, but it could not be traced to Dexter Bailey. Dexter may have won it in a poker game.

Paul Rose owned the Golden Pawn Shop in Tulsa, Okla. He had operated this business about 11 years at the time of the trial. He knew Brett Richard Bailey and had bought a lot of stuff from him. He testified that on Jan. 20, 1978, he sold a gun to Brett Richard Bailey; he had a journal of purchases which showed under No. 4473 that it was purchased and signed for by Brett Richard Bailey. The description of the gun was recorded as a .38 Colt Detective Special, serial number 750207. Brett Bailey signed this document in the presence of Paul Rose, who also signed the form, as required by the Federal government. There were no changes to the document since signed. He identified the gun and testified that he last saw it before the preliminary hearing when he sold it to Brett. Paul Rose testified that about three or four months before the preliminary hearing Brett talked with him about the gun. Rose told Brett the serial number and that two or three guys from O.S.B.I. had asked about it.

Brett Bailey testified that he was the brother of Kenneth Dexter Bailey and identified him in court. The next question was if he had ever done business with a pawn shop in Tulsa, the Golden Pawn Shop. Then he was asked about purchases there. The death gun was handed to him and he was asked to look it over carefully then he was asked if he recognized it. If his answer should be no or he was not sure, ask if he ever owned a gun similar to this one and ask him to describe the gun he owned (.38 Colt) and where he got it (Gold Pawn Shop). If he doesn't remember the name ask him about his preliminary hearing testimony where he testified that he had purchased the gun from Paul Rose. Then ask Brett if Paul Rose testified that he sold you a .38 Colt Detective Special with serial number 750207 on Jan. 20, 1978, would he be accurate. Then ask him to read the serial number of the .38 Colt handed to him. Where is the gun that you bought from Paul Rose? Is this the same gun that you bought from Paul Rose? If Brett's answer should be no, ask do you remember being asked the question at preliminary hearing located at Volume VI, page 6, line 25, "Question. All right. Do you know where that weapon that we had previously talked about here is today? Do you remember the answer you gave at preliminary hearing Volume VI, page 7, line 2? "I assume that is it."

Then ask what he did with the gun after he bought it from Paul Rose. If he says he shot it, ask if Dexter ever shot it. Ask when the last time was when he saw this gun. (March or April 1978 when he sold the gun at a flea market. If he comes up with the name of the purchaser ask why he didn't tell us his name at the preliminary hearing. Then ask if he had talked to Paul Rose since Jan. 20, 1978, about the gun which you bought from him. What did you ask Paul Rose about the gun (serial number)? Ask if he talked with O.S.B.I. agents during their investigation of this case; did he talk with anyone before talking with the O.S.B.I. agents (lawyer father of the defendant Kenneth Dexter Bailey) and what did that office tell you to tell the officers (I have no comment to make to you gentlemen). Ask Brett if he had anything to do with the killing of Ray Courtemanche. Ask if he kept any records of sales of guns at the flea market and if he held a license to sell guns and if he gave the gun to Dexter.

Tom Jordan testified about his position with O.S.B.I. and about items of evidence with which he had contact and what he did with each item. He explained his work and why he used homemade bullets for comparison.

There was a chart of all items of evidence which carefully traced the chain of custody.

After the testimony of Tom Jordan all items of evidence would be offered into evidence including the Death Projectile, 3 expended casings, the Death gun, a second gun, 3 sand-blasted projectiles and a photo of the bridge where the death gun was found.

At this point the State would Rest.

Then a demurrer would be entered, which was expected to be overruled. A demurrer is simply a request made by the defense to the court stating that even if everything set out were true that it would not be enough to move forward with the trial. It clearly would be expected that the court would overrule the demurrer.

Then it would be expected that the defense would move for a directed verdict which again would be expected to be overruled.

Then the defense would put on their case. If they had not made an opening statement, they would have the opportunity to do so before putting on evidence.

I had a list of the people subpoenaed by the defense. It contained 41 names. A supplemental list contained 11 names, some of which were duplications from the primary list.

Next, I had to "defend" the case. In other words, I had to prepare a case for the defense to be certain that I anticipated what each witness would testify to.

First, I considered the defense theory of defense.

1. The defendant was someplace else, K. D. Bailey's office, the bakery and the newspaper.

2. Someone else did it. Motion in Limine (a motion before a judge from which the defense is excluded) to exclude testimony.

3. Attack the State's case.

Ballistics. John Sadumas

Hypnosis. Dr. Diamond or Dr. Orne.

Guy who owed gambling debt.

Defendant Kenneth Dexter Bailey.

Defendant's hair.

Expected evidence in support of each theory:

O.S.B.I. did not suspect Dexter until the 4th and K.D. , defendant's father, didn't know until the 8th.

Cindy Thomas, County News. Preliminary Hearing transcript volume VIII 152.

Carla Jones, Peoples Bakery. Preliminary Hearing transcript volume VII 181.

Mary Bailey Romine, attorney in K.D. Bailey's office and the sister of K.D.

Ramona Belford, personal secretary for K.D. Bailey since 1966. Testify as to the time Dexter was in the office.

K.D. Bailey the father of Dexter and Brett Bailey. K.D. was in a lawsuit with Ray Courtemanche and had told one person that if Ray did not dismiss the lawsuit that it was going to turn into a dirty fight. Ask about the loss of sources of income within the past five years, which would have included rent from the welfare office after Kenneth Butler defeated him for the position of state senator.

Dennis Seacat was one of the lawyers in K.D. Bailey's law firm. He made a statement to a lawyer from Miami, Okla., who was not covered by the attorney-client privilege. Dexter made a TV appearance wherein he said "I am not innocent".

Darla Gayle, about one or two weeks before Ray was killed was in Style One Barber Shop in Morris, Okla., a small town about five miles east of Okmulgee past 9:00 A.M. Linda Beaver, the owner, and Ann (Bearden) Smith were cutting hair when a guy walked in from the north and said, "Mind if I use the phone? Have phone book?" He said he had a nine o'clock appointment with Ray Courtemanche, but he would have to miss it because his car broke down. Darla helped him find the number because he did not know how to spell Courtemanche though he had the "C" section open. He dialed direct. She did not hear the conversation. He paid 30 cents and walked out to the north. He was close to 30 years old, approximately 5' 10" looked to be in good shape, had blond hair about to the collar, she believed his hair covered his ears. Doesn't know about sideburns and not sure about mustache. He was not wearing glasses; he was wearing jeans or casual pants with a light weight short jacket. He did not look like Dexter, but she couldn't rule out that it might have been Dexter. He was in the shop about 10 minutes. Ask about her relationship with Dexter Bailey and Randy White (Sue Bailey's sibling). Is it common talk that you are dating Randy White?

Linda remembered the time as 9:10, the money to pay for the call as 38 cents composed of dimes, a nickel and pennies. She also remembered the guy's age at about 22 to 25, 5' 10", 180 Pounds, medium build.

Ann (Bearden) Smith also worked for the Farm Bureau in Okmulgee. Saturday morning about three weeks before Ray was killed, she worked in Style One Barber Shop in Morris, Okla., with Linda Beaver, they were both cutting hair. She drove to town from the east about 8:45 A.M. and saw a Red-Orange Sunbird Pontiac with a 2" yellow stripe approximately below the door handle. It was approximately two years old, clean, parked about 1 and 1/2 miles east of Morris on the north side of the road. She had to drive with care because the car was near a small bridge, and a car was coming. A guy came into the shop and said he had a 9:00 appointment, and someone in the shop said, "You have missed it because it's 9:10!" He didn't know how to spell the name, so Darla helped him find the number. She heard him say "unable to make appointment -talk later." The charge was 37 cents, and he paid with four dimes. He called, hung up, then got an answer. Also hung up, then grabbed quickly to catch the operator to get change. He had already called a friend to come get him. After he left, they talked about why he hadn't called Ray from the first phone. He was wearing blue jeans and a dark blue or green jacket with a zipper. The guy was about 5'8" and 150 pounds, age 24 or 25. He had mid brown hair to mid ear, parted in the middle, Linda thought it was parted on the side, no mustache or beard. Jacket was zipped part way up. Jacket was made of cotton blend with synthetic type material, if snagged would run and not pull out a hunk. Looked like a college guy. The day was cool and sunny. The composite picture was a lot like the guy in the shop; it was not Dexter.

Cross examination about details and relationships of witnesses.

I had copies of a couple of cases I might need at this point.

Defendant attack on the State's case.

Lester Neal testimony about the flat tire. On cross ask him to describe the damage to the tire.

John Sanders, former Chicago police officer who had done ballistics work for 35 years. He would be expected to testify about how he would usually conduct a ballistic examination. The O.S.B.I. did not allow him to use their equipment to conduct his own tests and he was not present when the O.S.B.I. conducted its exam, so he really didn't know what happened during the O.S.B.I. exam. He was asked why he did not come to examine the death gun when the court first authorized such examination but waited until the last minute. The examination would be extensive and detailed requiring detailed answers.

There was a chance that the defense would call Dr. Bernard Diamond or Dr. Orne to testify about hypnosis. I know this subject inside and out and had the transcript of Dr. Diamond's testimony, which could be used extensively to rebut his assertions. Whatever experts might be called I would have him explain what a Freudian slip is, a slip in speaking revealing what the speaker meant rather than what the speaker said, specifically relating to Dexter's TV interview where he said, "I am not innocent".

Continuing with witnesses the defense might call:

Emma O'Hern might testify that Kenneth Dexter Bailey had short hair, not over his ears. She, her brother and Randy White met Kenneth Dexter Bailey, the defendant's wife Sue at Oklahoma State Tech for lunch. Dexter's hair was combed over and he had no mustache that she remembers. She went to school with Randy White at Twin Hills. and he is about 33. She knows Mike Bailey; they have looked at cars at Bailey Motors. Her brother Jerry Flood went to school with a guy who works at Bailey Motors.

A person named Yearling might testify that Coleman's car was at the car wash right at dark, about 5:00. He got off work early that day and would not have washed his car as late as 9:00 PM.

A guy by the name of Chastain might testify that he doesn't remember if Dexter's hair was long or short and he was at the ball game the night before Ray Courtemanche was killed.

If the defendant Kenneth Dexter Bailey takes the stand to testify, I expected to ask questions including the following: Who else was at the Moose Lodge? Where did he get the 32? (in a poker game) Was he aware of a lawsuit between Ray Courtemanche and his dad K.D. Bailey and what was it over? (Politics) What race? (State Senator) Any benefits come with being the State Senator? (Job appointments and office rentals) If K.D. Bailey had won the Senate seat who would have been appointed tag agent? (Kenneth Dexter Bailey or his wife Sue) Did K.D. Bailey ever ask Ray Courtemanche to dismiss the lawsuit? How much did you earn last year? ($12,000 -$13,000) Has K.D. Bailey ever supplied any of the money you have lived on? Who is paying your legal expense? Did K.D. Bailey ever urge you to get out of the rodeo business? What jobs have you tried to get? (Creek Nation) Why didn't you get it? Did you ever make the statement that Ray Courtemanche cost you $200,000.00? How long have you been acquainted with the Courtemanche family? How many times were you at the home of Ray Courtemanche in February 1981? What did you talk to Ray about? Have you ever threatened anyone, pull a knife on someone? (Pine Knot) Did you ever ride a horse into the club at the Canterbury Inn? Took the bill from Charlie Martin to K.D. 's office? Dennis Seacat was one of your lawyers, did you ever appear with him on television in a newscast? In that TV press conference did you say "I am not innocent?"

These listed questions of defense witnesses are just questions to be considered and would be used, modified or not used as the trial testimony developed.

After the defense rests its case the State will have an opportunity to rebut the testimony that they put on.

Debbie Wells who worked in K.D. 's office knew on Feb. 3rd that Dexter was a suspect in the murder of Ray Courtemanche.

Paul Witt with the Okmulgee Police Department had been told by Chastain that he didn't know if the defendant's hair was long or short.

Dan Jones could testify about a knife being pulled by Dexter.

Terry George could testify about Dexter riding a horse into the club at the Canterbury Inn.

Dexter made the statement on TV, "I am not innocent".

Dick Gibbon could testify about K.D. commenting that Ray's law suite would be dropped or things were going to get dirty.

Debbie Rhodes, a girl working in K.D. Bailey's office told her aunt, "I knew when Dexter left the office, they didn't like my answer."

Ray Wallace saw Dexter driving toward the ranch in a pickup five to 10 minutes before 4:00 P.M.

Helen Courtemanche, Defendant's mustache was light colored, color of Ray's car and parked on the driveway when the jury viewed the house, and Dexter's hair was fuller.

Charlie Martin, horse training bill not delivered to Dexter until 4 days after Ray was killed. Dexter asked him if he had received a subpoena and wanted him to testify in his favor, but he refused because it was not so.

Jackie Roberts, mouth gets dry under hypnosis, and Billie Jean Dugger didn't see tag on front of car rather than no tag there.

Art Hackney, girl said orange car was a Pontiac.

Tom Jordan, Kansas City did their own test firing? Bullet dropped or rolled or otherwise damaged? Misaligned cylinder, Hole in flesh same size as bullet, Mistreated death projectile, Leading in barrel, Handling of projects.

Kate from Kansas City examined projectile and gun.

Lawyer Seacat: Did you conduct a press conference with Dexter? Was a TV station there? I do not want the words you said, but tell me the words Dexter said. Did you represent Mike Stacy or Richard Coleman, and how many times did you talk with them about their testimony? Who are all the lawyers who have been involved in the defense of this case? (Exclude David Thompson) What is meant by the attorney-client privilege? Does the attorney-client privilege extend to anyone other than the lawyers you have named? Have you had a conversation with a lawyer, other than those you have named, about this case? Did you make any comment to him about the guilt or innocence of the defendant, Dexter? Who was the lawyer? (from Miami).

Dian Beason from Pauls Valley, Okla., could testify about Dexter's earnings for the past 10 years.

I prepared an affidavit setting out the need for Dr. Martin Reiser, a necessary witness in this trial, which had been set for trial at 9:00 A.M. on Nov. 11, 1981.

A jury was selected being very careful to do what I could to get a fair trial.

Recently I made a trip to Okmulgee to review court dockets to be certain that my facts and memory were accurate. The docket book could not be found on the first trip. I wrote a letter to the Court Clerk explaining what I needed to review, and on the next trip the book was provided to me in an adequate work space in the law library. My memory is that in some cases the docket book contained a listing of witnesses called. I did not find such a list in this case, which took a number of days. I really do not remember if someone from the Court Clerk's office kept any notes during the trial or not. Certainly, we had a good reporter who recorded the trial word for word, and there are never enough employees to do everything desired. In this case the jury decided the case in favor of the defendant. Had the defendant been convicted there certainly would have been an appeal based on a completed transcript of the evidence presented at trial, and the District Attorney would have been provided with a copy of the transcript and undoubtedly, I could have found the actual word-for-word testimony given during the trial. I did not search for the reporter's notes which possibly could have been transcribed but for a different reporter to attempt to transcribe the original notes after 30 plus years would have been difficult and subject to errors, even if they could have been found. As District Attorney I could have appealed the case, but the defendant had been put in jeopardy and was not found guilty, and he could not have been retried. To spend public money for a transcript in this case would have been a misuse of public money.

STATE'S CLOSING STATEMENT TO THE JURY

INSTRUCTIONS WERE GONE OVER BY THE JUDGE WITH ATTORNEYS ON BOTH SIDES OF THE CASE

I reviewed the instructions with the jury.

I reviewed the evidence. I did point out that if the jury remembered any evidence differently than I did that the jurors should rely on their own memorirs of the evidence presented.

Helen Courtemanche, the wife of Ray Courtemanche, testified that the Defendant, Dexter Bailey, was at the Courtemanche house the day before the murder.

Kenneth Butler testified that Ray Courtemanche was a human being with a home, a wife, kids, a job, business interests, and Ray saw lots of people.

Cheryl Womble testified that Ray was at the office the very day he was killed.

Betty Reynolds testified that she had only met Ray a few days before he was killed. She saw Ray at the store between 4:00 and 4:35 PM.

Amos Dixon saw Ray at the store at 4:10 P.M.; he knew because he looked at his watch. He saw what he believed was Ray Courtemanche at the intersection of US 75 and the new Morris Road at 4:20 P.M.. He was watching the time closely because he couldn't return to the County Barn before 4:30, and it was 4:20 P.M. There was a red car following Ray at the time.

Patty Harris, the police dispatcher, received a call from EMSA, the ambulance service, at 4:32 P.M.; she logged every call and listed the time. Consequently we know just about when Ray was killed – within 12 minutes, between 4:20 P.M. and 4:32 P.M..

Billie Jean Dugger saw the killer run from the killing. She saw him look at her; he appeared surprised. She saw him put on a ski mask while he had a gun in his hand. She realized what the sound she had heard had been – a gunshot. She saw him jump down to where his car was parked and point the gun at her. I submit to you that her attention was focused on the man and the gun. She did realize that there was a red car – and was able to give some description of it, like the black behind the side windows. Her vision was not good, and she could not see the thin white stripe on the black tires. And remember it was the hub caps that were shinny. Even the expert on hypnosis testified that Billie Jean Dugger could not remember anything that her eye had not seen. Shortly after the shooting and before being hypnotized she gave Captain Rade a description of the killer, which matched the defendant. She gave Captain Rade a description of the car, which matched the description of the car the defendant was driving. You heard the hypnosis tape and have a transcript of what was said on the tape. You heard her explain that she was allowing her thoughts to flow to the hypnotist in an effort to be of help.

Remember the car was moving and she was looking for an Okmulgee tag on the back. Remember right after she said she couldn't see any tag on the front of the red car – she said she was losing her concentration, and the hypnotist had to take her back down into hypnosis. She never said there was a louver on the back window - she did say there was black around the window. And remember she identified the car two times, at Oklahoma State Tech and downtown. She told you that the composite was not right, but she quit because additional work was making the picture look less like the killer. The defendant matched the description of the killer, height, weight, age, athletic build. Also remember I asked Billie Jean Dugger to turn toward you as long as she saw the killer – you be the judge of what she saw.

Richard Powell saw the red car going South on Mission and saw the killer throw the ski mask into the back seat. He saw Billie Jean Dugger in front of her house. He saw the car again later and identified the driver as Richard Coleman – the man who lent the same red car to the defendant, Kenneth Dexter Bailey.

Hadley Cook saw the car speeding west on 36th street in the general direction of the Bailey ranch. I believe this is the same route you took to the ranch. You can look at the aerial photos to see the various routes the defendant may have taken once he reached US 75 to get to the ranch. He may have gone across 36th Street and taken the dirt road into the ranch, he may have gone around Wal-Mart, he may have traveled one of the streets north of Wal-Mart to get to Delaware and dash home.

Jim Newport saw Billie Jean Dugger and Ray after he was dead. They told you what they knew.

Dennis Grabel was the first police officer on the scene. He secured the scene and called for a detective.

Roy Fields was the first detective on the scene and took charge of the scene. He left once, with the crime scene in the care of Chief of Police Hodge. He took pictures during the evening and worked with O.S.B.I. Agent Roger Chrisco processing the scene. I believe it was his picture that showed the hand covering the bullct and then showed the bullet exposed when the hand had been moved. No one was looking for a bullet lying on the floor until it couldn't be found anywhere else, and apparently it got bumped a time or two before it was discovered.

Dr. Anderson made more pictures, which made the crime scene clear.

Perry Harkrider, police officer, found a .38 projectile in the defendant's back yard which may have been fired from the gun that killed Ray Courtemanche.

Don Connors found another .38 projectile in the defendant's back yard, which may have been fired from the death gun.

Oklahoma Highway Patrol Trooper Leon Hudson made a drawing of the inside and outside of the crime scene. He told you that the drawing is not to scale but that the measurements are accurate.

Roger Chrisco, an O.S.B.I. agent, worked with Detective Roy Fields. He picked up the death projectile. He talked with the defendant about 7:00 A.M. on Feb. 8, 1981, at the defendant's house. Defendant Dexter Bailey told him the he had been to the home of Ray Courtemanche on Feb. 2, 1981, to see about getting into court reporting school. Defendant Bailey also said that on Feb. 3, 1981, he left the ranch about 3:00 P.M., he borrowed the red car and he was going to his father's office to see about a horse bill. Defendant Bailey also told Agent Chrisco that about 4:00 or 4:15 P.M. he returned to the ranch, took a shower and shaved off his mustache. The people at his father's office said he was there from 4:00 to 4:30 P.M. or two or three minutes after that, and the body shop man even saw him in the street in front of the law office as late as perhaps 5:00 P.M..

Defendant Bailey had already told the officers that he had returned to the ranch between 4:00 and 4:15 P.M.. Defendant Bailey also told Agent Chrisco that he didn't remember when he last fired a pistol behind his house. Defendant Bailey gave the .38 pistol that could not be traced to him to the officers. HE USED THE WRONG GUN. Test drives were made, and it takes between 4 minutes 3 seconds and 5 minutes 25 seconds to drive from the home of Ray Courtemanche, the crime scene, to the ranch.

Dr. M.F. Merchant, Medical Examiner, told you that Ray was killed by the gun shot in the back of his head – he didn't die from anything else.

Jackie Roberts, O.S.B.I. agent and hypnotist, told you about the hypnosis. She was the only hypnotist who testified who saw Billie Jean Dugger.

Harvey Pratt, O.S.B.I. agent and artist, told you that the composite drawing was not a portrait of a person. It is only an approximation to use to exclude people who don't look anything like the killer.

Mike Stacy told of the defendant shooting a pistol in his back yard on the morning of the murder. He said the defendant left Feb. 4, 1981, and didn't return until Feb. 8, 1981. He had had a conversation with the defendant about silencers for guns. Mike said he had his own trash can and never burned trash. Defendant Dexter Bailey told him that he had had the gun a long time and wanted to know if it would still shoot. The defendant told the jury that he was practicing with a .22 so he could be better than his son.

Sue Bailey, the wife of the defendant, admitted that the defendant had burned something in the trash can about 4:30 -5:00 P.M. on the day Ray was killed. Sue also admitted that she asked Mrs. Stacy not to say anything to the officers about defendant Dexter shooting in the back yard on the morning of the killing.

Judy Stacy confirmed what Sue had said, and she testified that she saw the defendant Dexter Bailey shooting the morning of the killing. She also saw him open the cylinder of the gun and unload it. Defendant Dexter Bailey told the jury that he was shooting a .22 Western style single action pistol.

Richard Coleman testified that the defendant wanted to borrow the car because some fellow owed him money and was avoiding him, and he needed a vehicle that the guy would not recognize to get close to him.

O.S.B.I. agents Bob Powell and Jim Pratt found empty cartridges in the defendant's trash can. They had been fired in the death gun. Pratt also found the burned zipper in the trash can.

O.S.B.I. agent Kevin Ottwell showed the photo line up to Billie Jean Dugger. She could not identify anyone with certainty. Perhaps she was afraid of the man who shot and killed her neighbor in broad day light and then pointed the same gun at her.

Raymond Caudill found the death gun on the bridge that crosses the Deep Fork River west of Okmulgee. He found it on the side of the bridge. Remember it was the lawyer – Taylor – who said the gun was out in the middle. Was that an effort to confuse the jury?

Paul Rose, pawnshop owner from Tulsa, sold the death gun that killed Ray Courtemanche to Brett Bailey, the brother of defendant Kenneth Dexter Bailey. Remember this is the very same gun that Caudill found on the bridge the morning following the killings, just as day light was breaking. This is the same gun Brett sold one month after he bought it – but he doesn't know who the buyer was. Yet it is the same gun that fired the expended casings found in defendant's trash can and which fired the death projectile thru the head of Ray Courtemanche.

Tom Jordan examined weapons, empty shell casings and expended cartridges. Through the use of the facilities at the O.S.B.I. lab in Oklahoma City he was able to find that the death projectile was fired from the death gun to the exclusion of all other guns in the world. He was also able to find that the expended casings found in defendant's trash can were fired from the death gun to the exclusion of all other guns in the world. Tom Jordan followed the policy of his office and he was not allowed to let the defense expert use O.S.B.I. equipment. Tom Jordan did call the Oklahoma City Police department and the Tulsa Police department in an effort to help the defendant expert, and he was willing to travel with the evidence wherever the defendant's expert wanted to take the items to examine them.

As I recall the Defense called the following witnesses:

Randy White. He is the brother-in-law of the defendant, Dexter. Randy is married to the sister of Sue, Dexter's wife, and is a good friend of Dexter. He told you that defendant's hair was shorter than the hair in the composite drawing. Billie Jean Dugger told you that the hair in the composite drawing wasn't right, and the defendant may have even had on a wig at the time of the murder.

Bud Beasley testified that Defendant Dexter made a sudden call the night of the murder, he had to get his horse shod so he could leave town.

John Sadunas the defendant's ballistic expert from Chicago. You heard his testimony; how much weight do you want to give his testimony? He mishandled and dropped the death projectile.

Rex Albritton, Gerald Flood, and Emma Jean O'Hern are more friends of defendant Dexter who testified that Dexter had short hair. The defendant may still have had on a wig. Emma Jean could not remember whether or not defendant Dexter had a mustache, but she was sure about his hair.

Sonny Pickens and Steve Davis, friends of defendant Dexter who went to the rodeo with defendant Dexter right after the murder. Steve just remembered the good times when defendant Dexter won.

Linda Beaver, Darla Gayle, and Ann Bearden Smith, the girls at the barber shop in Morris. They all remembered a guy coming into the shop on Saturday two weeks before Ray was killed and that he called Ray Courtemanche and told him he would see him in two weeks. They all remembered different prices for the phone call and different combinations of coins paying for the call - 4 dimes; 25 cents, ten cents and three cents; five cents, ten cents and pennies. They were all sure of the amount and the combinations. Each described the guy differently as to age, height and weight. Darla Gayle admitted knowing Randy White, and she even admitted that there is common talk that she is dating Randy White, who is married to the defendant's wife's sister and is a friend of defendant Kenneth Dexter Bailey and goes to rodeos with him. Darla said the guy's car was orange red.

Steve Woolsey saw an orange red car with black louvers on the back.

That phone call and that car don't prove anything. The killer would not have made an appointment to kill Ray and let other people know of the appointment. If it happened it was just one of the many people that Ray saw. The killer's car was a Ford product.

Dale Ward a McAlester photographer put a Wyoming tag on a red-orange car that had nothing to do with the death car and took pictures of it as it looked to his eye, with the car standing still, with the car pointed directly at him, with him standing still, on level ground with no gun being pointed at him. This was an effort to mislead the jury as to what they wanted the jury to believe Billie Jean Dugger ought to have seen. No-one ever asked if Billie Jean Dugger was color blind. And she said she couldn't see that far.

Charles Lackey saw defendant Kenneth Dexter Bailey Jr at the Moose Lodge and told him of the death of Ray Courtemanche, and defendant Kenneth Dexter Bailey, Jr didn't act shocked. He already knew of the killing; he had just killed him!

Dr. Walter Bowlin hypnosis expert from Oklahoma City told you what a "Freudian slip" is - that is when a person says what he really thinks rather than what he meant to say. Defendant Kenneth Dexter Bailey, Jr told you when he went on TV "I am NOT innocent." That probably made him nervous. This expert never saw Billie Jean Dugger or even talked to Jackie Roberts. He did not see Billie Jean Dugger while she was hypnotized. He felt there was no tag on the car, but the tape and the transcript taken as a whole and her testimony make it clear that she just wasn't able to read a tag number.

Mike Chastin, another witness, spoke about the defendant's hair. The defendant may have had a wig on.

Employees in the office of Attorney K.D. Bailey, the father of defendant Kenneth Dexter Bailey:

Debbie Wells remembered defendant Dexter coming into K.D.'s office between 4:00 and 4:15 P.M. on the day Ray was killed but didn't know if the time was accurate. The very next day she knew that Dexter was a suspect in the killing of Ray Courtemanche because K.D. told her. But remember the officers didn't talk to Dexter until Feb. 8th when he returned from a rodeo. Remember Dexter told you that he would never forget that the officers told him on Feb. 8 that they had talked with 38 people, and they wanted to ask him some questions. The officers didn't even talk to Dexter until Feb. 8. Yet Debbie Wells knew on Feb. 4 that Dexter was a suspect because K.D. told her – Defendant Dexter must have told K.D. , or he would not have known to say anything.

Brenda Richie left at 4:30 P.M. and saw defendant Dexter at his father's office at 4:30 but Coleman saw defendant Dexter at the ranch at 4:30 P.M.

Ramona Belford is a loyal employ of attorney K.D. Bailey. She received the bill from the defendant Dexter at the very time of the killing. But the creator of the bill didn't even give the bill to defendant Dexter until after the killing. She had known the defendant Dexter all his life and is the office manager for attorney K.D. Bailey. Yet she didn't know defendant Dexter was a suspect until Feb 8th, even though K.D. had told Debbie on Feb 4th that Dexter was a suspect, the day after the killing.

Mary Bailey Romine, attorney and sister of K.D. Bailey, saw the defendant Dexter in the office at 4:20 P.M.

Dennis Seacat, one of the attorneys in K.D. Bailey's law firm saw defendant Dexter come into his father's office at 4:00 P.M. and saw him leave at 4:30, 4:31, 4:32 or 4:33 P.M. He said defendant Dexter was wearing a blue fluffy down jacket. He told me the District Attorney that I had filed on the wrong man – wouldn't you expect him to say his client who was paying him was not guilty. He was endorsed on the original information as a witness against the defendant – yet he continued to represent him until he withdrew as an attorney for the defendant during this trial so he could testify on behalf of his law partner's son. What is his interest?

Gibson Brooks saw defendant Dexter walking across the street in front of K.D. 's office between 4:30 and 5:00 P.M. on February 3, 1981, and he was wearing a blue jean jacket. That conflicts with the blue fluffy down jacket that Dennis Seacat said the defendant was wearing.

Hazel Sullivan saw a red car drive about medium fast along Mission – once from the north and once from the south. The killer's car was going fast. Richard Powell had to pull over there on Mission. She saw the car between 4 and 4:45 P.M. but only saw it for 2 seconds through trees. She is not even sure if she saw the same car both times.

Kenneth Dexter Bailey said he was nervous and scared on the stand. He did not act nervous or scared on the stand as you would expect a person to act who was on trial for murder first degree. REMEMBER THE FROIDIAN SLIP, "I AM NOT INNOCENT." Important: Defendant Dexter said he was in Indianapolis the weekend before Ray was killed and he didn't get home until 6:00 A.M. on Feb. 2, 1981. Defendant Dexter said Charlie Martin woke him up between 9:00 and 10:00 A.M. on Feb. 2, 1981 and gave him the bill he took to his father at the exact time Ray was killed. But remember Mr. Martin never remembered delivering bills on Sunday, and defendant Dexter wasn't at home on Sunday, Feb. 1, 1981. Mr. Martin delivered the bill between 12:00 noon and 3:00 P.M. Mr. Martin was in Sallisaw on Feb. 2 and Feb. 3, 1981. Mr. Martin attempted to deliver the bill once and had to go back to give it to him.

Mr. Martin had to deliver the bill after Ray was killed.

There was no bill for defendant Dexter to deliver to his father at the exact time of the killing. The defendant's defense is based on a lie! Defendant Dexter told you that he burned wet newspapers with kerosene right after he got back to the ranch right after the killing. What do you believe was burning in that trash can beside the zipper? Kenneth Dexter Bailey, Jr told the officers he couldn't remember when he shot a pistol in the back yard. At trial, nine months later, he remembered that 10 days before Ray was killed, he shot at a coyote and hit a trash can with a .38.

Attorney Steve Taylor asked defendant Dexter Bailey, "Did you kill Ray Courtemanche?" Remember how he looked! And just three or four months before trial, while his lawyers were working on preparing the very best defense they could, he traded off the .22 western style single action pistol that he now claims he shot on the morning of Feb. 3, 1981, so he didn't have the gun to bring to court to show you. The .22 is gone just like whatever was attached to the burned zipper. Defendant Dexter had the gun which couldn't be traced to him due to being won in a poker game. The death gun which was traced to brother Brett Bailey fired the casings found in defendant Dexter's trash can. Defendant Kenneth Dexter Bailey, Jr. used the wrong gun and gave the officers the wrong gun!

Charles Martin did not prepare the bill until after the end of the month. He never remembered delivering bills on Sunday. He was in Sallisaw Monday February. 2 and Tuesday Feb. 3, 1981. Defendant Dexter Bailey was out of state on Feb. 1 and didn't get in until 6:00 A.M. on February 2nd. The bill could not have been delivered until AFTER Ray was killed.

The State only has to prove its case just beyond a reasonable doubt. In this case the state proved its case far beyond a reasonable doubt!

Ray Courtemanche was murdered on a bright February afternoon. There sits the cold-blooded murderer!

Defendant Kenneth Dexter Bailey, Jr is not innocent. He is guilty as charged.

Additional items for argument to the jury:

I have a lot of faith in the common sense of the jury.

Bullet hole in the barrel is still silver after 10 months.

Defendant Dexter didn't bring the blue goose down jacket because he burned it up.

Commit murder in private.

Sick enough to have diarrhea - too sick to rope. He had just killed someone and had an eye witness; he probably did mess in his pants.

Hypnosis is used every day for weight loss and to stop smoking – no big deal. Are all those people unable to testify in court? Next we will hear that they can't contract or carry on everyday business.

Debbie Wells testified that she found out on the 4th that Dexter was a suspect.

Smell of death.

One resounding shot.

The argument that Dexter was a scapegoat isn't logical. Someone looking for a scapegoat would have chosen some poor boy without money, friends, or influence who couldn't fight.

Used the wrong gun – not a stolen gun but the gun that had been sold to his brother.

Political rivals. Loss of renting Welfare Office, etc. MAD.

Ray was asked to get a job for Dexter.

On a bright sunny afternoon defendant was a cold-blooded killer.

NOT Heat of Passion – practiced in the morning, borrowed a car, shot in the back of the head. Campbell v. State, Vol 52, No 39 of the Oklahoma Bar Journal, page 2576, Nov. 7, 1981.

Not unusual to not find fingerprints, tissue or fiber – not in the house on the day of the killing, and he was there only 45 seconds.

We are always hearing "Why don't they do something?" Police officers have done their job. Defense attorneys have done their job and will go home when this trial is over. The Judge has done his job. The D.A. has done his job. Now you the jury are THEY. You are the only ones left who have not yet done your job. I hope, and I feel confident, that when you finish your job that the citizens will feel safe and say, "They did their job well".

A farm boy had dreamed all his life of going to the circus. He had read everything he could find on circuses. Going to the circus was his life ambition. Flyers were posted of a circus coming to his town! 50 cents was hard to get. At last, his father agreed to find 50 cents if (1) the boy would do all of his chores early and well and (2) he would walk to town, the family was not going that early. On the day of the circus, he finished his work - walked then ran to town with 50 cents in his pocket. He saw a group of people on Main street. He saw animals, beautiful girls and friendly clowns walking by. The boy handed the clown 50 cents and said "Oh, thank you Mr. Clown" then walked home. He thought he had seen the circus, but he had only seen the parade. The defense has paraded witnesses but have you ever seen the show of truth from the defendant, or just a parade?

No-one would make an appointment with someone to murder them and let other people know about it.

The law should protect the rights of all people, but the paramount interest of the law should be to protect the rights of law-abiding citizens, especially as to life, liberty, and the pursuit of happiness.

ADDITIONAL CONSIDERATIONS

It should be noted that the defendant argued against hypnosis at the Preliminary Hearing then at trial switched to argue that the hypnosis was well done.

There can be found reports in hypnosis literature of a person who has been hypnotized without knowing it. I had to consider this as I heard the evidence from the defense, especially from the ladies who worked in the office of attorney K.D. Bailey, father of defendant Dexter Bailey. One of these ladies had worked for me in the past, and I was convinced that she was honest and would not have taken part in a plan to fabricate evidence. I could not find any evidence of fraud in their testimony, but I still believe they were mistaken about the time defendant Dexter Bailey was at his father's office. It is possible to hypnotize a person and change his or her memory as to time or some other fact and instruct him to forget being given this instruction. I found no evidence of any post hypnotic suggestion changing any evidence, but if it had happened it might have been impossible to discover.

If it happened or ever does happen that a witness is hypnotized, instructed to remember a different time etc., and instructed not to remember that he had been so instructed and such evidence were presented to the court, that would be a fraud upon the court, and there would be no statute of limitations.

I felt and continue to believe that the right person was charged and tried for the murder of Ray Courtemanche. ***The jury found the defendant not guilty.*** Therefore, there was no appeal. If there had been an appeal the defense would have purchased a transcript of the trial and I would have access to all of the exact words spoken during the trial as reported by the court reporter.

The case proceeded to trial very much along the lines of what I had set out in my trial notebook. After the evidence was presented to the jury the Judge read the instructions to the jury after they had been gone over by the lawyers out of the presence of the jury. Then the jury rendered its verdict after hearing arguments from the lawyers and deliberating their decision.

Errors in the Case

1 The first and major error was for the O.S.B.I. to snap up my only witness very quickly after the crime and hypnotize her. Hypnosis is a valuable tool for law enforcement when properly used. The very first consideration is that hypnosis should be used only after all other investigation has failed to develop facts that form the basis for a provable criminal charge. The O.S.B.I. hypnotist testified that people think of hypnosis as "Spooky!" This is certainly true and undoubtedly damaged the believability of the testimony of our only eye witness. The facts are that she gave the same report before and after hypnosis without any material difference. Her testimony should have carried great weight from the very beginning. There would have been no question about something spooky if she had not been hypnotized.

2. The O.S.B.I. artist was in a rush to finish his work to get to Weatherford, Okla. in the western part of the state. He rushed his work and as he continued to rush the picture got less like the killer.

3. The O.S.B.I. artist testified that a composite drawing is not intended to look like the killer but only to be a tool to rule out people who did not look like the killer. This seemed to be clearly understood by the O.S.B.I., but it did not seem to have been communicated to the citizens of Okmulgee. There should have been an effort to educate the public that the composite drawing was not intended to look like the killer but was intended only to rule out people who do not look like the killer. The citizens of Okmulgee seemed to be looking for the person in the picture, rather than just using it to rule out people who did not look like the killer.

OTHER CONSIDERATIONS

In law school we learned that if we had the facts on our side we should argue the facts, if we had the law on our side we should argue the law, and if we had neither on our side we should argue to confuse.

The prosecution presented and argued the facts and the law.

It seems to me that the defense presented and argued confusion.

It also became clear that some people in Okmulgee were afraid of the Baileys.

While in Okmulgee my family and I attended the First Baptist Church. On one occasion a preacher was called to preach with a view of being called to serve as pastor. My wife and I were the only people who voted against calling this individual. Everyone else voted to call him, and he became our preacher. What surprised me was the number of individuals who came to me in the next week or two and told me privately that they wished they had voted their convictions instead of just blindly going along with the recommendation of the search committee.

Shortly after I came to Okmulgee as an Assistant District Attorney, I observed that when someone would be cut or more likely killed in a cutting in a joint on Fifth Street that night everyone there could give full details. By the time for Preliminary Hearing memories were foggy and by trial those same people had trouble even remembering that they might have been there that evening. What memory remained amounted to the "fact" that the guy who lived rather than the guy who died was the good guy. At times it seemed to me that this same thinking prevailed throughout the entire community, not just on Fifth Street.

Of course, there are personal likes and dislikes that are commingled in the lives of the members of the jury. One time I received a lot of complaints from various organizations in Okmulgee that supported their individual organization's activities by inviting people to come and play bingo for a cash prize. The law allowed winning pots of up to $500.00. The complaints were that the Elks were awarding more than $500.00 so everyone went to the Elks, and the other organizations could not play within the law and compete. I sent a law enforcement officer to the Elks with the instruction to take names if there were violations. Things got out of hand when the officer started arresting people and had to call in other officers to manage the situation. My intent all along was that if violations were found that I would summons the lodge to my office to see what needed to be done to keep things within the law and that probably would have involved a fine, but the lodge should have been able to continue offering bingo. A lot of people were needlessly upset over the way things were handled that night at the Elks Lodge. Feelings like these can carry over to a jury trial.

REASON FOR WRITING THIS BOOK

First, older lawyers should share some of their experience with younger lawyers and the general public.

Second, the justice system should be aware of the possibility of testimony being given by witnesses who have been hypnotized, given an instruction to change a memory such as the time of some event and being given an instruction to forget that they had been given such instruction so that they could truthfully believe and testify about a changed memory. This would be a fraud upon the court and might be very difficult to detect.

The End

Made in United States
North Haven, CT
10 November 2026

22106111R00129